DECODING
MANHATTAN

DECODING MANHATTAN

ISLAND OF DIAGRAMS, MAPS, AND GRAPHICS

Antonis Antoniou and Steven Heller

ABRAMS, NEW YORK

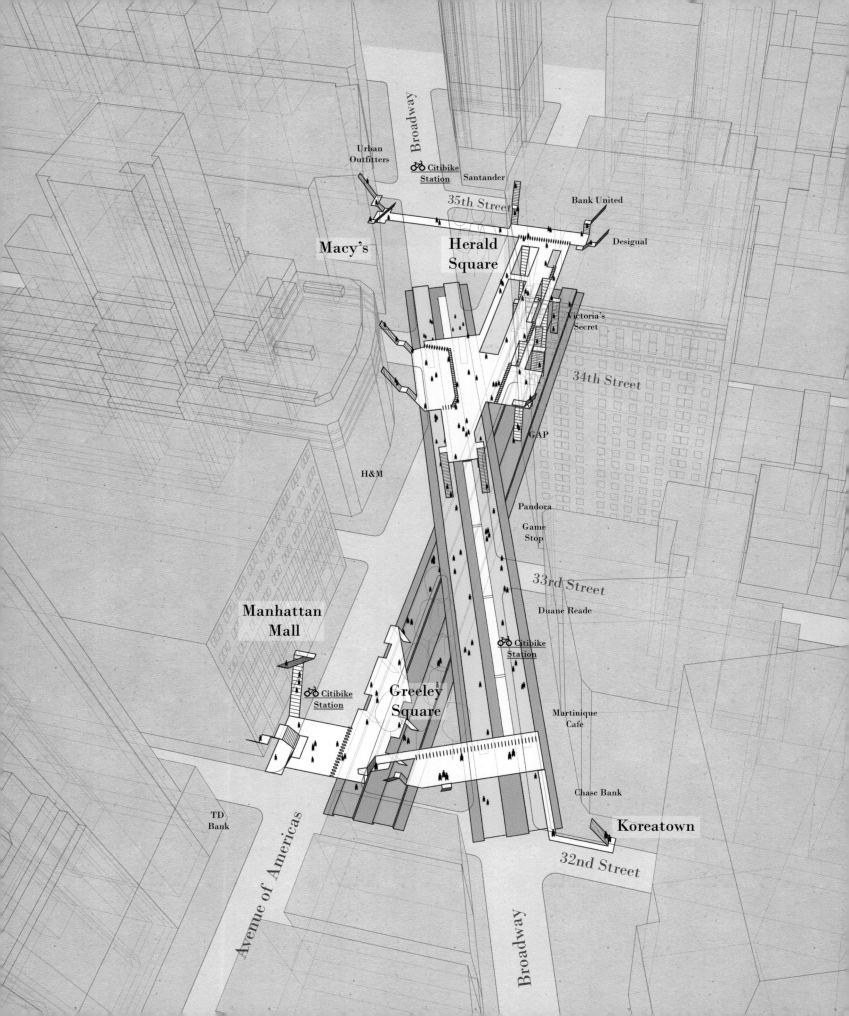

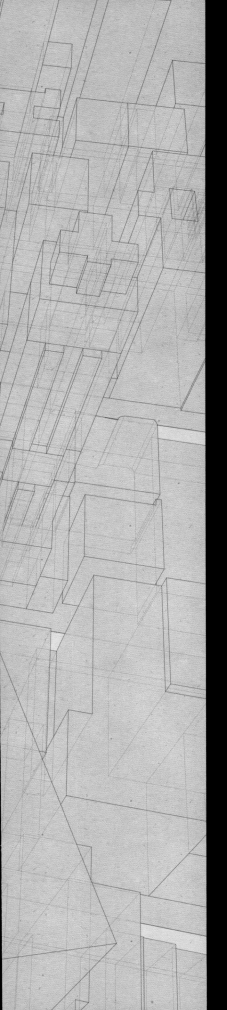

CONTENTS

INTRODUCTION
MANHATTAN
AS
DIAGRAM

EVEN A LONGTIME MANHATTANITE IS LIKELY TO SUFFER THE same geographical disorientation as a first-time visitor from time to time. When that happens, it can be surprisingly easy—one might say democratic—to correct one's internal GPS and quickly find a way to get from point A to point Z. Brooklyn, Queens, the Bronx, and Staten Island are mazes of streets, terraces, courts, plazas, boulevards, and culs-de-sac that defeat logical maneuvering; Manhattan's street grid is a wayfinding marvel. Aside from the quaint historic winding lanes, hidden cobblestone alleys, and converging intersections typical of vintage downtown Manhattan, most (but not all) of the borough was planned on such a rational formula, with numbered streets crossed by numbered (more or less) avenues, that getting around can be as simple as reading a street sign.

On maps and charts, Manhattan Island looks like an elongated chess board with various anomalous protrusions. Its matrix of orthogonal blocks, with a scattering of triangles, is largely filled in with rectangular building lots. This is the diagrammatic foundation that, just as it helps the wayfinder, shapes and shadows the charts, maps, graphics, cutaways, cross sections, and other comparative and contemplative graphic depictions of the city and its people, places, and things that you will find throughout this book. Here, diagrams are keys to the city, providing fascinating, and often surprising, insights into the inner and outer workings of Manhattan from diverse perspectives, often with condensed and intense detail to satisfy the most obsessive viewer. They show what is under the skin, behind the curtain, below ground, or floating in air.

No word brings together these eclectic images more cohesively and poetically than *diagram*. Diagrams have existed since the beginning of art making. In recent years—and notably with the advent of the computer—the genre has blossomed into a huge profession with its own specific conventions and aesthetics, practicing what is known in the current vernacular of design as data visualization and information graphics (and at times information architecture), inventing friendly and accessible ways to help us consume and digest our overabundance of data. In the end, however, the new data "viz" is just more diagrams. In this book, the best of the old and new sits side by side.

Diagrams explain the world, illuminating differences and similarities among all sorts of things. The simplest chart can provide a visual clue to help unravel the most convoluted phenomena, and yet, by virtue of visual logic, the most intricate rendering may reduce complexity into digestible forms. Further, we embrace diagrams not just to understand how things work, but to also understand how *we* work. These impersonal tools acquire indispensable personal meanings—they help us understand the mechanics of our lives, illuminating experience with criticism or humor. A Venn diagram will help us define our place in the world, a flowchart can guide us through a choice, a pie chart shows us how we spend our time and money—the applications of diagrams for self-exploration are limitless and wondrous.

In the newspapers and magazines where many of the diagrams in this book were originally published, they were used to edify *and* entertain by combining image and text within a single impactful graphic. As Manhattan's stories have been presented to the public through graphics for decades, this diagrammatic approach to journalism has shaped the global image of the city.

In 1910, the *New-York Tribune* wished to impress upon its readers the vast dimensions of the RMS *Titanic*, then nearing completion in Belfast, Ireland, and New York provided the perfect yardstick. Arthur Ragland Momand's illustration, *Where Can We Dock This Marine Monster When She Reaches the Port of New York?* (page 74), is a cutaway view of the behemoth, comparing its bulk to existing and passé modes of transportation, including a railroad train on her upper deck and Henry Hudson's square-rigged *Half Moon* resting crosswise, with her topmasts jutting into one of the *Titanic*'s dining rooms. The height of the steamship is measured against a landmark familiar to *Tribune* readers, the fourteen-story Postal Telegraph Building on Broadway and Murray Street. Even though it is now common to see huge oceangoing apartment-house-sized vessels docked on Manhattan's Hudson River, this diagram, which alerted the public that a new heavyweight contender was coming to the world's capital of bigness, has not lost any of its impact.

In another eye-catching comparative diagram celebrating bigness published in the *Scientific American* in 1906, illustrator C. McKnight-Smith showed the Singer Building, then under construction and the world's tallest on completion, dwarfing a group of world-famous monuments and looming over the city's skyline (page 66). As New York soared skyward, countless illustrations like this one, in newspapers, magazines, books, and posters, sought to help New Yorkers come to grips with their dramatically changing city. Indeed, changing New York claimed the Singer Building in 1969, making it the only structure illustrated in Smith's diagram to have been demolished.

As big as New York was proud to be, it could also be small and mean, and diagrams were also routinely used to agitate for social change. On July 1, 1865, *Frank Leslie's Illustrated Newspaper* addressed the "burning shame" of tenement living conditions under the rubric, *HOW THE POOR LIVE IN CROWDED CITIES—HOW PESTILENCE IS GENERATED—HOW THE PARENTS ARE DEMORALIZED AND THEIR CHILDREN DEPRAVED—THE GREAT SOURCE OF DESTITUTION AND CRIME* (pages 114–115). In addition to "an actual scene in one of the rooms, as witnessed by our artist," a panoramic cross section by Albert Berghaus shows the cramped block of Gotham Court, which would become one of New York's most notorious tenements, along with a ground plan of the building, showing its proximity to Murderers Alley. Like Jacob Riis's famously horrific photographs of Gotham Court published twenty-five years later in *How the Other Half Lives*, this infographic makes a strong case for reform of the city's living conditions.

Of course, not all diagrams are preoccupied with the highs and the lows. Many diagrams were and are created that simply document streetscapes. In 1899 the *New York Mail and Express* created a visual directory of Broadway, from Bowling Green to Columbus Circle (page 116). This was quite an effort, since each building, rendered by hand engraving, is precise down to the last window. The traditional building elevation diagram takes on extra meaning when the dimension of time is added, as in Julia Wertz's *Four Decades of CBGB & OMFUG at 315 Bowery in Manhattan,* which shows in crisp line drawings its

A. G. Racey, *The Man in the Moon*, from *Life*, September 18, 1902.
Racey adds a cosmic element to the repertoire of New York boosterism—and inadvertently predicts the recent spate of super-tall, narrow-footprint construction so prevalent in Manhattan wealthy real estate zones today.

(de)-volution from a bar-and-grill in the 1940s, to its opening as a club in 1973 and subsequent expansion in the 1980s, and finally its gentrification in the 2000s (page 51). In 1936, Marvin W. Auringer drew *Mid-town New York* in all its glory (pages 26–27): Here, the familiar is made intriguing to the viewer, thanks to the perspective, as diagrammatic aerial representations are extra pleasurable.

Humor is also a common trope used in data visualization past and present. The most famous of all is arguably Saul Steinberg's drawing, *View of the World from 9th Avenue*, which appeared on the cover of *The New Yorker* in 1976 (page 83), expressing a world view of New York's centrality that might not be shared by all. Steinberg sarcastically portrayed the country west of the Hudson as a bare patch of green and reduced the rest of the world to low hills on the horizon, while the most important real estate, the streets and avenues of New York, take up the lion's share of imagery. By the late nineteenth century, when the city was a mass of architectural styles piled on top of each other, a Victorian *Jetsons*, of sorts, the comic artist Grant E. Hamilton rendered it as a futuristic Tower of Babel in a drawing titled *What We Are Coming To* (page 30) in *Judge* magazine; his "Combination Apartment-House," with subway, railroad, roadways, and carnival midway, prefigured the smashed-together style of decades-later Post-modernism.

The skyscraper may be the signature image of New York, but diagrams taking the viewer behind the brick, mortar, and steel also exemplify its identity. *Popular Mechanic*'s axonometric view of the interior of Radio City Music Hall (page 130) from 1932 captures the ebb and flow of multitudes of people through the world's largest auditorium. And who cannot feel fondness for the cutaway of the Chelsea Hotel (page 134) drawn by Jim Flora for *Life* magazine in 1964? What makes these views so voyeuristically compelling is that they strip away the city's facades to expose remarkable, and occasionally not-so-savory, worlds.

Decoding Manhattan may not provide an answer to what makes the city tick, but it is filled with clues. It celebrates a rich visual language that can be technical and precise but is also exquisite, sensual, and witty. If that does not make sense, we will draw you a diagram.

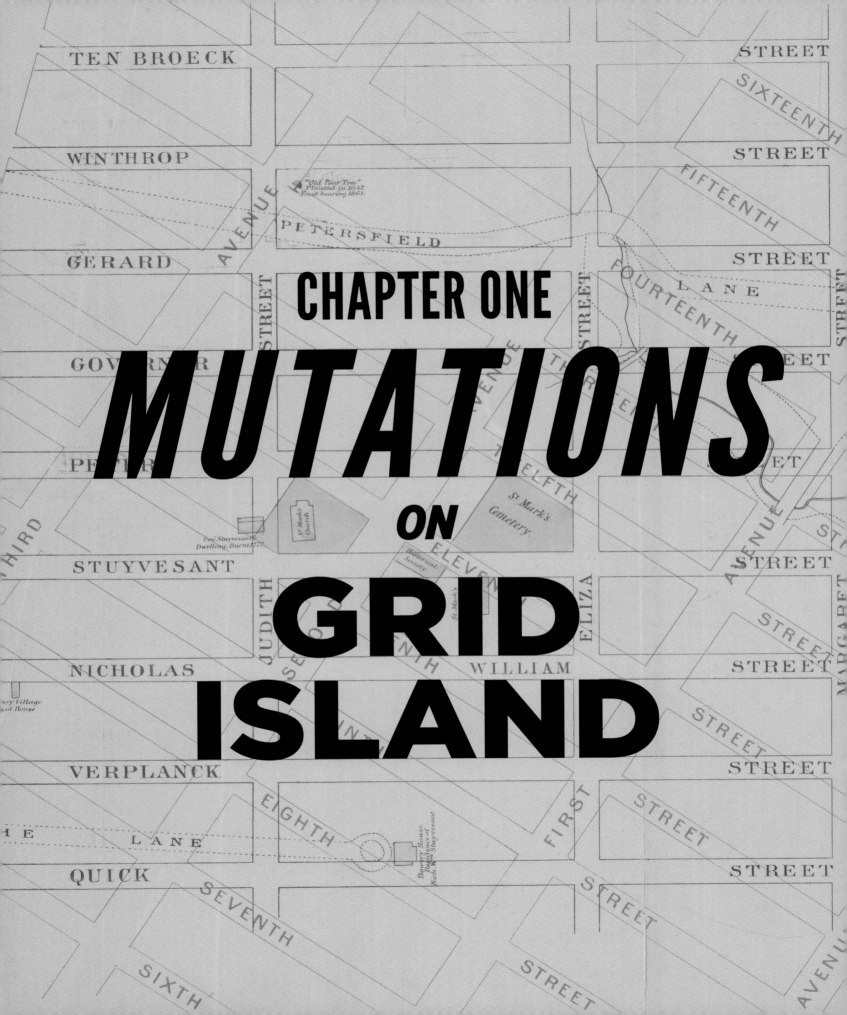

CHAPTER ONE
MUTATIONS
ON
GRID
ISLAND

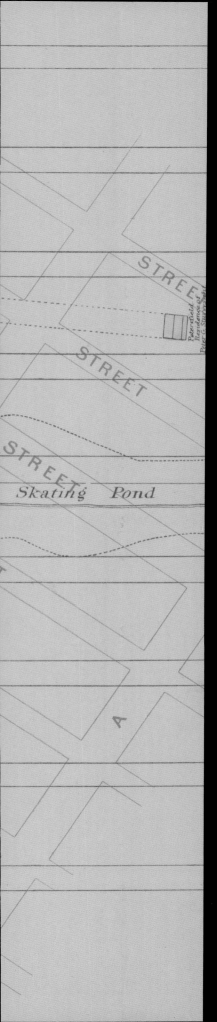

WHILE DEVELOPERS OPPORTUNISTICALLY DEVELOP and preservationists committedly preserve its legacy, the island of Manhattan maintains a mysterious aura above it all that comes into focus through diagrams that speak louder than photographs or words. Manhattan's greatness inheres in the island's familiar contours, highly adaptable to graphic commentary, such as J. Y. Pique's 1951 New York romance cover of *Park East* magazine (page 35); in grandly conceived, man-made engineering feats like its ingenious street grid, laid out in defiance of the natural hilly landscape, as illustrated in any number of Manhattan street maps (pages 16–17); and such planning strategies as the zoning laws that sculpted its emblematic skyline, as dynamically and dramatically captured by architect Hugh Ferriss's visual analysis of the 1916 New York zoning law (page 25). In our daily experience of the city, we see the surfaces produced by these facts and forces, while diagrams reveal underlying patterns and structure. In this chapter, we look at transformations and mutations: Time passes, and the grid expands and fragments, pushing outward against the edges of the land and upward against the sky.

A diagram does not always have to provide a functional outcome or adhere to convention. Manhattan is a place in space that requires navigation, but it also exists on higher planes that are best explored through abstract or metaphorical visual representation. Such are the timelines by chart maker Ward Shelley, *Andy Warhol-Chelsea Girls, ver. 1* (pages 44–45) and *Downtown Body, ver. 1* (pages 46–47), that show circulatory systems pumping data through the city as body.

Artists and designers have the means to record, reflect on, and re-envision the city's spirit and syncopated rhythms in pictures, sometimes by referencing familiar visual icons of the city. The *New York Journal and Advertiser's* 1897 comic The *Journal's Suggestion to Greater New York* (page 33) shows the Brooklyn Bridge as a bustling carnival attraction, prefiguring the massive street fairs and festivals so common today. Paula Scher's identity design for Manhattan Records (page 15) repurposes Piet Mondrian's *Broadway Boogie Woogie*, and in the process generates a logo formed by a three-by-three grid of simple building blocks. Maxwell J. Roberts's *New York Vignelli Circles* (page 43) riffs on Massimo Vignelli's famous subway diagram/map, taking its controversial abstraction of the shapes and size relations of the boroughs many steps further.

In transformation and mutation lies the beauty of these humble yet intricate works of art.

Plate 9.

EXPLANATION of Plate 9. These Columns corresponding to the 7 Sections, Showing the different Rocks as they are found at the Localities they represent their figure and title corresponding with the Number of Each Plate.

COLUMN of N. YORK Fig. 1.

Diluvium.	8.
Primitive Lime stone	7.
Serpentine.	6.
* Quartz Rock	5.
* Hornblende Slate	4.
* Gneiss.	3.
Sienite.	2.
Granite.	1.

* These 3 are at equal heights on our Island.

COLUMN OF THE PALISADOES Fig. 2.

Diluvium.	6.
Basalt or Trap.	5.
Green Stone Slate.	4.
Red Sandstone.	3.
Serpentine.	2.
Granite.	1.

COLUMN FROM THE HUDSON to the OCEAN. Fig. 3.

Beach Sand.	10.
Diluvium.	9.
Tertiary.	8.
Green Sand.	7.
Trap.	6.
Green Stone Slate.	5.
Red Sandstone.	4.
Serpentine.	3.
Gneiss.	2.
Granite.	1.

COLUMN of STATEN IS? Fig. 4.

Diluvium.	6.
Pea-iron ore.	5.
Trap.	4.
Red Sandstone.	3.
Serpentine.	2.
Granite.	1.

COLUMN of DONDEBERG Fig. 5.

Brick Clay.	5.
Transition Limestone.	4.
Talcose Slate.	3.
Gneiss.	2.
Granite.	1.

COLUMN of RHODE IS? Fig. 6.

Coal & Shale.	5. 6. 5. 6.
4 Varieties of Graywacke.	4.
Talcose Slate.	3.
Serpentine.	2.
Granite.	1.

COLUMN of NIAGARA Fig. 7.

Fresh Water Shells.	11.
Shales of Hamilton Group.	10.
Pyritiferous Rock of Eaton.	9.
Corniferous Limestone.	8.
Shale Belonging to the Salt Group.	7.
Limestone.	6.
Shale.	5.
Limestone.	4.
Red Marl & Sand-Stone.	3.
Medina, Sandstone.	2.
Red Marl.	

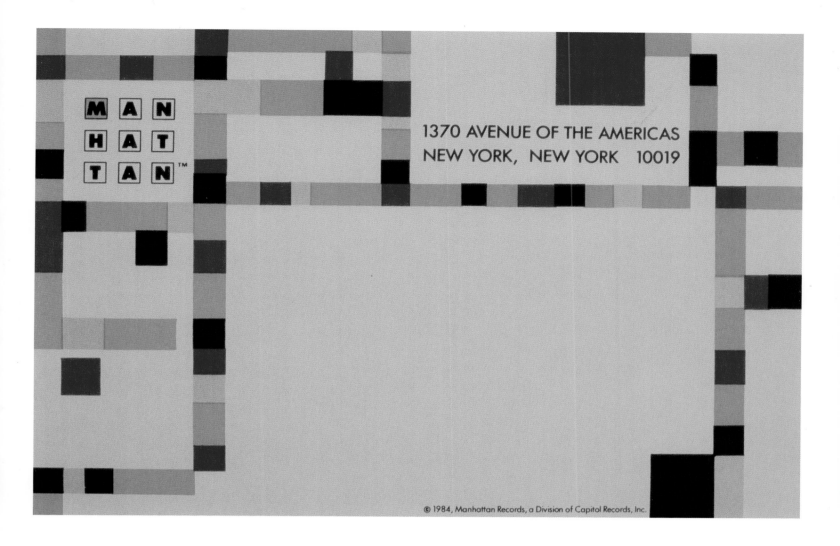

OPPOSITE

Plate 9, from *A Geological History of Manhattan or New York Island* by Issachar Cozzens, 1843.

Manhattan Island is metamorphic in many senses, and one is that if you were to scrape away its surface, what you would find is an undulating platform of its famous metamorphic bedrock: Manhattan schist. This gridded table is a key to plates showing geological cross sections of various sites on the island that appeared in Issachar Cozzens's book. The blocks in this grid, including "gneiss," as Manhattan schist used to be called, represent the different natural materials that lie underfoot. Manhattan's sturdy geological makeup (with a particularly muscular Midtown) bolstered the urge to build ever higher.

ABOVE

Paula Scher, *Identity for Manhattan Records*, 1984.

Designer Paula Scher repurposed Piet Mondrian's 1943 painting *Broadway Boogie Woogie*—which she called "an abstracted map of Manhattan"—to design a logo for Manhattan Records. "The logic for using this painting as an identity for Manhattan Records was obvious," she explained. "It ostensibly represented Manhattan and was inspired by music. But its strongest attribute was that the painting's color blocks could easily be reconfigured for a multitude of uses. I began considering the logotype as something that came out of the red, blue, and yellow boxes of the painting. A logo in a grid, like the city. The character count of the word Manhattan was perfect, allowing for three stacks of three-letter units: MAN, HAT, TAN. It was my first and only idea for the logo."

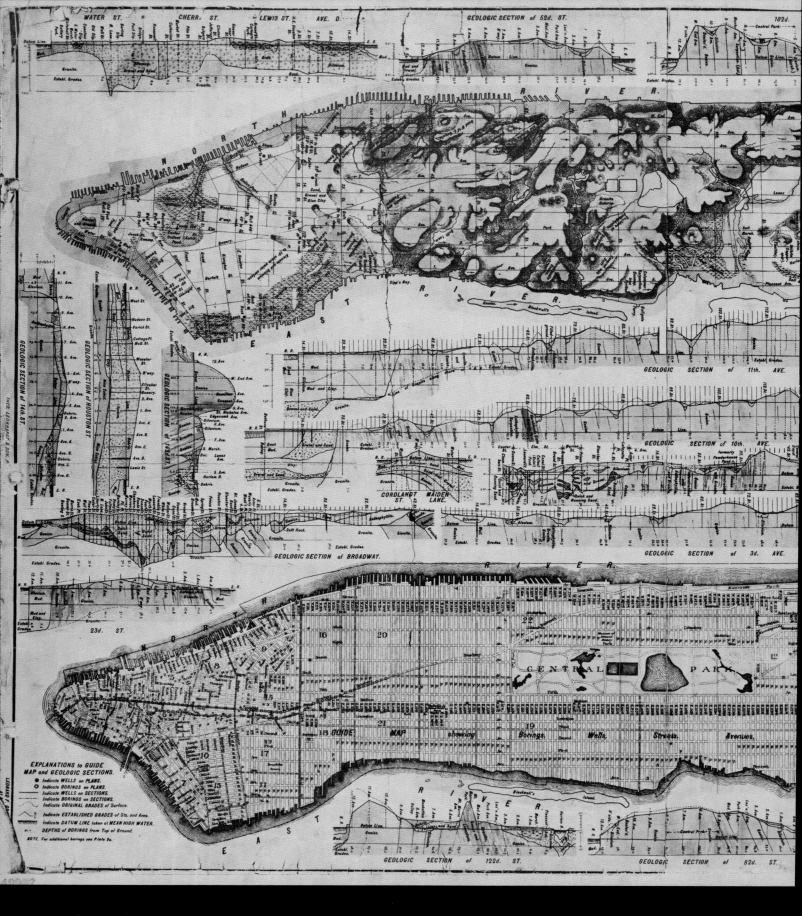

Leonard F. Graether, *Geologic Map and Sections of Manhattan Island, State of New York*, 1898.

Once an island of rolling hills, meadows, and swamps, Manhattan's topography today is almost completely defined by the grid. The imposition of the grid required a violent sculpting of its terrain, with waterways filled in and hills leveled. Before-and-after merge in these maps and sections, showing that streams became streets and salt marshes were turned into squares.

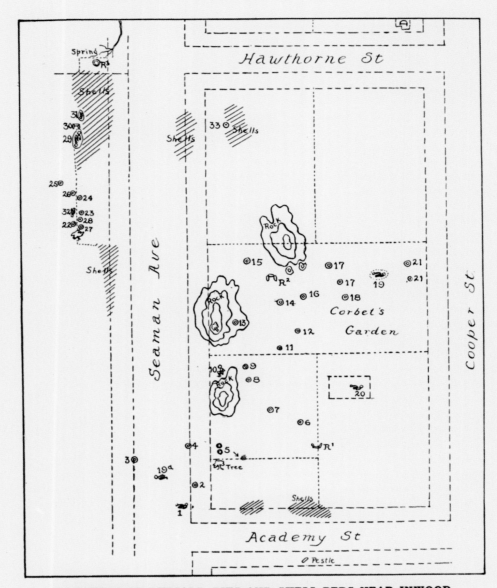

LOCATION OF BURIALS, PITS AND SHELL-BEDS NEAR INWOOD

1. Human remains. 2. Shell pit, deer antler. 3. Shell pit. 4. Shell pit, pottery. 5. Shell pits. 6. Shell pit, sturgeon below. 7. Shell pit, sturgeon scales. 8, 9. Shell pits. 10. Human remains. 11. Fire pit. 12. Shell pit. 13. Dog burial, puppy. 14. Shell pit. 15. Part of a jar. 16. Shell pit, fish and meat bones. 17. Shell pits. 18. Two dogs in shell pit. 19. Human skeleton, 1907. 19a. Female skeleton, 1908. 20. Human remains when house was built. 21. Small fire pits, Revolutionary. 22. Large shell pit. 23. Large shell pit. 24. Shell pit. 25. Dog burial. 26, 27, 28. Shell pits. 29. Two human skeletons, male and female. 30. Revolutionary fireplace "Royal Marines" and "17th." 31. Skeleton and infant, female. 32. Skeleton (Chenoweth, 1908). 33. Revolutionary fireplace. 71st, officers' buttons. D. Dyckman dwelling. R¹, R². Revolutionary fireplaces. R³. Revolutionary well.

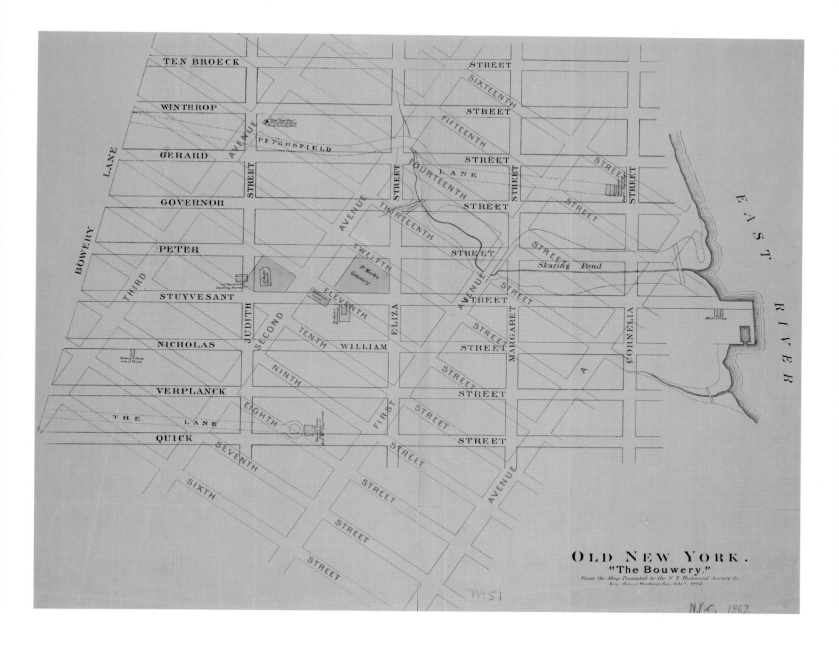

OLD NEW YORK.
"The Bouwery."
From the Map Presented to the N. Y. Historical Society by
Benj. Robert Winthrop Esq. Febr? 1862

N.Y.C. 1862

OPPOSITE

OPPOSITE

Location of Burials, Pits and Shell-Beds Near Inwood, from *Indians of Manhattan Island and Vicinity* by Alanson Skinner, 1921.

There is very little remaining archaeological evidence of the presence of the Native Americans called the Lenape who lived on Manhattan Island when the Europeans arrived. One encampment on the eastern edge of what is now Inwood Hill Park is well documented. Here, ethnologist Alanson Skinner maps findings in the Inwood section of Manhattan. The list is scattershot—human and animal remains, shell middens, and American Revolution–era fireplaces—suggesting how thoroughly the building up of the island obliterated the past. Some Lenape were still living in the area in the 1930s, when the park was completed.

ABOVE AND PAGE 12

Benjamin Winthrop, *Old New York, "The Bouwery," from Manual of the Corporation of the City of New York for 1862.* 1862.

A banker and antiquarian, Benjamin Winthrop deplored the new grid and its "despotic mathematical rules." Here, in a map showing a part of what is now the East Village, he lays the new street plan in red over doomed streets whose names conjure the Colonial past (a short stretch of Stuyvesant Street survived the realignment). At the corner of East 13th Street and Third Avenue stood Peter Stuyvesant's famous pear tree, "planted in 1647," which was destroyed in a vehicular collision in 1867. "Laborers were engaged in removing the limbs and trunk yesterday, which were proclaimed obstructions to travel," wrote the *New York Times* at the time. In 2003, a new tree was planted in its place.

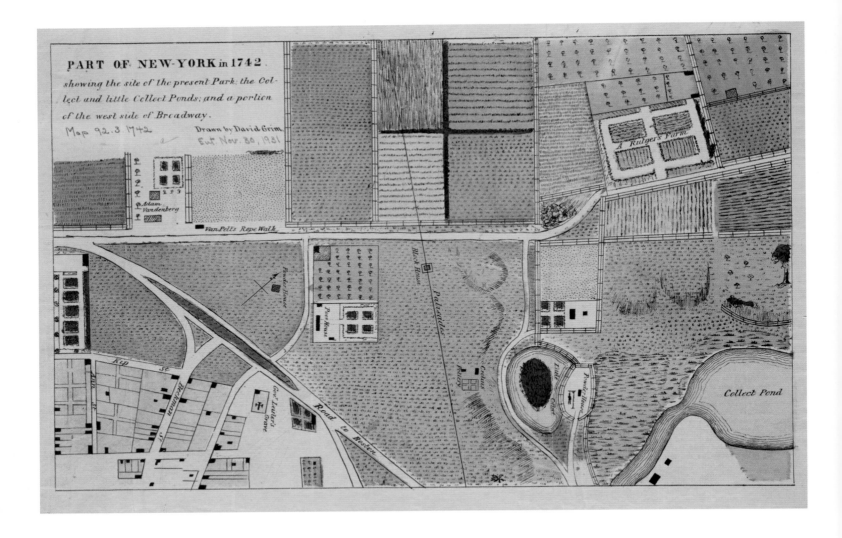

David Grim, *Part of New York in 1742*, c. 1813.

David Grim was about five years old in 1742; he drew this map, "showing the site of the present Park; the Collect and little Collect Ponds; and a portion of the west side of Broadway," from memory seventy years later, when he took to cartography as a serious pastime. Grim's map is oriented with west at the top, and it is true to his name, with its gallows, powder house, and poorhouse. Today, City Hall can be found roughly on the site of Grim's poorhouse.

Maps of Manhattan, c. 1890.

Three leaves from a booklet of charming Manhattan maps, probably made for readers of *The Sun*, show sections of the city as they looked in the late nineteenth century. Opposite: The Battery, the financial center around Wall Street, and the old seaport along the East River. Overleaf, left: The city's downtown nerve center—where communications, newspapers (including *The Sun*), and government were gathered together in a dense cluster. Overleaf right: The residential Upper West Side and Central Park.

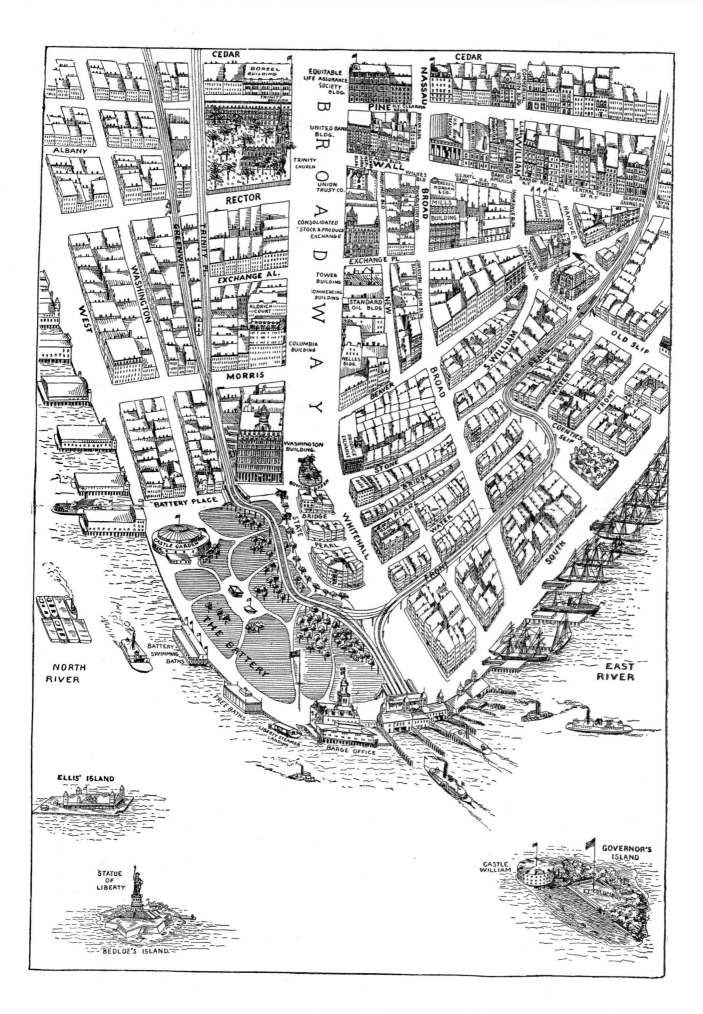

21

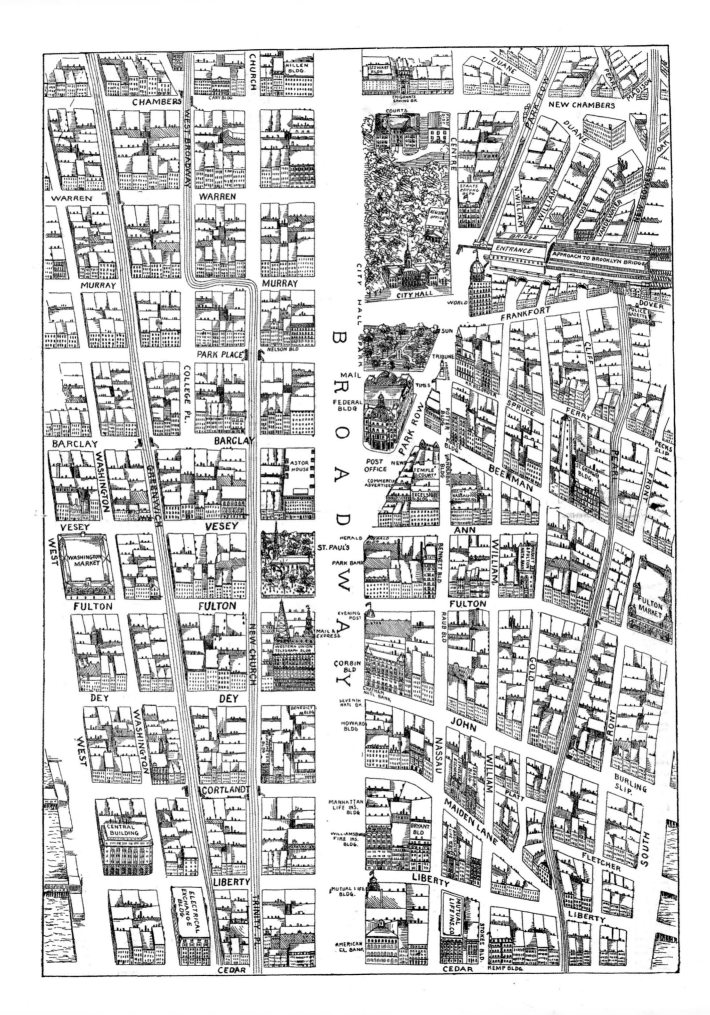

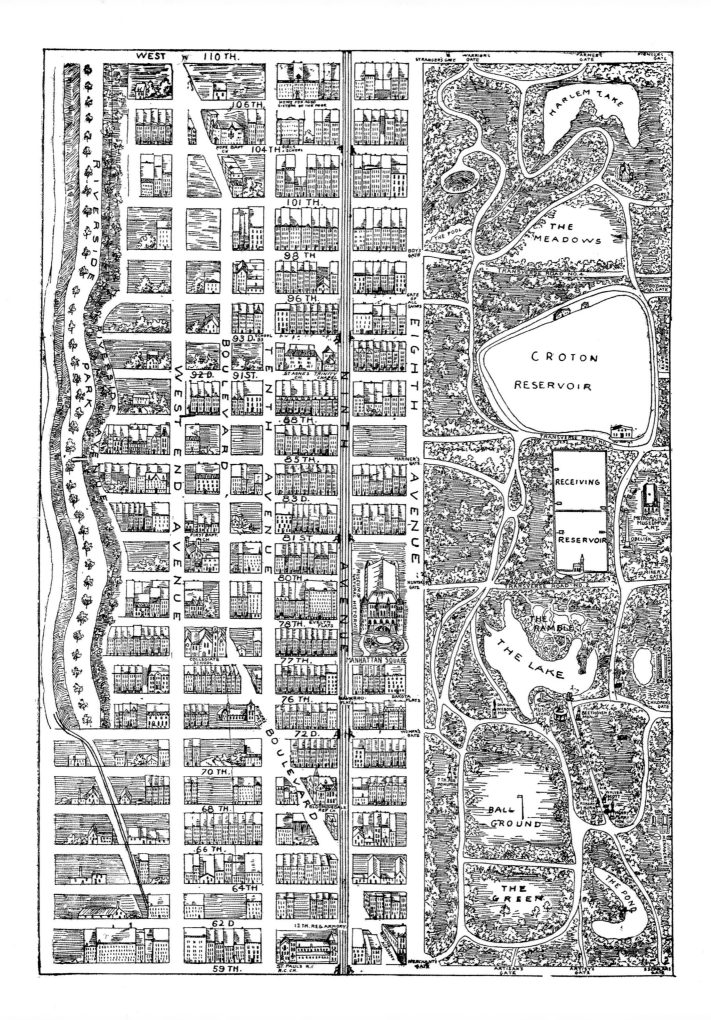

Hugh Ferriss, *Evolution of the Set-back Building*, 1922.
By showing four stages in a design process intended to result in
a building with the maximum allowable mass, with necessary
setbacks, under the 1916 New York zoning law, architect Hugh
Ferriss demonstrated how zoning requirements shaped the new
skyscrapers of the twentieth century. In his book *The Metropolis
of Tomorrow*, Ferriss wrote that, "the actual effect of the law was
to introduce what is often spoken of as no less than a new era in
American Architecture. The whole procedure constitutes another
example of the fact that the larger movements of Architecture
occur not as the result of some individual designer's stimulus but
in response to some practical general condition."

Marvin W. Auringer, *Mid-town New York. Theatres, Hotels & Shopping District*, 1936.

Midtown Manhattan is drawn with extraordinary precision in this axonometric massing diagram, where the landmark buildings are rendered in more detail. Twenty years after the 1916 zoning law, the stepped setbacks it required for buildings to attain maximum allowable height are clearly visible, especially around Broadway. The map border uses a continuous ribbon as both a decorative element and to name streets and avenues.

Mutations

The problem of transportation in the city of New York is rendered extremely difficult and costly by the fact that 2,000,000 of the people live upon, and as many more daily enter or leave, a long, narrow island, which is separated from the mainland by broad and deep rivers. To overcome this isolation public and private enterprise has built, during the past decade, no less than fourteen tunnels and three of the greatest long-span bridges of the world.

BIRD'S EYE VIEW OF MANHATTAN ISLAND, SHOWING NEW YORK'S ELABORATE SYSTEM OF BRIDGES AND TUNNELS.

Charles Figaro, *Bird's Eye View of Manhattan Island, Showing New York's Elaborate System of Bridges and Tunnels*, from *Scientific American*, December 5, 1908.

This view helps to explain why transportation in New York City is, as the caption under the illustration says, "extremely difficult and costly": each day, two million people must enter and leave "a long narrow island, which is separated from the mainland by broad and deep rivers." Figaro lays out, as if on an operating table, the isolated body of Manhattan, with its artificial limbs, both visible and hidden—including fourteen tunnels and "three of the greatest long-span bridges in the world" built in the decade before this dramatic aerial perspective

Gotham Has Many Bridges but May Get More in 1911, from the *New-York Tribune*, January 1, 1911.

A very deformed Manhattan is packed to the gills with bridges and tunnels, existing or planned. On the Hudson side, the 57th Street and 110th Street bridge proposals were pipedreams, as was a span between the Brooklyn Bridge and the Manhattan Bridge.

WHAT WE ARE COMING TO.
JUDGE'S COMBINATION APARTMENT-HOUSE OF THE FUTURE.

Grant E. Hamilton, *What We Are Coming To: Judge's Combination-Apartment House of the Future*, from *Judge*, February 16, 1895.

One of three leading satirical magazines in America (the others being *Life* and *Puck*), the Republican-leaning *Judge* would often produce comic commentary on the state of the city. One wonders if William Earle Dodge Stokes, the Upper West Side developer who built the turreted Ansonia Hotel, with its rooftop farm, soon after this cartoon was published, found inspiration here.

OPPOSITE

A. B. Walker, *Celestial Real Estate Company*, from *Life*, March 4, 1909.

Architect Rem Koolhaas was fascinated with this visionary cartoon from *Life*'s "Real Estate Number." It was, he raved in *Delirious New York*, "a theorem that describes the ideal performance of the Skyscraper: a slender steel structure supports 84 horizontal planes, all the size of the original plot. Each of these artificial levels is treated as a virgin site, as if the others did not exist, to establish a strictly private realm around a single country house and its attendant facilities, stable, servants' cottages, etc. . . .The building becomes a stack of individual privacies. Only five of the 84 platforms are visible; lower in the clouds other activities occupy remaining plots; the use of each platform can never be known in advance of its construction. Villas may go up and collapse, other facilities may replace them, but that will not affect the framework."

·LIFE·

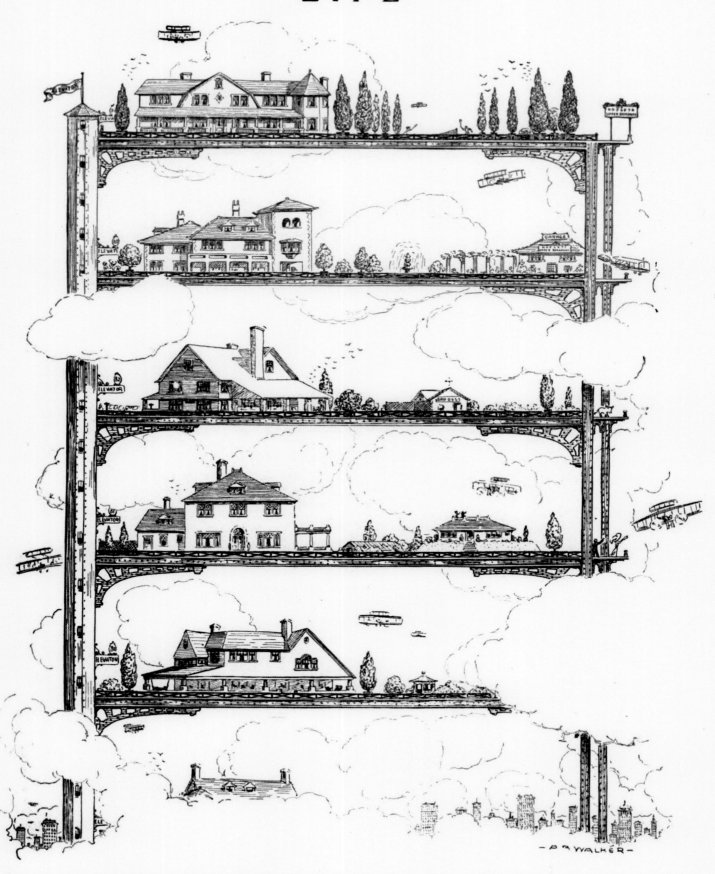

"BUY A COZY COTTAGE IN OUR STEEL CONSTRUCTED CHOICE LOTS, LESS THAN A MILE ABOVE BROADWAY. ONLY TEN MINUTES BY ELEVATOR. ALL THE COMFORTS OF THE COUNTRY WITH NONE OF ITS DISADVANTAGES."—*Celestial Real Estate Company.*

Grant E. Hamilton, *The Future Emigrant Lodging House*, from *Judge*, April 12, 1890.

In the 1890s, the anti-immigration nativist press frequently published cartoons using, and often debasing, the Statue of Liberty to defend traditional American values. In 1890, Bedloe's Island, home to the statue, along with Governor's Island and Ellis Island, were all proposed as potential sites for a new immigrant processing station to accommodate the influx of millions looking for a better future. Here, *Judge* magazine envisions the monument as an "International Tenement House," in a theme-park makeover packed with racist clichés. Instead, Ellis Island was chosen as the new site, and the following year the Immigration Act of 1891 passed, giving the Federal government control over immigration.

Walt McDougall, *The Journal's Suggestion to Greater New York*, from the *New York Journal and Advertiser*, October 24, 1897.

The Brooklyn Bridge is transformed into a festive capitalist spectacle in this front-page newspaper cartoon contemplating the corrupt monopolies of New York. The bridge originally had a cable-car system that carried commuters across, but by the 1890s, trolley companies in Brooklyn were pressing for trackage terminating on the Manhattan side, an immense political plum waiting to be plucked. Trolley service commenced in 1898, the year that the City of Greater New York came into being, but the bridge's majestic piers have been forever free of advertising.

THE FUTURE EMIGRANT LODGING HOUSE.

NO. 53. NEW YORK, SUNDAY, OCTOBER 24, 1897. Copyright, 1897, by W. R. Hearst.

THE JOURNAL'S SUGGESTION TO GREATER NEW YORK.

If the Trolley Companies Get the Right of Way, Why Not Give Other Companies a Chance?

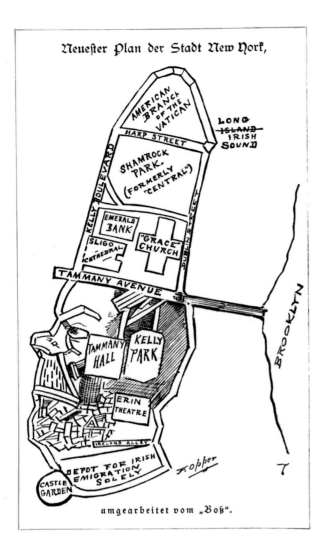

LEFT

Frederick Opper, *Neuester Plan der Stadt New Norf (Newest Plan for New York City)*, from *Puck* (German edition), November 24, 1880.

Frederick Opper's crude redrawing of Manhattan Island exploits German fears of Irish political clout, as the city fragmented into ethnic neighborhoods, each scratching for power. Foremost among Democratic Party "political machines" in American cities, New York's Tammany Hall played a major role in city and state politics, giving immigrants, most notably the Irish (after 1850 the great majority were Irish Catholics), a foothold in the power structure.

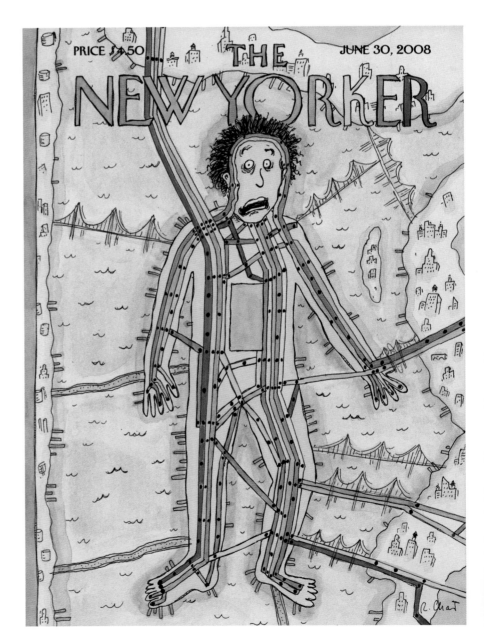

RIGHT

Roz Chast, *Subway Man*, cover for *The New Yorker*, June 30, 2008.

Cartoonist Roz Chast personifies the island as a terrified subway commuter, capturing the psychological dimension of the "difficult and costly" transportation system more realistically portrayed in the *Scientific American* precisely one hundred years earlier (see page 28).

J. Y. Pique, cover for *Park East: The Magazine of New York*, April 1951.

Spring is in the air and the boroughs come alive on this cover for *Park East* magazine, which, in chic tones, chronicled what was then anachronistically still called "the carriage trade." Like its competitor, the far more successful and substantive *New Yorker*, *Park East* used illustration on its covers.

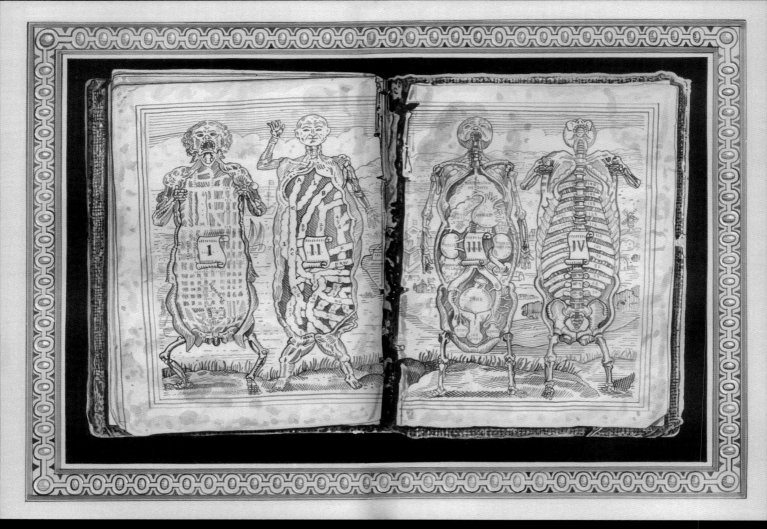

**Adam Dant, *Manhattan Dissected*, from his
Living Maps: An Atlas of Cities Personified, 2012.**

In a riff on Renaissance anatomy manuals, four gruesome corpses
representing the body of Manhattan are dissected to reveal different
systems: grid plan, subway, neighborhoods, and crosstown transit. "As
scientists, historians, and general gawkers dissect and schematically
map out the cadaver of the greatest city in the world," Adam Dant
wrote, "the wonder of seeing its construction revealed layer by layer
almost compensates for the fact that it is condemned to end up 'on the
slab' as a breathless pile of concrete and steel."

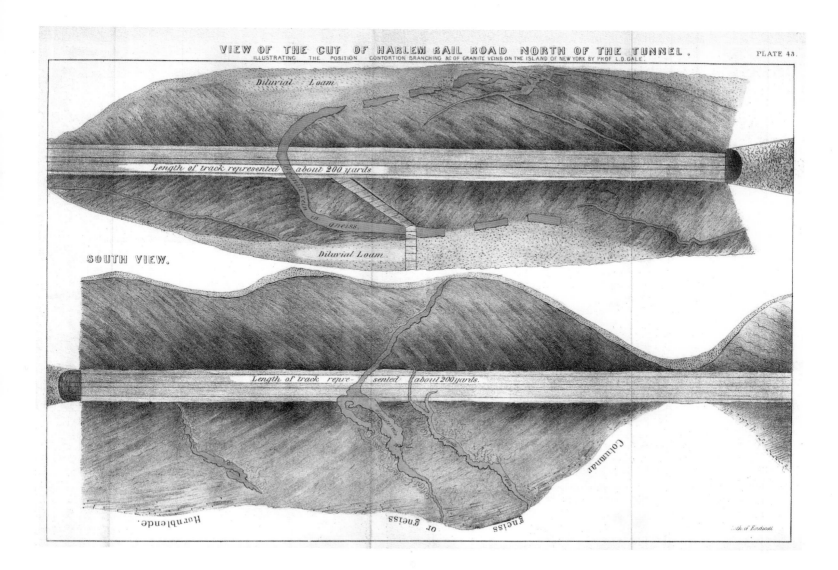

William Mather, *View of the Cut of Harlem Rail Road North of the Tunnel* and *South View*, from *Geology of New York* by James Hall, 1842.

When the Harlem Rail Road, running north along what would one day become Park Avenue, dug a tunnel under Yorkville from East 86th Street to East 96th Street in the late 1830s, the deep cuts at either end gave geologists in the late 1830s a clear view of the island's bedrock. Here, in a view from above, the cuts, crisscrossed by veins of granite and covered by a layer of loam, are flattened out, looking like nothing so much as two fish swimming across the sheet.

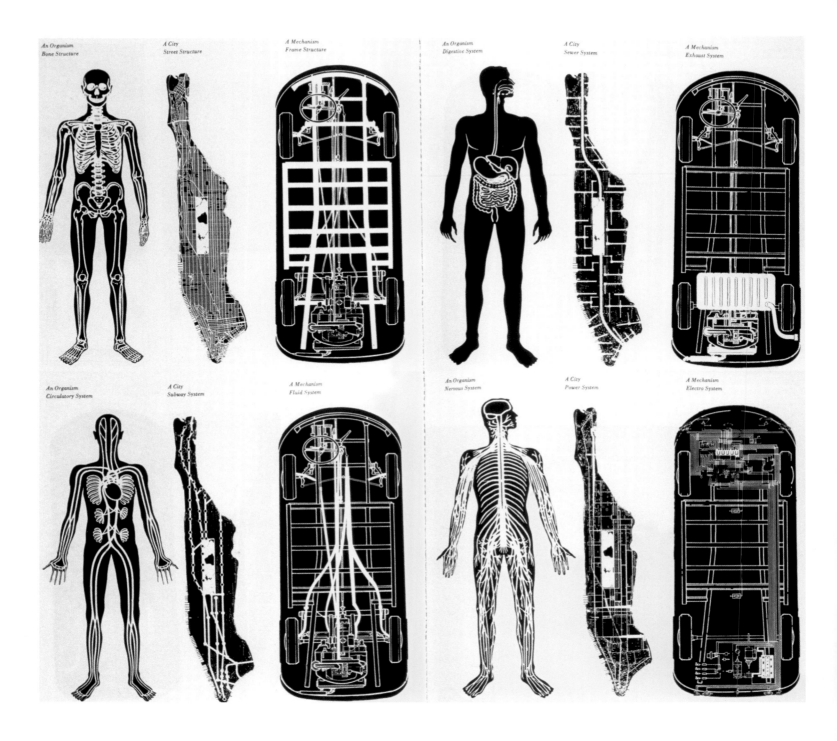

ABOVE

Oswald Mathias Ungers, *City Metaphors*, 1976.

Architect Oswald Mathias Ungers draws analogies between systems in the human body, the car, and the island of Manhattan. As he explained in his 1982 essay, "Designing and Thinking in Images Metaphors and Analogies," "Everyday language abounds in phrases and expressions of metaphorical character such as: straight from the horse's mouth, the tooth of time, or the tide of events, a forest of masts, the jungle of the city. Metaphors are transformations of an actual event into a figurative expression, evoking images by substituting an abstract notion for something more descriptive and illustrative."

OPPOSITE

Saul Steinberg, untitled drawing for *The New Yorker*, February 22–March 1, 1999.

Romanian-born artist Saul Steinberg was entranced by his adopted city. In this whimsical combination of hand mnemonics and palmistry, he gives you Manhattan in the palm of your hand.

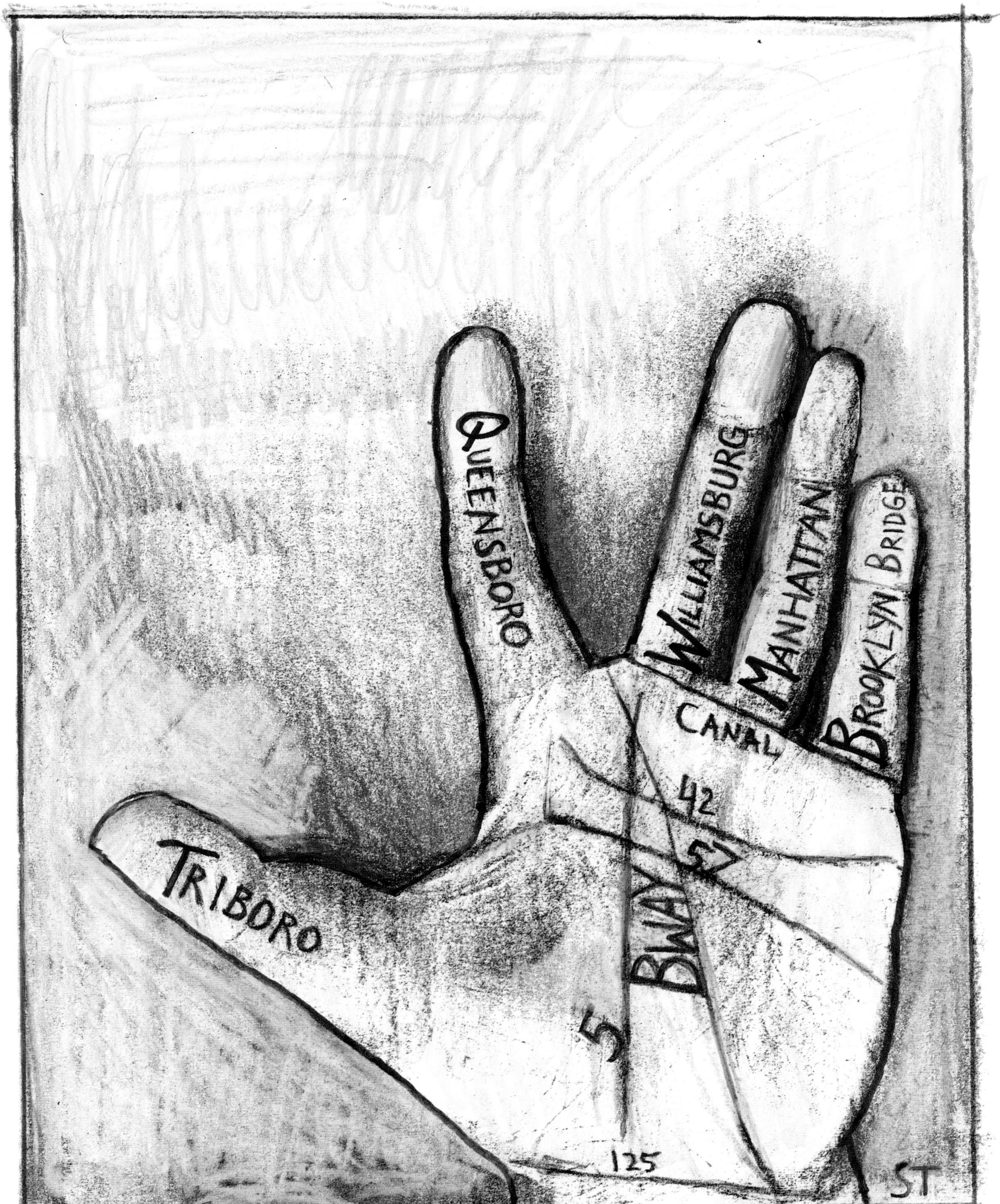
QUEENSBORO
WILLIAMSBURG
MANHATTAN
BROOKLYN BRIDGE
TRIBORO
CANAL
42
57
BWAY
BWAY
5
125
ST

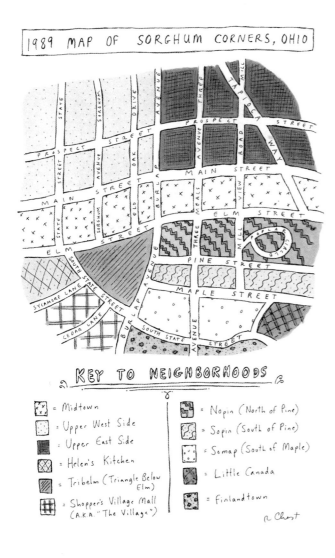

1989 MAP OF SORGHUM CORNERS, OHIO

KEY TO NEIGHBORHOODS

= Midtown
= Upper West Side
= Upper East Side
= Helen's Kitchen
= Tribelm (Triangle Below Elm)
= Shopper's Village Mall (A.K.A. "The Village")

= Nopin (North of Pine)
= Sopin (South of Pine)
= Somap (South of Maple)
= Little Canada
= Finlandtown

R. Chast

ABOVE

Roz Chast, *1989 Map of Sorghum Corners, Ohio*, 1988.
Chast brings big-city Manhattan neighborhood nomenclature to a fictional Ohio small town, in a parody mash-up of New York's acronym fever and rural clichés, with a playful use of the farm patterns often employed in maps.

RIGHT

Jonathan Wolstenholme, *London on the Hudson*, from *Punch*, August 18, 1989.
Another mash-up, this time of London and Manhattan, was accompanied by an irreverent text by Janet Abrams. Instead of Penn Station ("the second circle of hell") topped by Madison Square Garden, there was Wembley Stadium perched above Paddington Station. The Barbican Centre replaced Lincoln Center, "for opera, ballet and theatre in late-Mussolini-stripped-classical style architecture, hub of the chic condominium district." Nelson's Column stood in for the Statue of Liberty, while the British Museum played the New York Public Library. "Enter Bryant Park at your peril," advised Abrams.

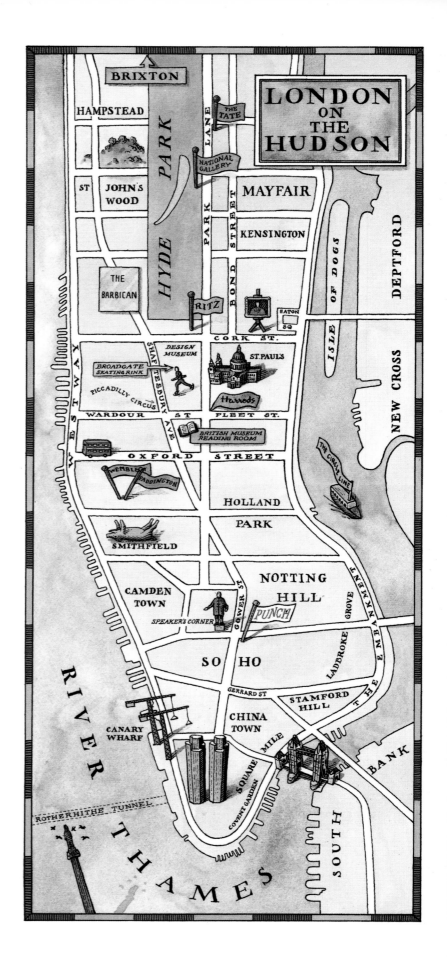

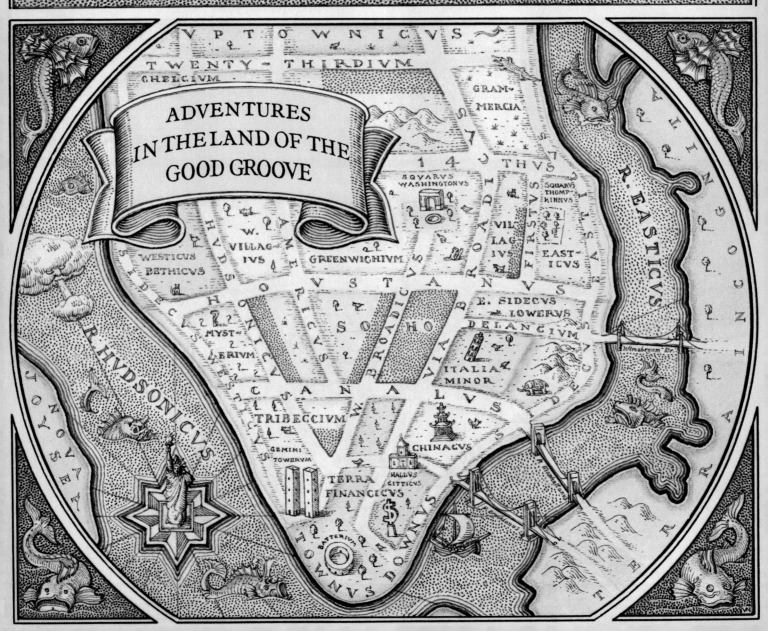

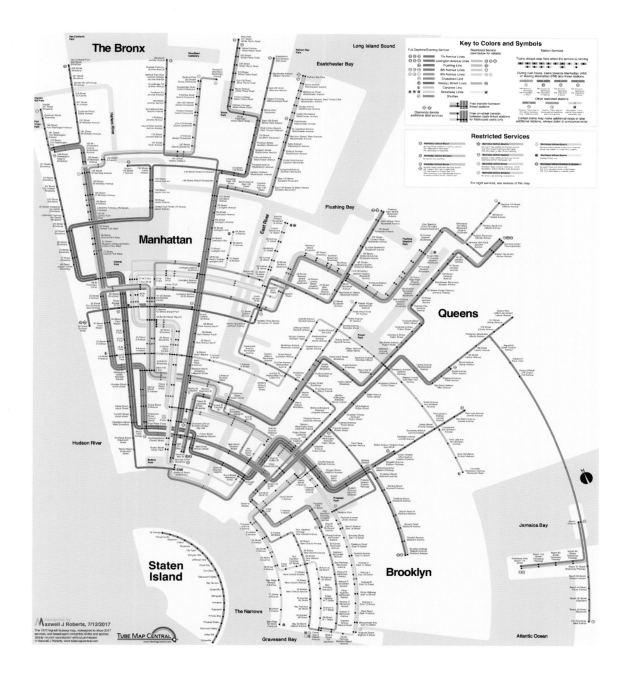

Triboro (David Heasty and Stefanie Weigler),
***Wrong Color Subway Map*, 2016.**

In 2009, David Heasty and Stefanie Weigler designed the "One-Color Subway Map": It was, in their words, a "graphic paradox," which broke new ground in subway wayfinding. In 2016, they one-upped themselves with the "Wrong Color Subway Map." Their hope: "We think through this project we have presented some interesting ideas that could inform a redesign of the M.T.A. map." Alas, the M.T.A. never called.

Maxwell J. Roberts, *New York Vignelli Circles*, 2017.

Among the many official maps of the New York subway system, the diagrammatic approach taken by Massimo Vignelli (working with Bob Noorda at Unimark International) in 1972 was the most impactful. Graphic designers loved it, but many New Yorkers were dismayed that the city's geography was so heavily abstracted. A psychologist and cartographer, Maxwell J. Roberts took Vignelli's approach to one logical conclusion: He retained the typography, but tidied up the designer's abstracted geography into a neat semicircle. "New York shouldn't work in this style at all," Roberts noted, "it is a grid city, not a radial city, and you can see which parts I got into a fight with, but overall it is quite striking. Diagram purists (such as Vignelli fans) will love it, geographical purists will be after my blood!"

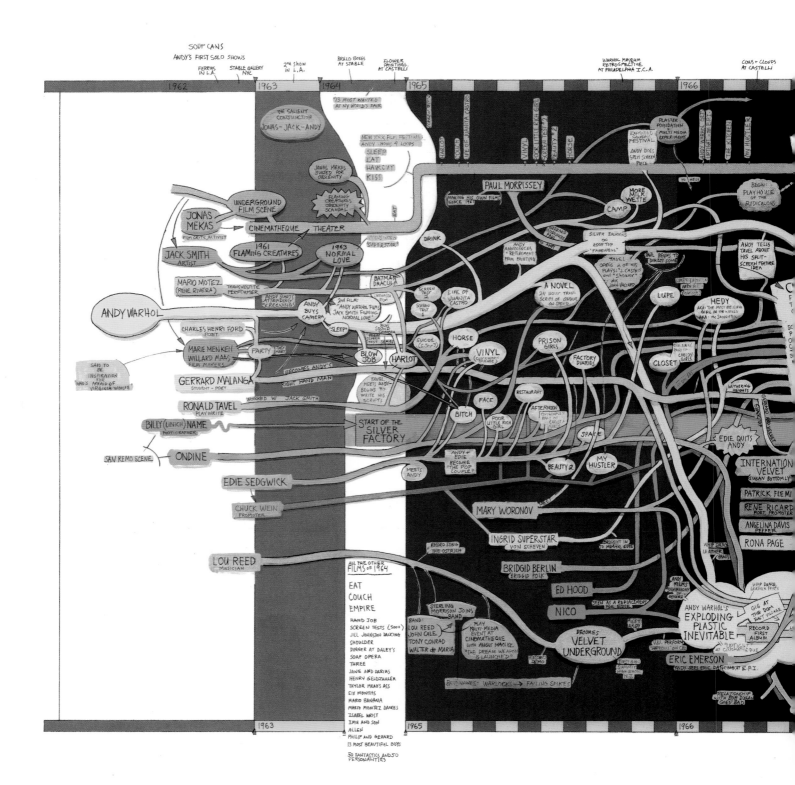

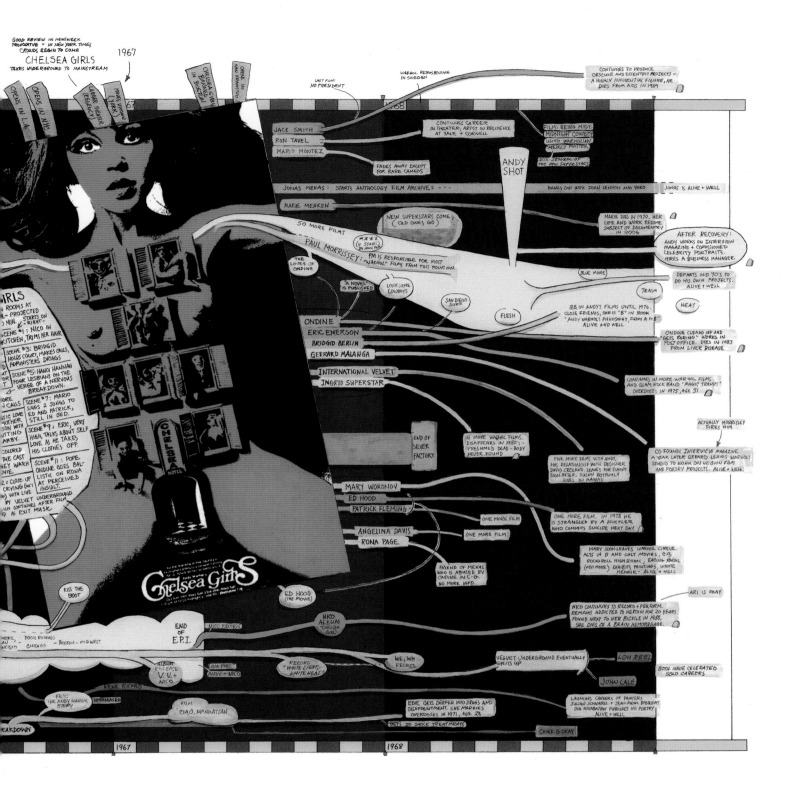

ABOVE

Ward Shelley, *Andy Warhol-Chelsea Girls, ver. 1*, 2008.

The Warholian universe unfurls in this 1960s timeline, centered around the artist's film *Chelsea Girls* and mapping his vast network of collaborators. Lifelines crisscross and tangle, to merge on the film's poster. "My paintings/drawings are attempts to use real information to depict our understandings of how things evolve and relate to one another," Ward Shelley writes. "They are 'wide-screen,' with all [the] information available to the interacting eye at every moment."

FOLLOWING SPREAD

Ward Shelley, *Downtown Body, ver. 1*, 2008.

Here Shelley tackles a bigger subject: The story of New York's Downtown-based avant-garde unfolds over a tumultuous century in a tour de force of narrative painting.

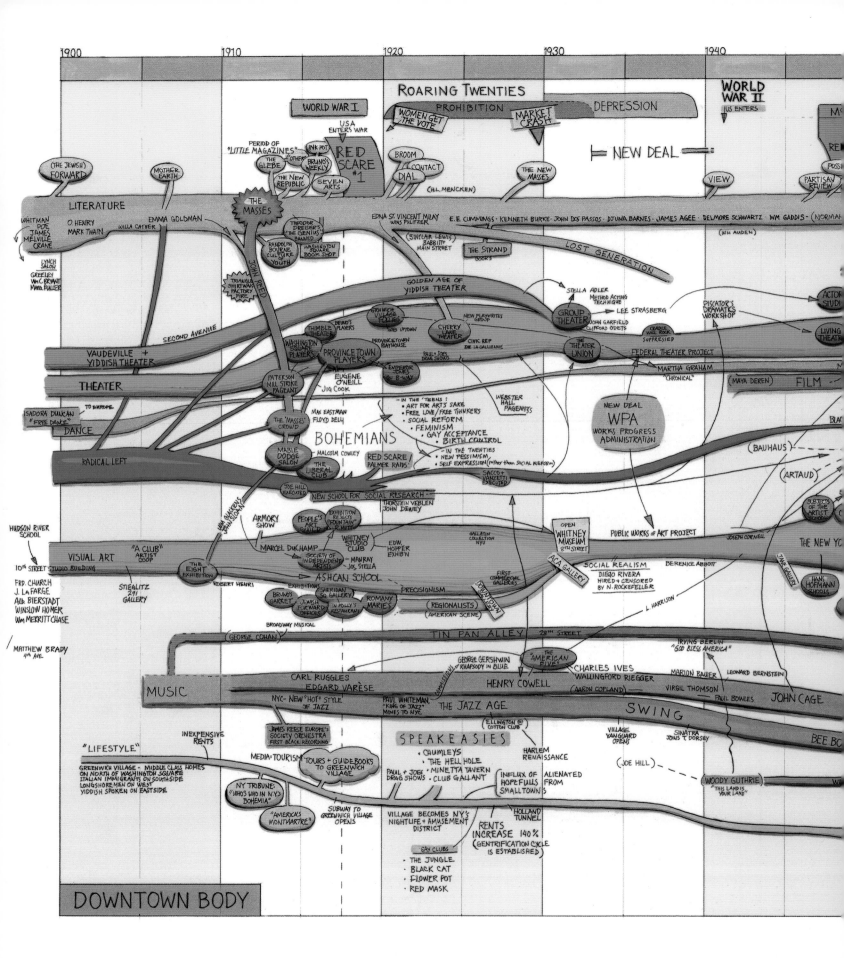

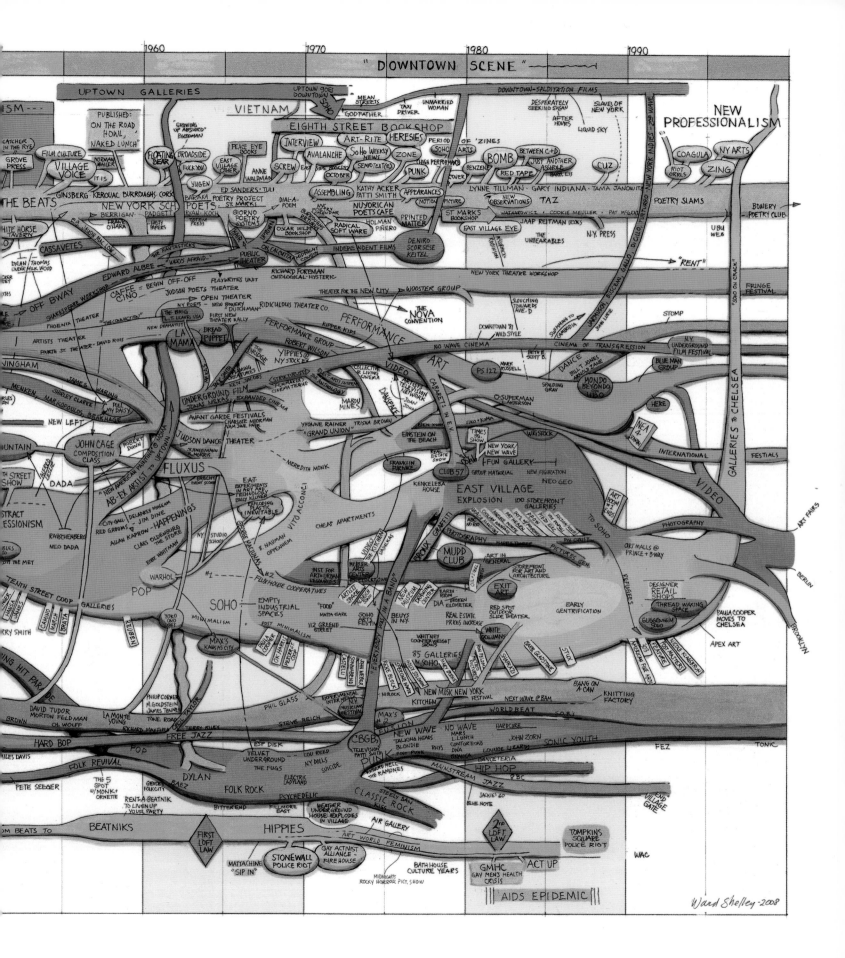

PHILIP
JOHNSON
1961

RICHARD
MEIER

FRANK
GEHRY

PHILIP
JOHNSON
1961

TOP

Steven Guarnaccia, *The Empire's New Clothes*, from *SPY*, May 1991.

Architect Philip Johnson wielded enormous influence on the selection of architects for major New York building projects in the 1980s. Here, in an exercise in counterfactual illustration, Steven Guarnaccia offers an all-star postmodernist roster of Johnsonian choices for an alternative Empire State Building.

RIGHT

Thomas Nast, *New York in a Few Years from Now. View from the Bay*, from *Harper's Weekly*, August 27, 1881.

When the premier American editorial cartoonist Thomas Nast drew this illustration, Trinity Church's spire, at 281 feet, was the tallest structure in Manhattan. Nast's vision of densely packed, stretched-out buildings in the architectural styles of the period, dwarfing the church, predates the term "skyscraper"— first used in 1893 by *Harper's Weekly*—by more than a decade.

OPPOSITE

Winsor McCay, *What Cities Will Rise?* from the *Chicago Herald Examiner*, February 19, 1928.

The great poet of the comic strip Winsor McCay takes aim at Manhattan's real-estate boom in an image that magically conjures the island's idyllic past, prosaic present, and terrifying future.

whomever he pleased was the Empire State Building—it was finished in 1931, just as the precocious
nson's mood, the building might have looked like this:

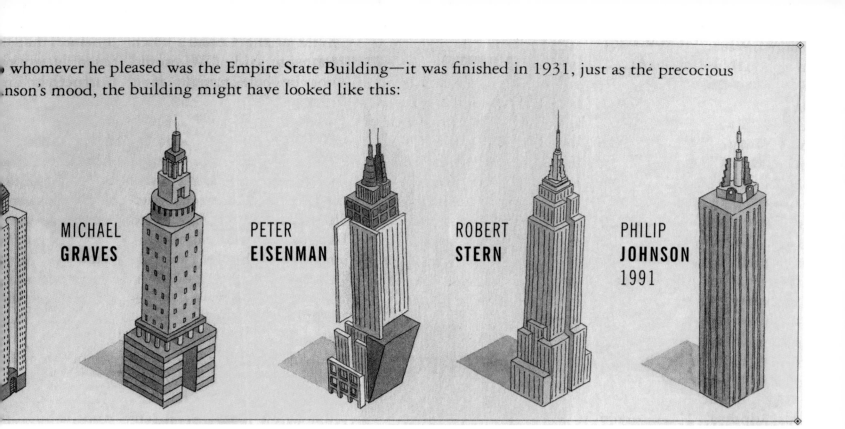

MICHAEL
GRAVES

PETER
EISENMAN

ROBERT
STERN

PHILIP
JOHNSON
1991

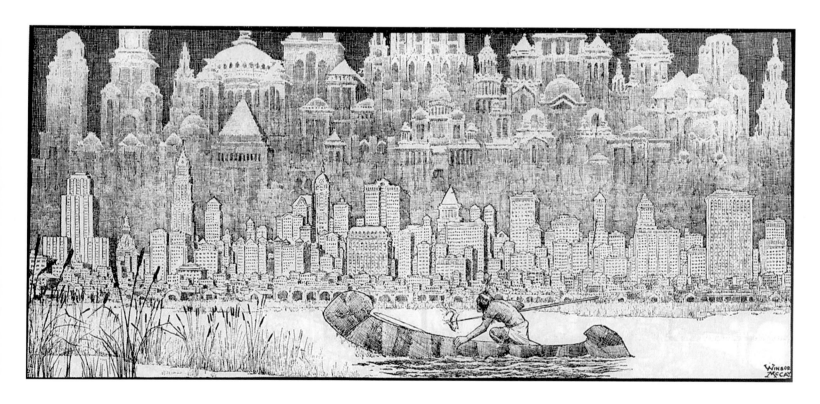

OPPOSITE

Richard McGuire, *Time Warp*, cover for *The New Yorker*, November 24, 2014.

Crossing a Manhattan avenue into several temporal dimensions at once, the bearded Richard McGuire looks quizzically out at the viewer. "As I walk around the city, I'm time-travelling, flashing forward, planning what it is I have to do," he said. "Then I have a sudden flashback to a remembered conversation, but I notice a plaque on a building commemorating a famous person who once lived there, and for a second I'm imagining them opening the door."

RIGHT

Julia Wertz, *Four Decades of CBGB & OMFUG at 315 Bowery in Manhattan*, from her *Tenements, Towers & Trash: An Unconventional Illustrated History of New York City*, 2017.

Like a god come down to Earth to inhabit a mortal body, CBGB, the spiritual home of American Punk Rock, endows an ordinary New York building with a fleeting aura of immortality. "I'm trying to show people a different way to engage with the city as they walk through it," Julia Wertz said.

FOLLOWING SPREAD

Giorgia Lupi, *Mondrian Abstract Paintings*, 2013.

A champion of using data visualization to further our understanding of humanistic projects, Giorgia Lupi created a visual timeline of the evolution of shapes, sizes, colors, and techniques in Mondrian's paintings, culminating in the pixelated visual jazz of the artist's paean to New York City, *Broadway Boogie Woogie*. The chart is surprisingly resonant with the transformation of Manhattan from an organic to an orthogonal physical environment.

Mondrian's abstract paintings

The visualization explores the evolution of Mondrian's abstract paintings over the years. Visualized for each painting are the main shapes (e.g., line types, line features, shape features), the relative canvas size, the main colors, and the painting technique.

total artistic production

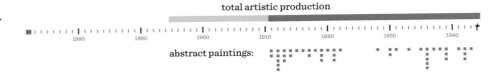

abstract paintings:

1. *Landscape with Trees*

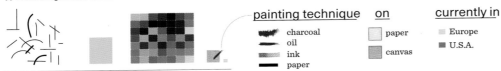

painting technique
- charcoal
- oil
- ink
- paper

on
- paper
- canvas

currently in
- Europe
- U.S.A.

visual features size
main shapes and line types

color palette
built dividing the canvas in 49 cells, with each cell is colored according to the prevalent color for that area of the painting

2. *Still Life with Ginger Jar I*

8. *Tableau III*

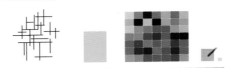

14. *Composition*

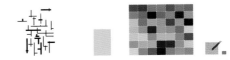

3. *Self-Portrait*

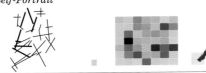

9. *Oval Composition*

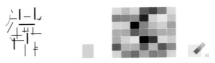

15. *Composition in Color A*

4. *Apple Tree in Flower*

10. *Church at Damburg*

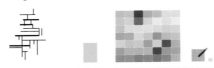

16. *Composition with Color Planes No. 3*

5. *The Grey Tree*

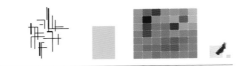

11. *Composition No. 6*

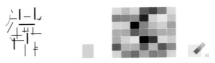

17. *Lozenge with Grey Lines*

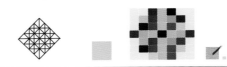

6. *Trees in Blossom*

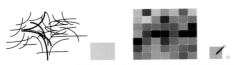

12. *Composition No. 9, Blue Façade*

18. *Composition: Checkerboard, Dark Colors*

7. *Composition Trees II*

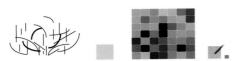

13. *Composition No. 10 (Pier and Ocean)*

19. *Composition: Light Color Planes with Grey Contours*

20. *Composition: Light Color Planes with Grey Lines*

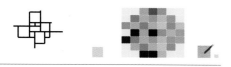

21. *Composition with Red, Blue and Yellowish-Green*

22. *Composition*

23. *Tableau I*

24. *Composition with Red, Yellow, Blue and Black*

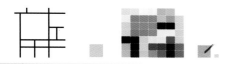

25. *Composition 2*

26. *Composition with Red, Yellow and Blue*

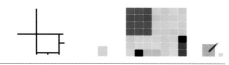

27. *Composition II with Black Lines*

28. *Composition with Blue, Red and Yellow*

29. *Composition with Two Lines*

30. *Composition with Yellow Lines*

31. *Composition with Red and Grey*

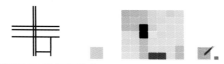

32. *Composition with Red and Blue*

33. *Vertical Composition with Blue and White*

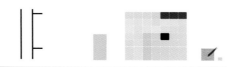

34. *Composition III with Blue, Yellow and White*

35. *Composition with Red*

36. *Composition with Red and Black*

37. *Composition with Blue*

38. *Composition with White, Red and Yellow*

39. *Composition*

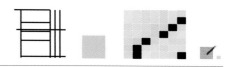

40. *Composition with Red, Yellow and Blue*

41. *Composition with Black, White, Yellow and Red*

42. *New York, New York*

43. *New York City I*

44. *New York City II*

45. *Broadway Boogie-Woogie*

46. *Victory Boogie-Woogie (unfinished)*

1973 NOVEMBER 1973

SUN	MON	TUE	WED	THU	FRI	SAT
First Quar. 3rd	Full Moon 10th	Last Quar. 17th	New Moon 24th	OFF 1	2	ON 3
4	5	6	7	8	9	10
11	12	13	14	15	16	17
18	19	20	21	22	23	24
25	26	27	28	29	30	

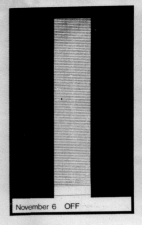

November 6 OFF   November 7 ON

Proposal for Manhattan Skyline   World Trade Center - Evening   Allan Wexler

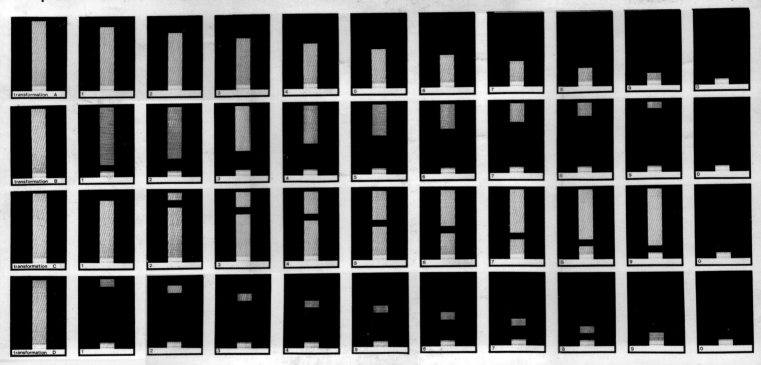

Allan Wexler, *Proposal for the Manhattan Skyline, World Trade Center*, 1973 and 1976.

The year artist Allan Wexler moved to New York City, the World Trade Center was nearing completion, and the towers' vast facades struck him as blank canvases waiting to be filled. "I am interested in simple solutions that make a big impact," he said, "so I proposed the redesign of the surfaces of the towers using only the light switches, the window shades, and the labor of the cleaning staff. Each evening the cleaning person consults a calendar positioned at each window of the building to determine if a light is to be left on or a window shade adjusted. ON/OFF—the binary system in operation."

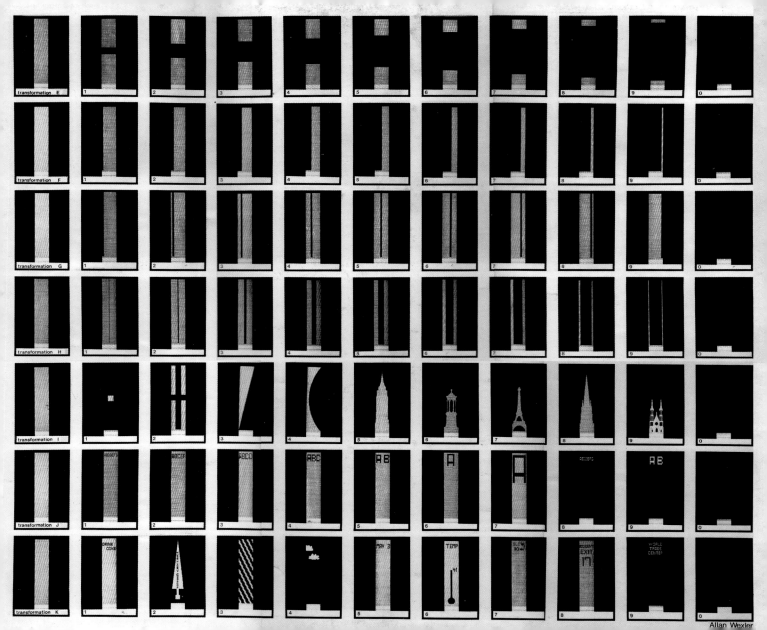

transformation E

transformation F

transformation G

transformation H

transformation I

transformation J

transformation K

Allan Wexler

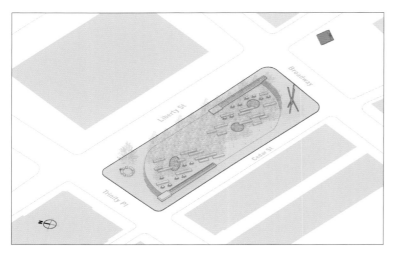

Zuccotti Park on September 15, 2011, prior to the occupation. Base axonometric, showing layout of park furniture and trees.

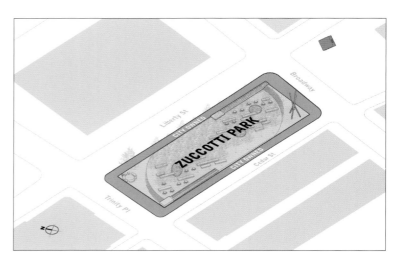

Property lines, September 15, 2011.

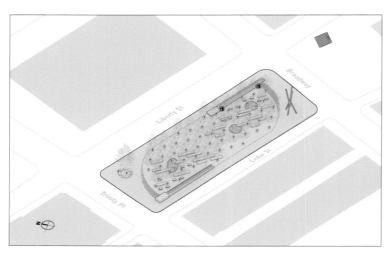

Water and power outlets, September 15, 2011.

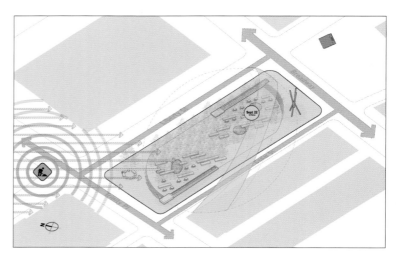

Climate overlay, September 22, 2011.

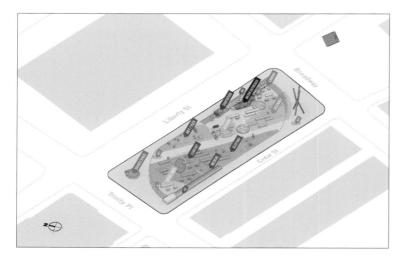

Functional zoning plan, October 14, 2011.

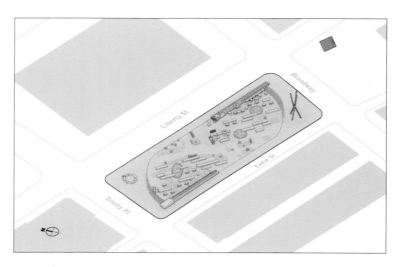

Operations plan, October 14, 2011. Illustration shows the kitchen, medic tent, desks, tarps and bins, drumming areas, Freedom Tower Wi-Fi, information tables, schedule, sandwich board, sanitation station.

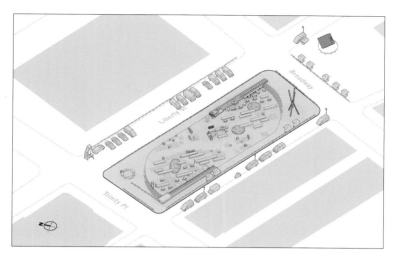

Composite operations plan, October 14, 2011. Showing food trucks, media vans, barricades, and police vehicles.

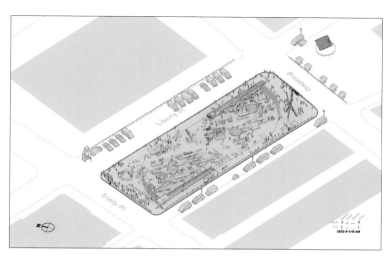

Activity plan, October 22, 2011. Shows participants standing, sitting and sleeping throughout the park.

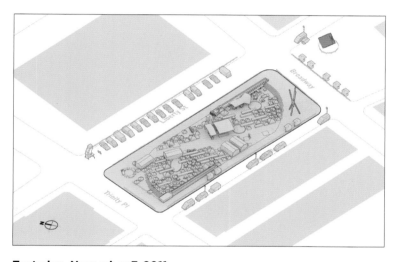

Tent plan, November 7, 2011.

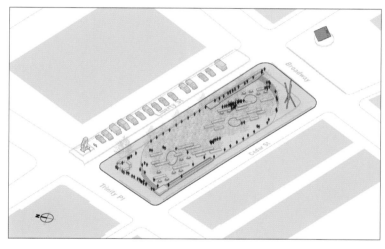

Post-Occupation Plan, November 15, 2011. After police evicted protesters and barricaded the park.

Jonathan Massey and Brett Snyder, *Mapping Liberty Plaza Diagrams*, 2012. Research and visualization assistance from Andrew Weigand and Grant D. Foster.

For two months in the fall of 2011, activists of the Occupy Wall Street movement seized the block-sized Zuccotti Park in Lower Manhattan in protest against economic inequality. Here, wrote Jonathan Massey and Brett Snyder, maps drawn at six points in time, "track the transformation of a staid corporate plaza into a testing ground for radical ideas about the reorganization of state and society."

CHAPTER TWO

THE

BIGGEST

APPLE

"**THERE ARE EIGHT MILLION STORIES IN THE NAKED CITY,**" famously utters the narrator of director Jules Dassin's 1948 noir police drama of the same name. The film's tagline, "The Most Exciting Story of the World's Most Exciting City!" suggests Manhattan's outsized reputation and the bragging rights that come with it. No other major metropolis comes close. New York's architectural marvels, cultural genius, technological sophistication, and human buoyancy are seen in many diagrammatical forms— all grandiose in one way or another. *Manhattan Superlatives* (page 67) claims that "every block of the Manhattan grid is unique, of course, but some rise above the rest." Individual blocks have characters and personalities, like Park and Lex at East 71st–72nd Streets, dubbed "Most Likely to Succeed" on account of its population of wealthy people, and 10th–11th Avenues at West 25th–26th Streets, labeled the "Most Artistic" thanks to "its grid-leading 49 galleries."

Scale is a guidepost. One of the most incredible (if kind of frightening) perspectives could be found in the *Scientific American* in 1907, where C. McKnight-Smith drew the New York skyline relative to the heights of Victoria Falls and Niagara Falls (opposite and page 70). Diagrams like this scenario for a disaster movie were intended to provide a satisfying jolt of terror.

If nature was the only adequate measure for Manhattan, then Manhattan, which set its own standard for man-made scale, could itself become a measure for other things in quirky comparative diagrams. In 1903, the editors of *Scientific American* believed that it would be enlightening for the reader to visualize the value of books and periodicals printed in the United States as being equal to a solid silver column almost as tall as the Statue of Liberty (page 73). Six years later, Beverly Towles drew a diagram in the same periodical that used New York buildings as scale markers dropped surrealistically into glass containers that represented the amount of glass used for different purposes in the national economy (page 72). Perhaps the magazine's most imaginative diagram, in 1912, sought to visually convey "the enormous quantities of material handled in building the Panama Canal" by showing a row of sixty-three pyramids equal in bulk to the Great Pyramid of Egypt stretching from the Battery to Harlem (page 71).

In 1910, in the face of a regional drought, the *New-York Tribune* asked, "How Much Water Can Gotham Afford to Give to Thirsty Neighbors?" (page 75). The diagram accompanying this serious question amusingly calibrates Manhattan's daily water consumption (510,000,000 gallons) as filling up Fifth Avenue from Washington Square to the Harlem River. Equally surreal was "The Great New York Octopus—Politics on Manhattan Island" from *Harper's Weekly,* which showed how the monstrous Democratic machine of 1877 had its tentacles in every facet of city infrastructure. In this last example, the comparative scale portrayed was purely symbolic, as was the octopus (page 80).

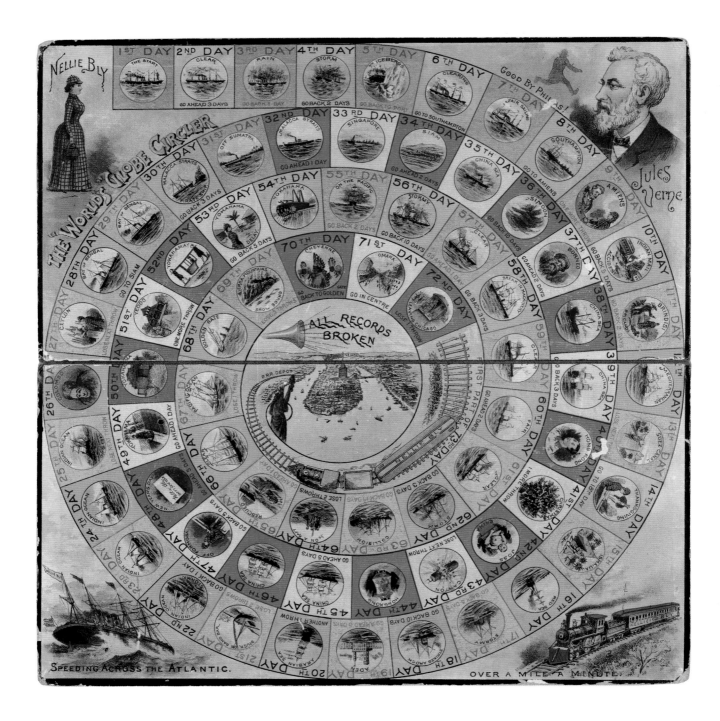

ABOVE

Round the World with Nellie Bly, 1890.

Intrepid journalist Nellie Bly's seventy-three–day trip around the
world in 1889–1890 was inspired by Jules Verne's *Around the World
in 80 Days* and sponsored by Joseph Pulitzer's *New York World*, which
created a board game so that readers could experience it vicariously.
A spiral timeline maps the places, means of transportation, setbacks,
and events—like meeting Jules Verne in Amiens, France (see "9th day"
on the squares)—of Bly's real race against both the fictional Phileas
Fogg and competing reporter Elizabeth Bisland of *Cosmopolitan* magazine. Manhattan and the Statue of Liberty stand at the center of this
whirlwind adventure as symbols of a grand victory.

OPPOSITE

**Distance & Direction of Various Places from New York as
Measured upon the Surface of the Artificial Globe**, from
**Comprehensive Atlas Geographical, Historical & Commercial
by Thomas G. Bradford, 1835.**

The globe as a spoked wheel with New York as its hub.

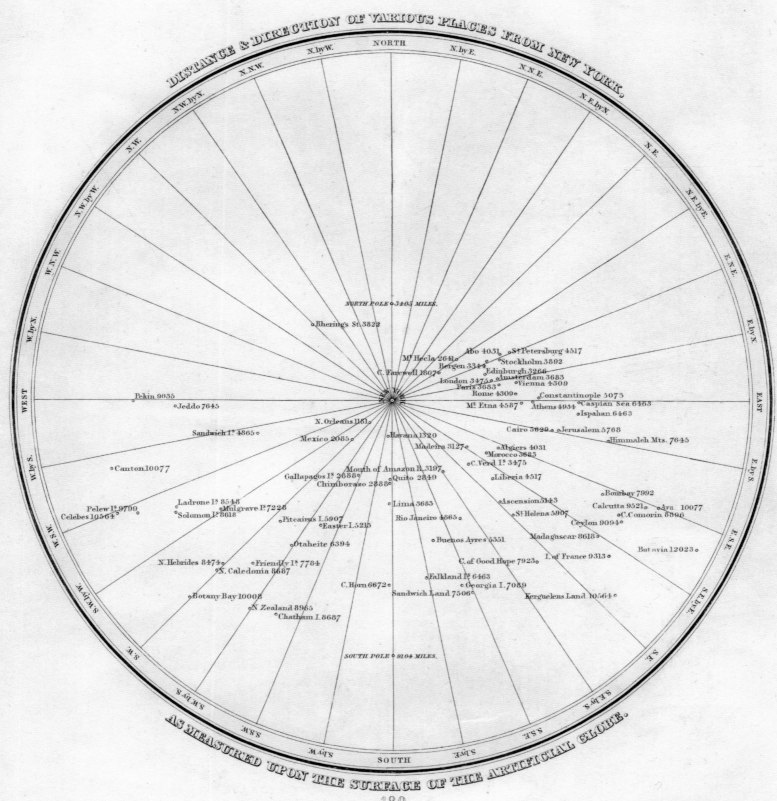

DISTANCE & DIRECTION OF VARIOUS PLACES FROM NEW YORK, AS MEASURED UPON THE SURFACE OF THE ARTIFICIAL GLOBE.

NORTH

NORTH POLE ○ 3407 MILES.

○ Bhering's St. 3822

Mt Hecla 2641 ○   Abo 4031 ○   ○ St Petersburg 4517
Bergen 3344 ○   ○ Stockholm 3892
C. Farewell 1807 ○   Edinburgh 3266 ○
London 3475 ○   ○ Amsterdam 3683
Paris 3683 ○   ○ Vienna 4309
Rome 4309 ○   ○ Constantinople 5073
Pekin 9035 ○   Mt Etna 4587 ○   Athens 4934 ○   ○ Caspian Sea 6463
○ Jeddo 7645   ○ Ispahan 6463

N. Orleans 1161 ○   Cairo 5629 ○ ○ Jerusalem 5768
Sandwich Is 4865 ○   Havana 1320 ○   ○ Himmaleh Mts. 7645
Mexico 2085 ○   Madeira 3127 ○   Algiers 4031 ○
Morocco 3683 ○
○ C. Verd Is 3475
Canton 10077 ○   Mouth of Amazon R. 3197 ○   ○ Liberia 4517
Gallapagos Is 2688 ○ ○ Quito 2849   Bombay 7992 ○
Chimborazo 2888 ○   Ascension 5143 ○   Calcutta 9521 ○   ○ Ava 10077
Ladrone Is 8548 ○   Lima 3683 ○   St Helena 5907 ○   ○ C. Comorin 8596
Pelew Is 9799 ○   Mulgrave Is 7228 ○   Ceylon 9094 ○
Celebes 10564 ○   ○ Solomon Is 8618   Rio Janeiro 4865 ○   Madagascar 8618 ○
Pitcairns I. 5907 ○   Batavia 12023 ○
○ Easter I. 5213   Buenos Ayres 5351 ○
Otaheite 6394 ○   ○ I. of France 9313
N. Hebrides 8474 ○   ○ Friendly Is 7784   C. of Good Hope 7923 ○
○ N. Caledonia 8687   Falkland Is 6463 ○
Botany Bay 10008 ○   C. Horn 6672 ○   ○ Georgia I. 7089   Kerguelens Land 10564 ○
○ N. Zealand 8965   Sandwich Land 7506 ○
○ Chatham I. 8687

SOUTH POLE ○ 9104 MILES.

SOUTH

180

The BUSIEST HOUR ON EARTH

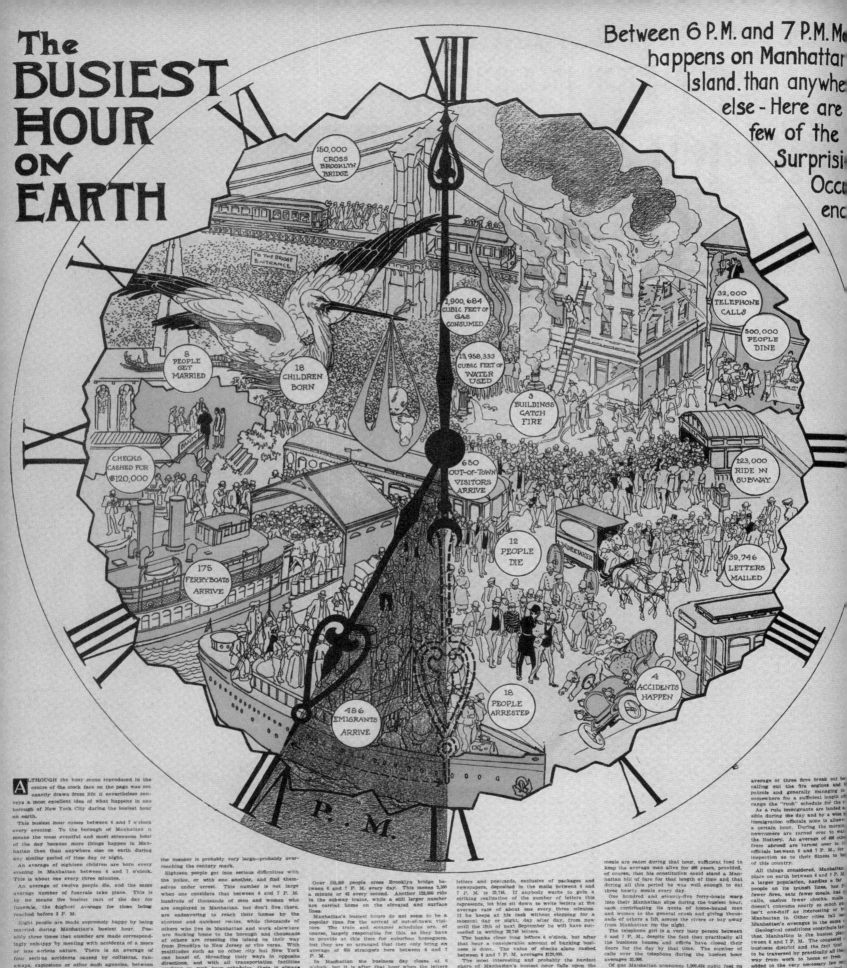

Between 6 P.M. and 7 P.M. Mo... happens on Manhattan Island, than anywhe... else - Here are ... few of the ... Surprisi... Occu... eno...

Labels in illustration:

150,000 CROSS BROOKLYN BRIDGE

TO THE BRIDGE ENTRANCE

1,900,684 CUBIC FEET OF GAS CONSUMED

13,958,333 CUBIC FEET OF WATER USED

3 BUILDINGS CATCH FIRE

32,000 TELEPHONE CALLS

500,000 PEOPLE DINE

8 PEOPLE GET MARRIED

18 CHILDREN BORN

650 OUT-OF-TOWN VISITORS ARRIVE

123,000 RIDE IN SUBWAY

CHECKS CASHED FOR $120,000

12 PEOPLE DIE

UNDERTAKER

39,746 LETTERS MAILED

175 FERRYBOATS ARRIVE

18 PEOPLE ARRESTED

4 ACCIDENTS HAPPEN

486 EMIGRANTS ARRIVE

P. M.

ALTHOUGH the busy scene reproduced in the centre of the clock face on the page was not exactly drawn from life it nevertheless conveys a most excellent idea of what happens in one borough of New York City during the busiest hour on earth.

This busiest hour comes between 6 and 7 o'clock every evening. To the borough of Manhattan it means the most eventful and most strenuous hour of the day because more things happen in Manhattan then than anywhere else on earth during any similar period of time day or night.

An average of eighteen children are born every evening in Manhattan between 6 and 7 o'clock. This is about one every three minutes.

An average of twelve people die, and the same average number of funerals take place. This is by no means the busiest part of the day for funerals, the highest average for them being reached before 2 P. M.

Eight people are made supremely happy by being married during Manhattan's busiest hour. Possibly three times that number are made correspondingly unhappy by meeting with accidents of a more or less serious nature. There is an average of four serious accidents caused by collisions, runaways, explosions or other such agencies, between 6 and 7 P. M. every day. There is no record of the number of small accidents which occur, but as this is the busiest hour of the whole twenty-four the number is probably very large—probably over-reaching the century mark.

Eighteen people get into serious difficulties with the police, or with one another, and find themselves under arrest. This number is not large when one considers that between 6 and 7 P. M. hundreds of thousands of men and women who are employed in Manhattan, but don't live there, are endeavoring to reach their homes by the shortest and quickest routes, while thousands of others who live in Manhattan and work elsewhere are flocking home to the borough and thousands of others are crossing the island on their way from Brooklyn to New Jersey or vice versa. With multitudes such as no other city but New York can boast of, threading their ways in opposite directions, and with all transportation facilities working on rush hour schedules, there is always sure to be more or less confusion. And confusion sometimes leads to contradictions and contradictions to conflicts and conflicts to incarceration.

Over 150,000 people cross Brooklyn bridge between 6 and 7 P. M. every day. This means 2,500 a minute or 42 every second. Another 123,000 ride in the subway trains, while a still larger number are carried home on the elevated and surface lines.

Manhattan's busiest hours do not seem to be a popular time for the arrival of out-of-town visitors. The train and steamer schedules are, of course, largely responsible for this, as they have to provide at this time for suburban homegoers, but they are so arranged that they only bring an average of 650 strangers here between 6 and 7 P. M.

In Manhattan the business day closes at 6 o'clock, but it is after that hour when the letters written, addressed and stamped during the day are turned over to the postal authorities to be forwarded to their destinations. The total number of letters and postcards, exclusive of packages and newspapers, deposited in the mails between 6 and 7 P. M. is 39,746. If anybody wants to gain a striking realization of the number of letters this represents, let him sit down to write letters at the average rate of about one every three minutes. If he keeps at his task without stopping for a moment day or night, day after day, from now until the 10th of next September he will have succeeded in writing 39,746 letters.

The banks close long before 6 o'clock, but after that hour a considerable amount of banking business is done. The value of checks alone cashed between 6 and 7 P. M. averages $120,000.

The most interesting and probably the hardest share of Manhattan's busiest hour falls upon the transportation lines and the restaurants and hotels.

Everybody seems to want to eat between 6 and 7 P. M. In Manhattan Borough alone half a million meals are eaten during that hour, sufficient food to keep the average man alive for 466 years, provided, of course, that his constitution could stand a Manhattan bill of fare for that length of time and that during all this period he was well enough to eat three hearty meals every day.

One hundred and seventy-five ferry-boats warp into their Manhattan slips during the busiest hour, each contributing its quota of home-bound men and women to the general crush and giving thousands of others a lift across the rivers or bay away from Manhattan for the night.

The telephone girl is a very busy person between 6 and 7 P. M., despite the fact that practically all the business houses and offices have closed their doors for the day by that time. The number of calls over the telephone during the busiest hour averages 32,000.

Of gas Manhattan consumes 1,900,684 cubic feet on an average between 6 and 7. The water consumption averages 13,958,333 cubic feet.

To add to the busy appearance of the island an average of three fires break out be... calling out the fire engines and ... patrols and generally managing to ... somewhere for a sufficient length of ... range the "rush" schedule for the ...

As a rule immigrants are landed ... sible during the day and by a wise ... immigration officials none is allow... a certain hour. During the morni... newcomers are turned over to wa... the Battery. An average of 486 oth... from abroad are turned over to th... officials between 6 and 7 P. M., for ... inspection as to their fitness to be ... of this country.

All things considered, Manhatta... place on earth between 6 and 7 P. M... a larger population, handles a far ... people on its transit lines, has f... fewer fires, eats fewer meals, has ... calls, cashes fewer checks, mails ... doesn't consume nearly so much ... isn't one-half as interesting or b... Manhattan is. Other cities call M... Manhattan's averages in the same ...

Geological conditions contribute ... that Manhattan is the busiest ... tween 6 and 7 P. M. The congest... business district and the fact that ... way from work to home or from ... added to the very necessary fro... every ferry and railroad terminal ... to the borough's strenuosity and ... pearance.

NEW YORK'S FINEST HOUR 6-7PM

The Busiest Hour on Earth, from The World Magazine, June 17, 1906.

Novelist Nicholson Baker and his wife, Margaret Brentano, rescued a rare collection of Joseph Pulitzer's *Sunday World* magazines, and published a selection of treasures from it in their book, *The World on Sunday*, including this gem: "An hour of Manhattan life on a clock face: Eighteen children are born, brought in by a stork at ten o'clock, and eighteen people are arrested, walked off the street by a policeman at five o'clock. One hundred and seventy-five ferryboats arrive in a jammed terminal at eight o'clock, and five hundred thousand people dine in a cutaway upstairs restaurant shortly after two o'clock. In the shadow of the hour hand, between six and seven o'clock, 486 immigrants arrive."

Seymour Chwast, *New York's Finest Hour, 6–7 PM*, 2005.

Thirty-two children born, forty-six emails sent, three buildings catch fire, seventy-eight planes land, and so on and so forth.

Life's Three Biggest Moments as New York City Experiences Them, from The Evening World, August 1, 1921.

A marriage every six minutes and thirty-nine seconds, a birth every three minutes, a death every seven minutes.

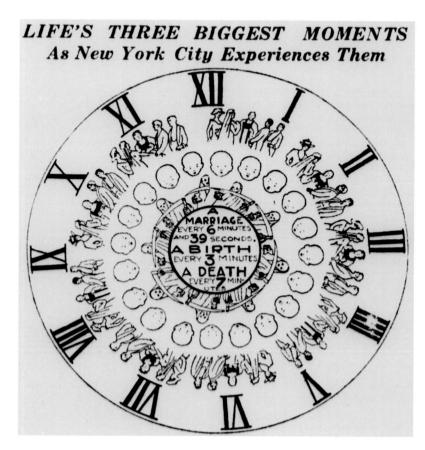

LIFE'S THREE BIGGEST MOMENTS
As New York City Experiences Them

MARRIAGE
EVERY 6 MINUTES
AND 39 SECONDS.
A BIRTH
EVERY 3 MINUTES
A DEATH
EVERY 7 MIN-
UTES

In This Number:
A BAROMETER
FOR THE BLUES.

The World Magazine
SECTION

For the Week of
SUNDAY, JANUARY 20, 1907.
(Copyright, 1907, by the Press Publishing
Company, New York World.)

How Far Can New York Climb Into the Sky?

"FURTHEST SKYWARD"
IN THE METROPOLIS.

This composite picture shows the evolution of the New York skyscraper from the first, the 60-foot Fraunces's Tavern of 1853, to the newest, the 658-foot, 46-story Metropolitan Building.

Drawn Especially for
the Sunday World by
LOUIS BIEDERMANN.

The 100-Story Building Possible and Probable.

By EDWARD S. MURPHY, Superintendent of Buildings.

THERE is no legal limit to the height of buildings now, and, so far as I can see, there is no need for any such limit. Just so long as builders comply with all the regulations of the department controlling the size and depth of the foundations they can go on raising their structures in the air until they more than double their present height.

The 100-story building I believe to be not only possible, but practicable. Certainly on all grounds of safety there will not be any objection to a structure of that height.

To prophesy for the future a little, it seems to me that the era of tall buildings has just begun. Tall as the forty-six-story building to be built by the Metropolitan Life Insurance Company may seem at present, I am positive we shall often see it equalled, beaten and perhaps actually doubled in size.

By Architect F. L. V. Hoppin.

WHAT is New York's skyscraper limit? Theoretically there is no limit. Practically we are closely approaching the useful if not the danger limit. We have one skyscraper, the tower of the Metropolitan Life Insurance Company's building in Madison Square, that is planned for forty-six stories, 658 feet high. This is very close to the limit.

I doubt if it will ever be practical to build higher than fifty stories, though, of course, it could be done.

Every New York man who has lived for a generation can remember when Trinity Church steeple punctured the atmosphere at what then seemed an incredible height. All New York could then be seen from Trinity's apparently dizzy height. It was an architectural marvel in 1846.

Where is it now? Overshadowed everywhere by tremendous hives of business that loom up in the air for twenty and more stories.

But Trinity held its prestige a long time. Then elevators came in and the six-story office building or hotel was possible. In 1881 the Produce Exchange Building was completed. From its lofty tower all New York lay below. The Tower Building at No. 50 Broadway was built in 1888—the first of the modern steel constructed buildings. In another year the Pulitzer Building took away first honors, its great gold dome rising 375 feet and 6 inches above the street.

In 1900 came the Park Row Building, even to-day the tallest in New York, just 382 feet above the sidewalk. Now they are building the Singer Building, with forty-one stories and 500 feet of elevation. But the new Metropolitan Life Insurance Building, which will rise on the site of Dr. Parkhurst's old church, is to pierce the air for 75 feet more—the tallest building ever built by man—658 feet high.

There are many things which must eventually make a limit to the modern skyscraper. To begin with, there are the problems of construction. We might assume that a building under the newest methods of steel construction could be reared to any height; but there are the practical considerations.

For example, there are considerations of wind pressure, fire, available water supply, elevator service, sufficient staircases, foundations.

When we have dug deep enough to be satisfied that there is no rock we lay a great bed of concrete, all strengthened with steel beams. On that great mass, which is really rock itself, we raise our structure.

The problems, the practical ones, come afterward. For example, while a fifty-story building might be just as feasible on a lot 100 feet square as one on a whole block, one would pay and the other wouldn't. The reason is simple.

The people who are expected to occupy these great skyscrapers demand the ordinary convenience. Here it would be the elevator service. There would have to be a complicated system of elevators, locals and expresses.

City water cannot reach the tops of such skyscrapers. This must be pumped to tanks on top. It is needed for general uses, to say nothing of the grave necessity for plenty of water in case of fire. The higher the building the larger the tank, for more water is needed. You are bound to reach the point, then, where the weight of this tank would be so great as to preclude its use.

Wind pressure is another item that must be seriously considered. The one with its narrow face toward the prevailing wind can be built higher than the one that must bear all the brunt of the winter's blasts full in its widest facade.

Therefore it is not unfair to assume that we are very near the high-building limit here in New York.

THE FORTY-SIX STORIES for the NEWEST SKYSCRAPER WILL BE WITHIN FOUR STORIES of the LIMIT, DECLARES ARCHITECT HOPPIN, but the NEW YORK BUILDING SUPERINTENDENT Says ONE HUNDRED STORIES ARE POSSIBLE.

1. METROPOLITAN LIFE 658 FEET
2. SINGER TOWER 500 FEET
3. PARK ROW SYNDICATE 382 FEET
4. PULITZER BUILDING 375 ½ FEET
5. AMERICAN SURETY 308 FEET
6. PRODUCE EXCHANGE 275 FEET
7. TRINITY CHURCH 284 FEET
8. TOWER BUILDING 140 FEET
9. FRAUNCES TAVERN 60 FEET

PERSPECTIVE KEY
TO THE
SKY SCRAPER
COMPOSITE

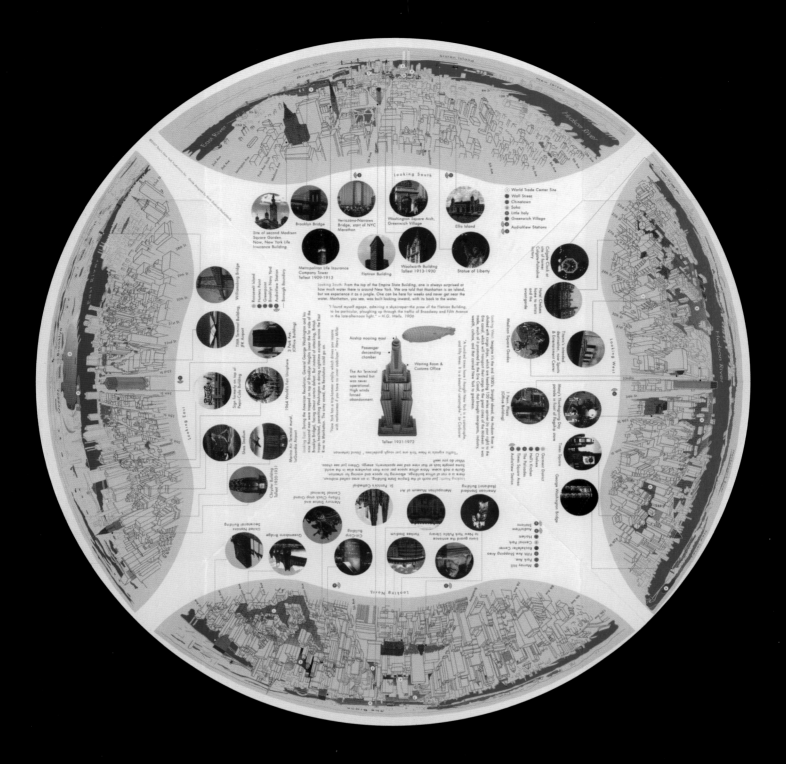

OPPOSITE

**Louis Biedermann, *How Far Can New York Climb Into the Sky?*
from *The World Magazine*, January 20, 1907.**

Manhattan's structures gather round from different corners of the island for this family portrait under the sun, made possible by Joseph Pulitzer's state-of-the-art, high-speed color presses. According to the article, the answer to the question its headline posed was one hundred stories—at a time when the Metropolitan Life Insurance Company Tower, the city's tallest, was forty-six stories. It would take the city only another twenty-four years to reach this benchmark, with the Empire State Building.

ABOVE

**Keith Godard/StudioWorks, *Empire State Building:
A Guide to the Views*, 2007.**

For anyone who grew up in New York in the twentieth century, it's startling to realize that when all of the buildings under construction at the time of printing this book are completed, the Empire State Building will be the seventh tallest in the city. Thanks to its iconic status and central location on the island, it's a good bet, however, that the view from its Observation Deck will always map a collective vision of Gotham.

The Biggest Apple   **65**

ABOVE, LEFT

C. McKnight-Smith, *An Office Building 612 Feet in Height, Now Under Construction in Lower New York*, from *Scientific American*, September 8, 1906.

"The effect of this stupendous structure upon the already remarkable skyline of New York City will be to dwarf the immensity of surrounding buildings and deceive the eye as to their already lofty altitude," announced this venerable magazine, with visual proof to boot. Completed in 1908, the Singer Tower, architect Ernest Flagg's second headquarters for the company, lasted just one year as the world's tallest—finally freeing New Yorkers of their Washington Monument envy—and became a tragic protagonist again sixty years later as the tallest building to be demolished.

ABOVE, RIGHT

C. McKnight-Smith, *A Twentieth Century Campanile in New York*, from *Scientific American*, March 30, 1907.

In 1909, the Metropolitan Life Insurance Company Tower claimed the title of tallest from the almost completed Singer Building. The article accompanying this illustration grouping together misty monuments concluded that, "There can be little doubt that this stupendous marble shaft, when completed, will be an object of decided architectural grandeur and beauty. Its heavenward lift is such that full one-half of its bulk will rise absolutely clear even of the cornice line of New York City's loftiest building." In *Delirious New York*, Rem Koolhaas declared the moment as, "Building becomes Tower, landlocked lighthouse, ostensibly flashing its beams out to sea, but in fact luring the metropolitan audience to itself." The Woolworth Building rose above Metropolitan Life in 1913.

OPPOSITE

Interboro Partners, *Manhattan Superlatives*, from *The Guide to the Grid*, 2012. Project team: Pippa Brashear, Michael Piper, Frank Ruchala Jr, and Sarah Williams.

According to this cheeky graphic, "every block of the Manhattan grid is unique, of course, but some rise above the rest."

MANHATTAN SUPERLATIVES

Every block of the Manhattan grid is unique, of course, but some rise above the rest. Below are some of the the grid's best and most distinct pieces. Some results are surprising, some are confounding. Just like the city itself.

Pippa Brashear, Michael Piper, Frank Ruchala Jr, Sarah Williams

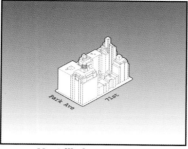

Most likely to Succeed
Park-Lexington avenues, East 71st-72nd streets

If money is a measure of success, this block leads the pack. Tied with eight others, this one won by having the largest population (of very wealthy people).

(most populous of highest per capita income blocks 2010 census)

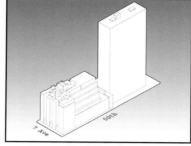

Most Popular
6th-7th avenues, West 50th-51st streets

Block 1003 was the most checked-in place on both Facebook and Foursquare. For the life of us we can't figure out what makes this block so special?

(most check-ins on facebook (31,978) & foursquare (4,786), 7/5-11/2011)

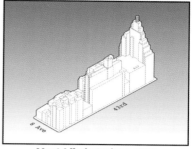

Most Likely to be a Star
7th-8th avenues, West 43rd-44th streets

Many people move to New York to make it big. They stand the best chance to make it on Block 1015 which has the most modeling and casting agencies in the City.

(NAICS code 711410, 2006 Economic Census)

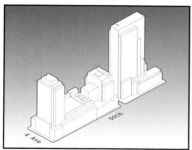

Most Photogenic
5th-6th avenues, West 50th-51st streets

Say Cheese, Block 1266! More photos of this block were uploaded to the web than any another block. Having Radio City Music Hall probably doesn't hurt.

(gettyimages database 4,909 photos, 2006-2007 data)

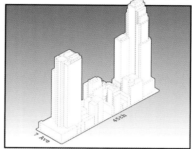

Manliest Block
6th Avenue-Broadway, West 45th-46th streets

Check it out ladies, if you want the best male-female odds on the grid (without going to a prison), move on over to Block 998; 2.1 men for every woman.

(2010 census)

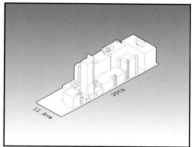

Most Artistic
10th-11th avenues, West 25th-26th streets

Remember those nerdy art kids in school? They're now likely showing their work on Block 697, with its grid-leading 49 galleries, and getting paid handsomely!

(galleries, NAICS 712110 and 453920, 2006 economic census)

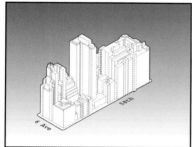

Nicest Smile
5th and 6th avenues, West 58th-59th streets

With 57 dentists on call, you'll never have a cavity again on Block 1274. The view from Central Park from the dentist chair might be the great selling point.

(dentist offices, NAICS 621210, 2006 Economic Census)

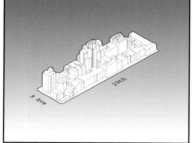

Whiniest
8th-9th avenues, West 29th-30th streets

New York is a big, tough city. Some people like to call 311 to complain about it. This block had the most calls in 2008. Hey buddy, move to Jersey if you got a problem.

(41 complaints in first 6 months of 2006)

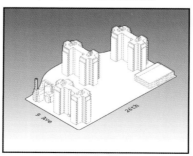

Least likely to find/keep a roomate
1st-2nd avenues, East 10th-11th streets

Heard most often on Block 452: "Another rough night?" "Yeah, those do look like bed bug bites." "Wait, you can't move out! What about the lease???"

(most complaints, bedbugregistry.com)

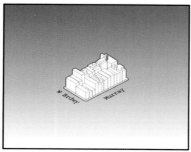

Life of the Party
Church-West Broadway, Murray-Warren streets

Five bars - one block. We really thought it would be more, and somewhere else. But nondescript Block 133 is the grid's inexplicable party capital.

(bars/alcohol selling drinking & eating establishments, NAICS 722410, 2006)

Most Rebellious
8th-9th avenues, West 26th-28th streets

Some blocks break rules. Block 751 Breaks Them All! The grid's very own James Dean has curved edges, blocks off surrounding streets and is full of towers in the park. Shine on you crazy diamond.

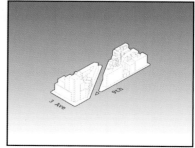

Separated at Birth
2nd-3rd Avenues, East 9th-10th Street

The 1811 grid typically erased what existed before it. Not here. Stuyvesant Street, a farm road once owned by the Stuyvesant family, split Block 465 in two from the very beginning. Literally separated at birth.

(reference http://en.wikipedia.org/wiki/Stuyvesant_Street_(Manhattan)

splendid structures of

NEW YORK CITY

	NAME
ROW 1 .0028 inches per foot	Height
ROWS 2-3 .0035 inches per foot	Address
ROW 4 .0069 inches per foot	APPROX YEAR CONSTRUCTION STARTED · PRIMARY ARCHITECTURAL STYLE
ROWS 5-7 .0090 inches per foot	

ONE WORLD TRADE CENTER
1792 ft
1 World Trade Center
2006 · CONTEMPORARY

EMPIRE STATE BUILDING
1454 ft
350 5th Avenue
1930 · ART DECO

432 PARK AVENUE
1396 ft
432 Park Avenue
2011 · CONTEMPORARY

BANK OF AMERICA TOWER
1200 ft
1 Bryant Park
2004 · DECONSTRUCTIVIST

4 TIMES SQUARE
1143 ft
1472 Broadway
1996 · POSTMODERN

CHRYSLER BUILDING
1046 ft
405 Lexington Avenue
1928 · ART DECO

NEW YORK TIMES BUILDING
1046 ft
620 8th Avenue
2003 · STRUCTURAL EXPRESSIONIST

CITIGROUP CENTER
915 ft
601 Lexington Avenue
1974 · MODERN

NEW YORK BY GEHRY
870 ft
8 Spruce Street
2006 · DECONSTRUCTIVIST

30 ROCKEFELLER CENTER
850 ft
30 Rockefeller Plaza
1930 · ART DECO

METLIFE BUILDING
808 ft
200 Park Avenue
1960 · INTERNATIONAL

WOOLWORTH BUILDING
792 ft
233 Broadway
1910 · GOTHIC REVIVAL

TIME WARNER CENTER
750 ft
10 Columbus Circle
2000 · CONTEMPORARY

SOLOW BUILDING
689 ft
9 West 57th Street
1966 · INTERNATIONAL

SONY TOWER
647 ft
550 Madison Avenue
1981 · POSTMODERN

WALDORF ASTORIA NEW YORK
625 ft
301 Park Avenue
1930 · ART DECO

HEARST TOWER
597 ft
300 West 57th Street
1926/2003 · STRUCTURAL EXPRESSIONIST

388 BRIDGE
590 ft
388 Bridge Street
2007 · CONTEMPORARY

MANHATTAN MUNICIPAL BUILDING
580 ft
1 Centre Street
1907 · BEAUX-ARTS

33 THOMAS STREET
551 ft
33 Thomas Street
1967 · BRUTALIST

HEADQUARTERS OF THE UNITED NATIONS
544 ft
405 East 42 Street
1948 · INTERNATIONAL

375 PEARL STREET
540 ft
375 Pearl Street
1975 · BRUTALIST

SEAGRAM BUILDING
516 ft
375 Park Avenue
1956 · INTERNATIONAL

WILLIAMSBURGH SAVINGS BANK TOWER
512 ft
1 Hanson Place
1927 · ART DECO

ST. PATRICK'S CATHEDRAL
330 ft
460 Madison Avenue
1858 · GOTHIC REVIVAL

LEVER HOUSE
307 ft
390 Park Avenue
1950 · INTERNATIONAL STYLE

ST. REGIS NEW YORK
306 ft
2 East 55th Street
1901 · BEAUX-ARTS

STATUE OF LIBERTY
305 ft
Liberty Island
1875 · NEOCLASSICAL

FLATIRON BUILDING
285 ft
175 5th Avenue
1901 · CHICAGO SCHOOL

TRINITY CHURCH
281 ft
75 Broadway
1839 · GOTHIC REVIVAL

THE STANDARD, HIGH LINE
261 ft
848 Washington Street
2006 · MODERN

PLAZA HOTEL
250 ft
768 5th Avenue
1905 · FRENCH RENAISSANCE REVIVAL

CATHEDRAL OF ST. JOHN THE DIVINE
232 ft
1047 Amsterdam Avenue
1892 · GOTHIC REVIVAL

CARNEGIE HALL
201 ft
881 7th Avenue
1890 · ITALIAN RENAISSANCE REVIVAL

NEW MUSEUM
175 ft
235 Bowery
2005 · CONTEMPORARY

BROOKLYN MUSEUM
130 ft
200 Eastern Parkway
1895 · BEAUX-ARTS

MADISON SQUARE GARDEN
150 ft
4 Pennsylvania Plaza
1964 · MODERN

PORTER HOUSE
150 ft
366 West 15th Street
1905/2002 · CONTEMPORARY

PRISON SHIP MARTYRS' MONUMENT
149 ft
Fort Greene Park
1907 · CLASSICAL

UNISPHERE
140 ft
11101 Corona Avenue
1962 · FUTURIST

41 COOPER SQUARE
135 ft
41 Cooper Square
2005 · DECONSTRUCTIVIST

METROPOLITAN MUSEUM OF ART
130 ft
1000 5th Avenue
1874 · BEAUX-ARTS

GRAND CENTRAL TERMINAL
130 ft
89 East 42nd Street
1903 · BEAUX-ARTS

NEW YORK STOCK EXCHANGE
110 ft
18 Broad Street
1901 · NEOCLASSICAL

THE DAKOTA
110 ft
1 West 72nd Street
1880 · FRENCH RENAISSANCE REVIVAL

NEW YORK PUBLIC LIBRARY
98 ft
5th Avenue at 42nd Street
1902 · BEAUX-ARTS

METROPOLITAN OPERA HOUSE, LINCOLN CENTER
95 ft
30 Lincoln Center Plaza
1966 · MODERN

NEW YORK CITY HALL
95 ft
City Hall Park
1803 · FRENCH RENAISSANCE REVIVAL

GUGGENHEIM
92 ft
1071 5th Ave at 88th Street
1956 · MODERN

SOLDIERS' AND SAILORS' ARCH
80 ft
20 Grand Army Plaza
1889 · NEOCLASSICAL

WASHINGTON SQUARE ARCH
77 ft
Washington Square Park
1890 · NEOCLASSICAL

FEDERAL HALL NATIONAL MEMORIAL
51 ft
26 Wall Street
1833 · CLASSICAL

TWA FLIGHT CENTER
16 ft
Terminal 5, John F. Kennedy International Airport
1956 · NEOFUTURISTIC

WYCKOFF HOUSE
27 ft
5816 Clarendon Road
1652 · COLONIAL

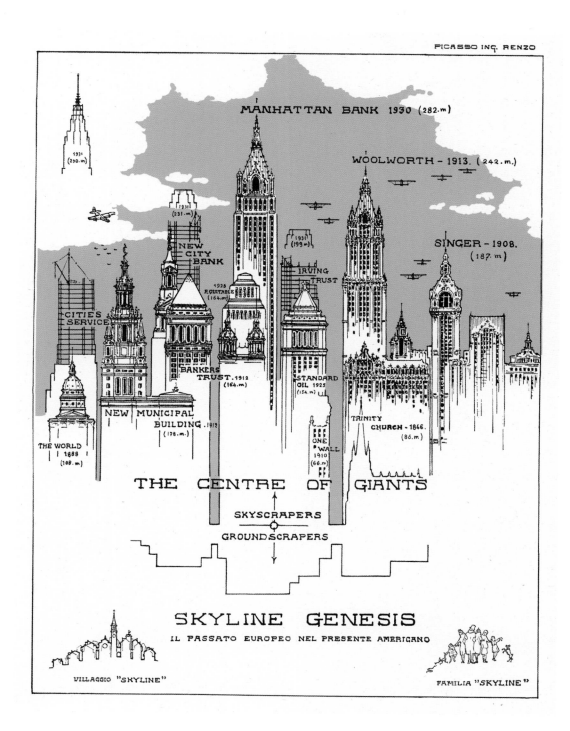

The Centre of Giants image contains the following labels:

PICASSO ING. RENZO

MANHATTAN BANK 1930 (282.m)

1931 (290.m)

WOOLWORTH - 1913. (242.m.)

1931 (231.m)

NEW CITY BANK

1931 (199.m)

SINGER - 1908. (187.m)

1928 EQUITABLE (164.m)

IRVING TRUST

CITIES SERVICE

BANKERS TRUST. 1912 (164.m)

STANDARD OIL 1925 (154.m)

NEW MUNICIPAL BUILDING .1912 (178.m.)

TRINITY CHURCH - 1846. (86.m)

THE WORLD 1888 (108.m)

ONE WALL 1910 (66.m)

THE CENTRE OF GIANTS

SKYSCRAPERS
GROUNDSCRAPERS

SKYLINE GENESIS

IL PASSATO EUROPEO NEL PRESENTE AMERICANO

VILLAGGIO "SKYLINE"

FAMILIA "SKYLINE"

Pop Chart Lab, *Splendid Structures of New York City*, 2015.
New York's unique tectonic species, clad in a crisp blueprint aesthetic, rise in elevation as they climb higher on the chart. They are drawn to scales that intelligently vary from row to row in order to accommodate their arrangement in height families and give space to the smaller structures, starting from the 1,792-foot One World Trade Center and closing with the 27-foot Wyckoff House in Brooklyn. Clearly, Midtown gets the lion's share. Each structure is additionally described by its location, year of construction, and architectural style.

Renzo Picasso, *Skyline Genesis—The Centre of Giants*, 1929.
The twentieth-century Empire City dazzled the world with its soaring skyscrapers. Among their biggest admirers was Renzo Picasso, a Genoese architect, engineer, inventor, urban enthusiast, dreamer, and planner. This is a montage of buildings, both complete and under construction, in Lower Manhattan. For comparative purposes, Picasso has drawn, bottom left, the skyline of a typical Italian village, and, bottom right, the "skyline" of a typical Italian family.

C. McKnight-Smith, *Victoria Falls as Compared with Niagara*, from *Scientific American*, June 29, 1907.

In the pages of *Scientific American,* even an article about waterfalls became an occasion for New York sizeism: "A comparison of Niagara and Victoria Falls is pictured in the front-page illustration, which shows at a glance how vastly greater is the African falls. . . . To illustrate the magnitude of the African waterfall, we have depicted against it the sky-line of New York from Battery Park to Worth Street. Not a building projects above the crest of the falls excepting only the tower of the Singer Building, which is now in process of erection."

RIGHT

The Great Engineering Works of New York City, from *Scientific American*, November 19, 1892.

A medley of imagery—combining elevations, sections, a planimetric map, a watershed map, a bird's eye view, and detailed renderings—suggests that Manhattan is at once a playground for great engineering feats and a graveyard of ideas, as many of the projects shown were never realized.

OPPOSITE

Pictorial representation of the enormous quantities of material handled in constructing the Panama Canal, from *Scientific American*, November 9, 1912.

Whether submerged in water or buried in dirt, Manhattan bears up under its weighty responsibility to be the measure of all things.

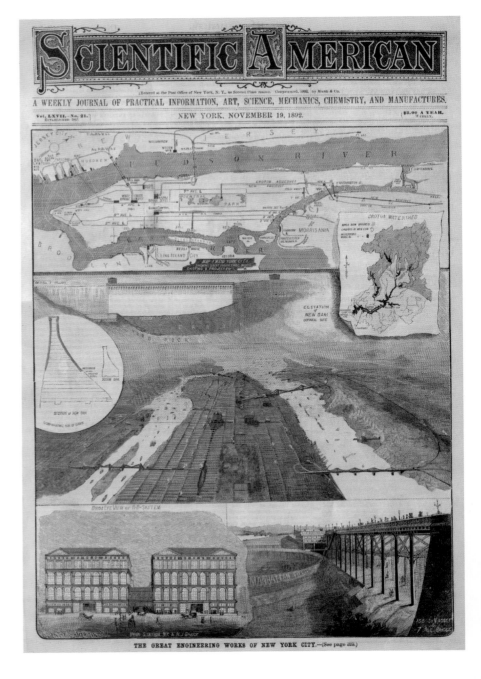

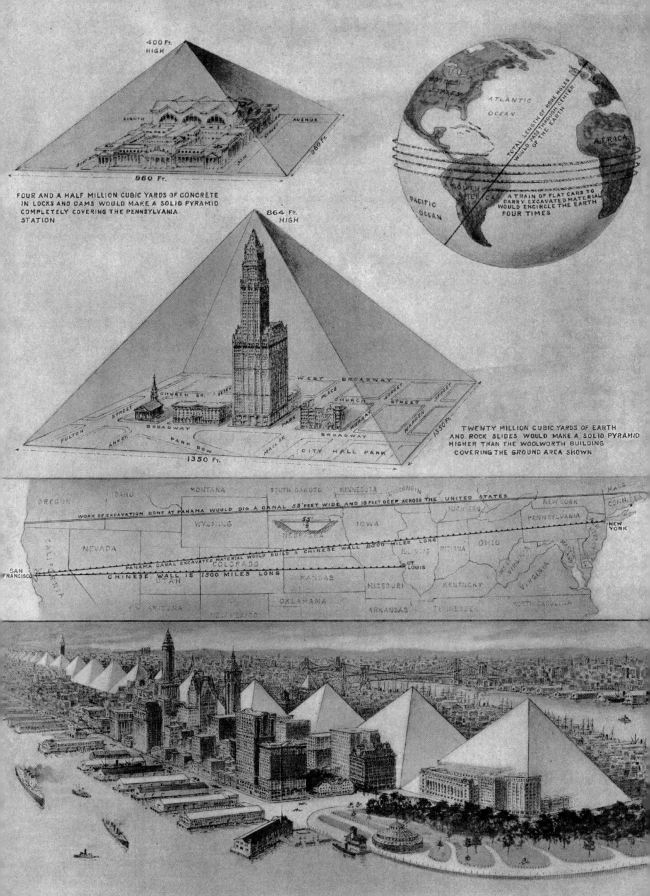

400 FT. HIGH

960 FT.

960 FT.

FOUR AND A HALF MILLION CUBIC YARDS OF CONCRETE
IN LOCKS AND DAMS WOULD MAKE A SOLID PYRAMID
COMPLETELY COVERING THE PENNSYLVANIA
STATION

ATLANTIC OCEAN

AFRICA

SOUTH AMERICA

PACIFIC OCEAN

TOTAL LENGTH OF BORE HOLES WOULD PASS THROUGH CENTER OF THE EARTH

A TRAIN OF FLAT CARS TO
CARRY EXCAVATED MATERIAL
WOULD ENCIRCLE THE EARTH
FOUR TIMES

864 FT. HIGH

1350 FT.

WEST BROADWAY

TWENTY MILLION CUBIC YARDS OF EARTH
AND ROCK SLIDES WOULD MAKE A SOLID PYRAMID
HIGHER THAN THE WOOLWORTH BUILDING
COVERING THE GROUND AREA SHOWN

WORK OF EXCAVATION DONE AT PANAMA WOULD DIG A CANAL 55 FEET WIDE AND 10 FEET DEEP ACROSS THE UNITED STATES

PANAMA CANAL EXCAVATED MATERIAL WOULD BUILD A CHINESE WALL 2500 MILES LONG
CHINESE WALL IS 1500 MILES LONG

EXCAVATED MATERIAL FROM THE PANAMA CANAL WOULD MAKE A LINE OF 63 PYRAMIDS, EACH ONE THE EQUAL OF THE GREAT PYRAMID OF EGYPT.
REACHING FROM THE BATTERY TO HARLEM, A DISTANCE OF NINE MILES

Surreal diagrams trumpet the great triumphs of American know-how. New York's structures—especially the tallest du jour—were popular measuring units to awe the readers of *Scientific American*. During its brief reign as tallest during 1908–09, the Singer Tower was used to visualize statistics for paper consumption and glass industry production—for the latter, it had to be bottled up. Its successor, the Metropolitan Life Insurance Tower, can be spotted in a still life dwarfed by mammoth ears of corn on Madison Square. The notoriously costly Woolworth Building turns into a neo-Gothic fire hydrant to show the annual outlay for new cars and their upkeep in the burgeoning US automobile industry.

ABOVE, LEFT
Charles Figaro, *The Civilized World's Consumption of Paper Presented in Graphical Form*, from *Scientific American*, October 10, 1908.

ABOVE, RIGHT
Beverly Towles, *The Giant Glass Industry*, from *Scientific American*, April 24, 1909.

OPPOSITE, TOP LEFT
Beverly Towles, *The Enormous Crops of 1909*, from *Scientific American*, December 18, 1909.

OPPOSITE, TOP RIGHT
Vincent Lynch, *A Graphical Representation of the Magnitude of the Automobile Industry*, from *Scientific American*, January 6, 1917.

OPPOSITE, BOTTOM
Amount of Material Consumed Annually in the Manufacture of Books and Periodicals in the United States, from *Scientific American*, November 14, 1903.

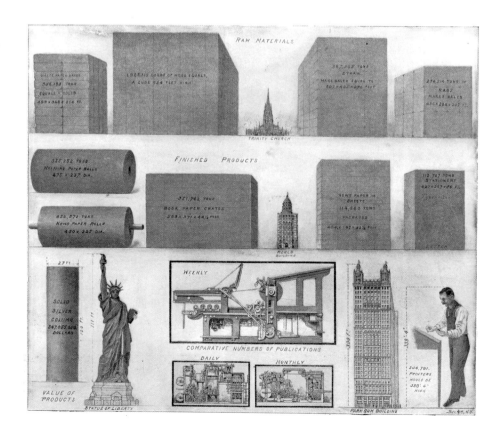

WHERE CAN WE DOCK THIS MARINE MONSTER WHEN SHE REACHES THE PORT OF NEW YORK?

Cross section of the White Star Steamship Titanic, now almost ready to be launched. A $12,000 model of her has been put on exhibition in this city. She is 882 feet 6 inches long and Manhattan's longest pier is 57½ feet shorter.

If her vast hull were empty, thirty-six full sized replicas of Hudson's famous Half Moon could be laid crosswise in her, under full sail, and still leave 270 feet of unoccupied tapering space at bow and stern; or twenty-eight full-sized replicas of

Fulton's Clermont could be piled up like cordwood inside her, without utilizing 282 feet and 6 inches of tapering space fore and aft, where several more could be stowed away. An ordinary railroad locomotive with tender, and drawing

eight Pullman sleepers, could be laid upon her deck abaft the spot near the captain's bridge, where our artist has cut her in two. From keel to funnel top she is nearly as tall as the Postal Telegraph Building, fronting on City Hall Park.

HALF MOON

ARTHUR RAGLAND HOWARD

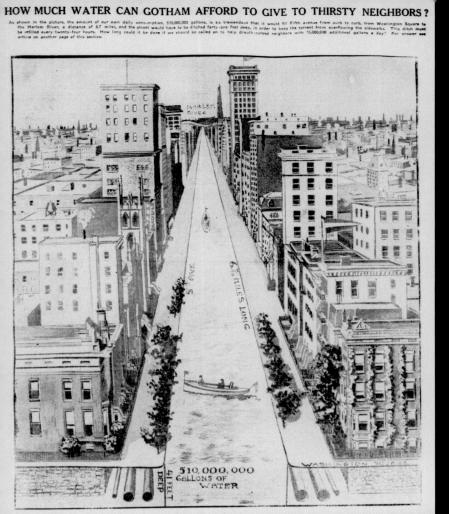

HOW MUCH WATER CAN GOTHAM AFFORD TO GIVE TO THIRSTY NEIGHBORS?

As shown in the picture, the amount of our own daily consumption, 510,000,000 gallons, is so tremendous that it would fill Fifth avenue from curb to curb, from Washington Square to the Harlem River, a distance of 6.7 miles, and the street would have to be ditched forty-one feet deep, in order to keep the torrent from overflowing the sidewalks. This ditch must be refilled every twenty-four hours. How long could it be done if we should be called on to help drouth-cursed neighbors with 15,000,000 additional gallons a day? For answer see article on another page of this section.

PICTORIAL DIAGRAM SHOWING HOW THE SEA WILL HAVE EN-CROACHED ON OUR ATLANTIC SEABOARD CITIES TEN THOUSAND YEARS FROM NOW, IF THE SUBSIDENCE OF OUR COAST LINE CONTINUES AT THE SAME RATE AS IT HAS DONE IN THE PAST.

OPPOSITE

Arthur Ragland "Pop" Momand, *Where Can We Dock This Marine Monster When She Reaches the Port of New York?* from the *New-York Tribune*, November 27, 1910.

"Cross section of the White Star Steamship *Titanic*, now almost ready to be launched. A $12,000 model of her has been put on exhibition in this city. She is 882 feet 6 inches long and Manhattan's longest pier is 57 ½ feet shorter." So begins the caption of this cutaway view of the leviathan, bringing together Henry Hudson's *Half Moon*, Robert Fulton's *Clermont*, "an ordinary railroad locomotive," and the Postal Telegraph Building from lower Broadway in a surreal scenario with a tragic denouement.

ABOVE, LEFT

How Much Water Can Gotham Afford to Give to Thirsty Neighbors?, from the *New-York Tribune*, November 6, 1910.

Whatever factoid was being communicated here, it certainly paled against the fun of seeing Fifth Avenue turned into a canal.

ABOVE, RIGHT

Arthur Ragland "Pop" Momand, *Fish May One Day Feed Among Sea-Crumbled Towers of Manhattan*, from the *New-York Tribune*, January 22, 1911.

Deep-sea divers are at work below the ruins of the Singer Building in this "pictorial diagram showing how the sea will have encroached on our Atlantic seaboard cities ten thousand years from now, if the subsidence of our coast line continues at the same rate it has done in the past." An ominously droll spectacle that is nevertheless a realistic possibility these days. Ten thousand years seem to have passed in a flash.

FOLLOWING SPREAD

Lucille Corcos, *Christmas at Macy's*, from *Fortune*, December 1954.

A cutaway of the block-long department store in all its consumerist glory.

MAXIMUM OCCUPANCY

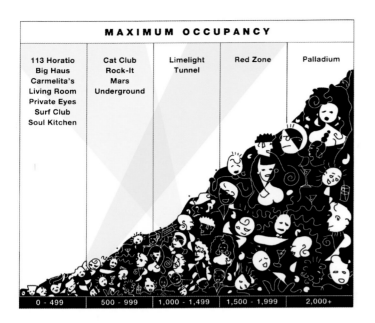

113 Horatio Big Haus Carmelita's Living Room Private Eyes Surf Club Soul Kitchen	Cat Club Rock-It Mars Underground	Limelight Tunnel	Red Zone	Palladium
0 - 499	500 - 999	1,000 - 1,499	1,500 - 1,999	2,000+

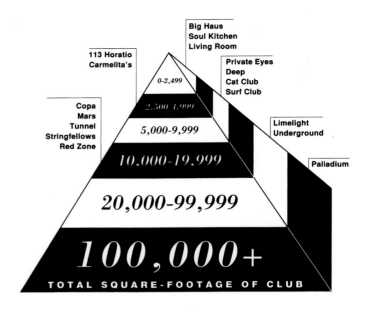

113 Horatio
Carmelita's
0-2,499

Big Haus
Soul Kitchen
Living Room

Copa
Mars
Tunnel
Stringfellows
Red Zone
2,500-4,999

Private Eyes
Deep
Cat Club
Surf Club

5,000-9,999

Limelight
Underground

10,000-19,999

Palladium

20,000-99,999

100,000+

TOTAL SQUARE-FOOTAGE OF CLUB

AVERAGE MILES TRAVELED TO CLUB

Mars
Underground
Private Eyes
Tunnel
Big Haus
Soul Kitchen
Deep
Carmelita's
Surf Club
113 Horatio
Living Room

Big Hunt Club
Sound Factory
Robots
M.K.
Nell's
Copa
Wild Pitch
Pyramid
Choice
Stringfellows
Rock-It

Bedrox
Love Transporter
Cat Club

Regine's

Palladium

Au Bar
Limelight
Peggy
Sue's

0+   10+   25+   100+   500+   1000+

MANHATTAN

BROOKLYN

JERSEY

UPSTATE

MIDWEST

EUROPE

COST OF A DRINK

	Absolut & Tonic	Premium Long-Necked Beer	Perrier	Sex-on-the-Beach
$12.00+	Regine's		Regine's	Regine's
$9.00				
$8.50	Stringfellows, Au Bar			Au Bar, M.K., Nell's, Stringfellows, Copa
$7.00				
$6.50	Red Zone, Private Eyes, Big Hunt Club, Limelight, Cat Club, M.K., Nell's, Surf Club, Mars, Underground, Carmelita's, 113 Horatio, Robots, Copa, Peggy Sue's, Palladium, Big Haus, Tunnel	Au Bar, Palladium, M.K., Nell's, Stringfellows, Copa, Red Zone	Au Bar	Limelight, Palladium, Tunnel, Big Haus, Soul Kitchen, Carmelita's, 113 Horatio, Private Eyes, Red Zone, Underground, Bedrox
$5.00				
$4.50	Living Room, Soul Kitchen, Deep, Rock-It, Pyramid, Bedrox	Underground, Cat Club, 113 Horatio, Living Room, Private Eyes, Big Haus, Limelight, Surf Club, Big Hunt Club, Mars, Bedrox	Palladium, Cat Club, 113 Horatio, M.K., Nell's, Stringfellows	Living Room, Cat Club, Surf Club, Pyramid, Rock-It
$3.50				
$3.00	Love Transporter	Love Transporter, Carmelita's, Rock-It, Tunnel, Pyramid, Soul Kitchen, Deep, Wild Pitch, Peggy Sue's	Big Haus, Carmelita's, Big Hunt Club, Mars, Sound Factory, Surf Club, Copa, Red Zone, Pyramid, Bedrox, Peggy Sue's, Living Room	
0				

Percentage of Men & Women Wearing Big Black Shoes

	Men	Women
Mars	30%	25%
Underground	50%	40%
Private Eyes	0	0
Tunnel	40%	20%
Big Haus	0	0
Love Transporter	75%	75%
Soul Kitchen	30%	60%
Deep	30%	30%
Carmelita's	60%	30%
Limelight	10%	10%
Palladium	30%	30%
Cat Club	40%	30%
Surf Club	0	0
113 Horatio	60%	60%
Living Room	0	0
Au Bar	0	0
Rock-It	0	0
M.K.	75%	0
Nell's	70%	0
Big Hunt Club	80%	45%
Sound Factory	80%	20%
Robots	30%	90%
Regine's	0	30%
Stringfellows	0	0
Copa	70%	30%
Wild Pitch	7%	5%
Red Zone	40%	35%
Pyramid	20%	40%
Choice	0	0
Bedrox	3%	0
Peggy Sue's	0	0

Percentage of Men & Women with Ponytails

	Men	Women
Mars	8%	12%
Underground	0.5%	2.5%
Private Eyes	10%	0
Tunnel	1%	3%
Big Haus	10%	5%
Love Transporter	15%	3%
Soul Kitchen	5%	20%
Deep	10%	30%
Carmelita's	15%	25%
Limelight	30%	30%
Palladium	8%	18%
Cat Club	70%	30%
Surf Club	15%	10%
113 Horatio	30%	30%
Living Room	15%	15%
Au Bar	5%	15%
Rock-It	2%	10%
M.K.	0.1%	0
Nell's	5%	5%
Big Hunt Club	5%	10%
Sound Factory	0	0
Robots	0	0
Regine's	0	0
Stringfellows	0	15%
Copa	0	0
Wild Pitch	0	0
Red Zone	15%	15%
Pyramid	3%	2%
Choice	20%	30%
Bedrox	0.8%	7%
Peggy Sue's	0	10%

BATHROOM CLEANLINESS

< spotless · spotty >

| Sound Factory Regine's Au Bar | Big Hunt Club M.K. Tunnel Private Eyes Stringfellows | Wild Pitch Nell's Palladium Red Zone Copa | Living Room Limelight Underground Bedrox | Surf Club Big Haus | 113 Horatio Carmelita's Love Transporter Rock-It | Deep Soul Kitchen Choice Peggy Sue's | Mars | Cat Club | Robots |

Natasha Tibbott (illustrator), Hal Rubenstein (editor), and Douglas Riccardi (art director), *A Clubography of New York*, from *Egg*, March 1990.

Egg, a short-lived magazine that covered the downtown Manhattan scene, produced this big basket of infographics for a feature about nightclubs. Evidently, there weren't enough hipsters interested in the square footage and maximum occupancy of their favorite haunts to sustain the magazine. One analyst said, "It was a downtown magazine for uptown people."

NEW YORK'S NEW SOLAR SYSTEM.

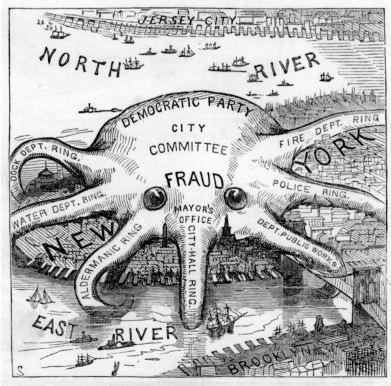

THE GREAT NEW YORK OCTOPUS—POLITICS ON MANHATTAN ISLAND.

THE TAMMANY TIGER STUDYING THE NEW MAP.

THE ROGUE'S MARCH.—*Arranged for the Piano-forte by* M. Woolf.

Political cartoonists wield popular tropes of the Gilded Age—the solar system, the octopus, and the music sheet—to evoke the power of Tammany Hall in the city's affairs. Richard "Boss" Croker is the burning sun of this "solar system."

OPPOSITE, TOP
Udo J. Keppler, *New York's New Solar System,* from *Puck*, March 30, 1898.

OPPOSITE, BOTTOM LEFT
***The Great New York Octopus—Politics on Manhattan Island,* from *Harper's Weekly*, December 1877.**

OPPOSITE, BOTTOM RIGHT
McNeill, *The Tammany Tiger Studying the New Map,* from *Twinkles,* April 24, 1897.

ABOVE
M. Woolf, *The Rogue's March,* from *Harper's Weekly*, November 18, 1871.

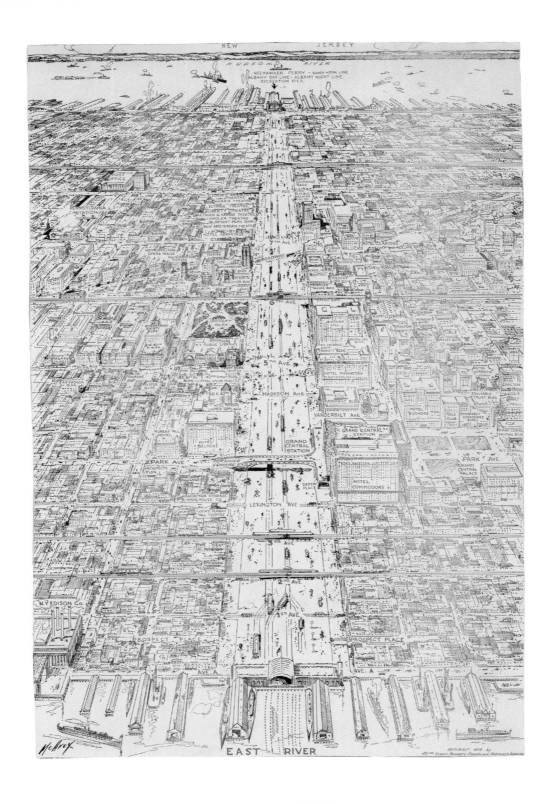

**McAvoy, map for the 42nd Street Property Owners
& Merchants Association, 1919.**

With an eerie premonition of Saul Steinberg's *View of the World from
9th Avenue*, a map for the 42nd Street Property Owners & Merchants
Association surveys the artery from east to west, vastly exaggerating
its width for marketing purposes. But 42nd Street did loom that large
in the national imagination.

**Saul Steinberg, *View of the World from 9th Avenue*, 1976.
Reproduced on the cover of *The New Yorker*, March 29, 1976.**

Probably the most famous, infamous, New York–centric, and
parodied of *New Yorker* covers.

CHAPTER THREE
RAPTUROUS *MOTION*

"**M**OVEMENT WAS THE ESSENCE OF MANHATTAN," WROTE THE travel writer Jan Morris in *Manhattan '45*. "It had always been so, and now its sense of flow, energy, openness, elasticity as Charles Dickens had called it, was headier than ever. Half the city's skill and aspirations seemed to go into the propagation of motion." Manhattan is a ballet on steroids. And all of us dancers are moving in syncopated chaos to the percussive rhythms from above and below.

The incredible *Relative Glare along Broadway, New York City, as Shown by Three Exposures of a Moving Camera* (page 90) captures lightning in a bottle—the explosive visual bursts of raw electricity as traffic zips from place to place. The Italian Futurist Fortunato Depero appears to be in awe of the flows, vibrations, idiosyncratic rhythms, and claustrophobic patterns of the dense conveyor-belt environment that is the Times Square subway station (page 87).

In a city known for its monumentality, human scale as experienced by the pedestrian is a virtue. Lots of walks here, including Saul Steinberg's witty drawing of his morning stroll for a *New Yorker* cover (page 109) and Christoph Niemann's *New York Cheat Sheets* (pages 110–111), showing, "a few handy charts that will, I hope, help readers to improve their lives." Then there is Jason Logan's route in and around Manhattan (page 107) to capture the scents of the city, which invest communities with aromas of food and nature. A favorite is Andrew DeGraff's 2014 *Paths of the Ghostbusters*, a condensed schematic of Manhattan showing where the fictional *Ghostbusters* characters from the sci-fi comedy film tracked their poltergeist prey (page 92). And a simple plan for *Roof Piece* by the Trisha Brown and Group dance company is evidence that even schematics can be expressive and emotional (page 94).

The mores of motion are portrayed in Wendy MacNaughton's *Jaywalkers of New York* (page 108) and in charts of parking violations by diplomats that turn into engaging visualizations (opposite and pages 104–105)—New Yorkers are somewhat obsessed with diplomats who fail to pay their parking tickets.

Kinetic communication, too, is a central feature of the city. An 1885 diagram of *The Pneumatic System of the Western Union Telegraph Company* (page 88); Matthew Leibowitz's 1946 surrealistic collage revealing the invisible motion of electromagnetic TV signals (page 91); and a cutaway of the United Nations General Assembly translation system from 1953 (pages 98–99) illuminate varied technological wonders.

The wealth of diagrams that document in static form the constantly shifting city—its people, transportation, and communications—is a testament to Manhattan's moveable feast.

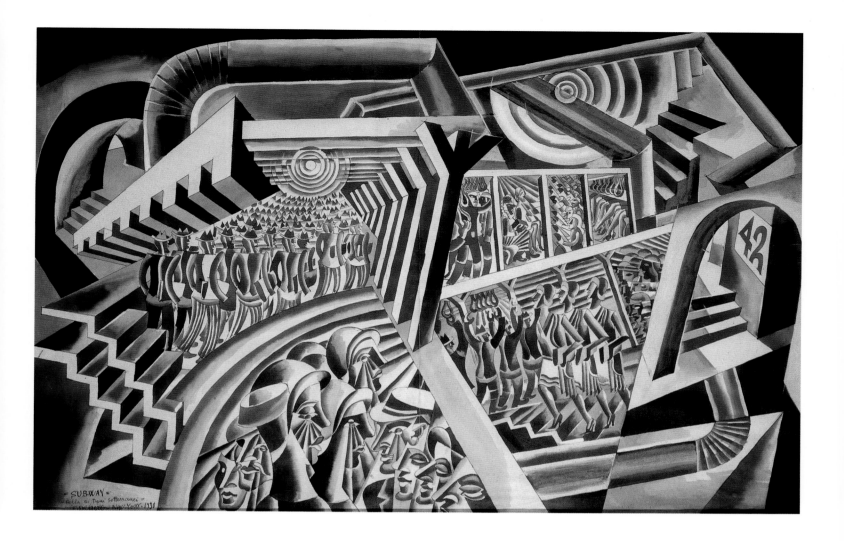

OPPOSITE
David Klein, *Fly TWA New York*, c. 1960.
A montage of colored planes produces a dreamlike picture of Times Square at night in the mind's eye. From 1955 to 1965, David Klein designed numerous award-winning travel posters, many of which are now considered emblematic of the 1960s "Jet Age," like his one for Howard Hughes's Trans World Airlines (TWA).

ABOVE
Fortunato Depero, *Subway, Crowd to the Underground Trains*, 1930.
Fortunato Depero, the Italian Futurist painter, illustrator, and scenic designer, captures Midtown crowds caught in a hermetic world. The stairways and passageways of the dungeonlike 42nd Street subway station are almost all empty; people are trapped in interstitial spaces with no means of entrance or egress.

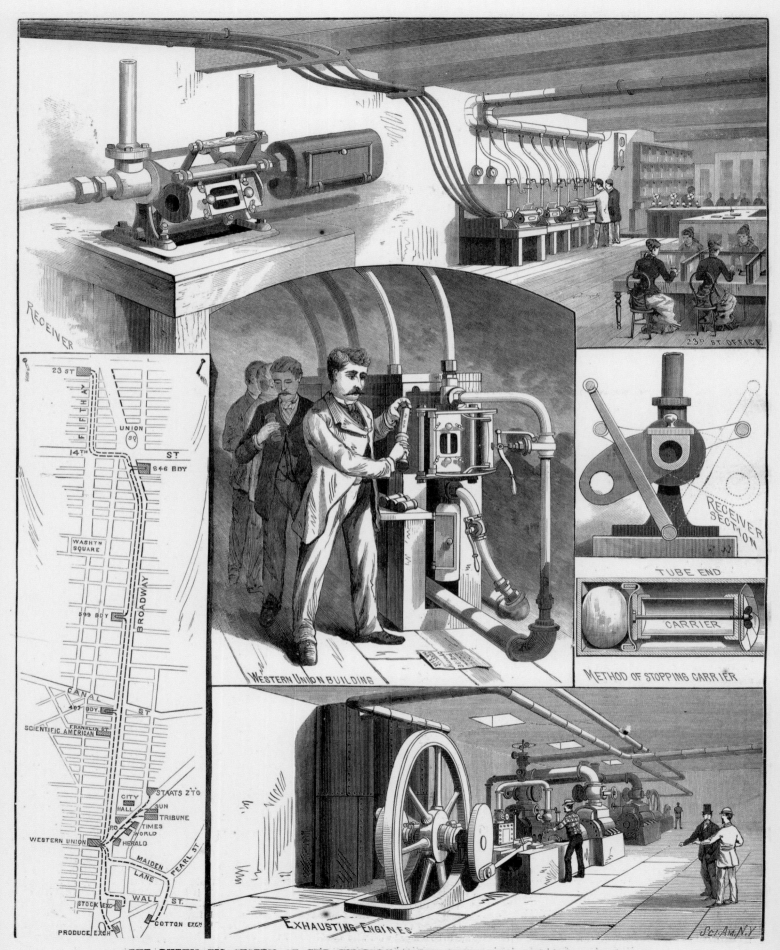

THE PNEUMATIC SYSTEM OF THE WESTERN UNION TELEGRAPH COMPANY.—[See page 100.]

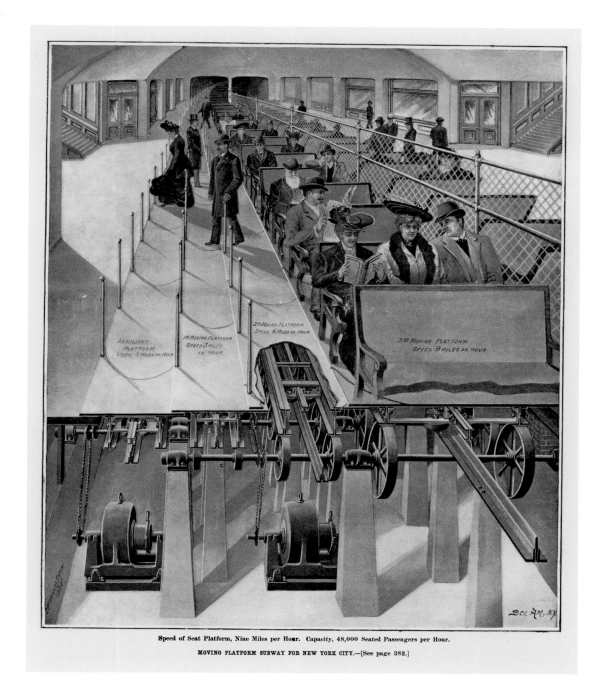

Speed of Seat Platform, Nine Miles per Hour. Capacity, 48,000 Seated Passengers per Hour.

MOVING PLATFORM SUBWAY FOR NEW YORK CITY.—[See page 382.]

OPPOSITE

The Pneumatic System of the Western Union Telegraph Company, from *Scientific American,* **February 14, 1885.**

Senator Ted Stevens of Alaska was only 150 years late when he described the Internet as a "network of tubes" in 2006. In the nineteenth century, the Western Union Telegraph Company headquarters, the Google of its day, on lower Broadway, was able to send messages in capsules propelled by compressed air to the main exchanges and newspapers scattered through the city. The company used a system of underground pneumatic tubes that stretched as far north as 23rd Street.

ABOVE

Moving Platform Subway for New York City, from *Scientific American,* **May 13, 1905.**

The moving sidewalk or platform has been one of the most stubbornly proposed and consistently rejected ideas in the history of public transportation. Starting in 1871, when an "endless-travelling sidewalk" above Broadway was proposed, and patented, by a New Jersey wine merchant, the idea popped up frequently in discussions of New York's transit woes. The "sectional perspective view" presented here comes from an amusingly impractical 1905 proposal for a crosstown moving platform below 34th Street. The idea never died, and moving sidewalks finally found a place in the world's airports.

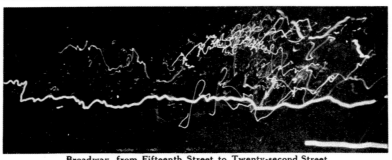

Broadway, from Fifteenth Street to Twenty-second Street

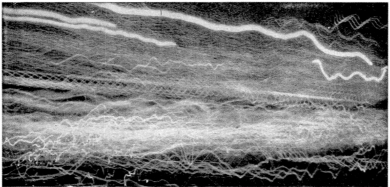

Broadway, from Twenty-fourth Street to Thirty-first Street

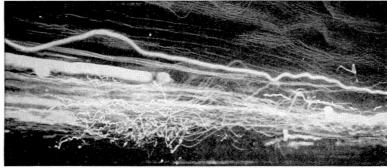

Broadway, from Thirty-fourth Street to Forty-first Street

RELATIVE GLARE ALONG BROADWAY, NEW YORK CITY, AS SHOWN BY THREE
EXPOSURES OF A MOVING CAMERA

ABOVE

Relative Glare along Broadway, New York City, as Shown by Three Exposures of a Moving Camera, from Popular Electricity in Plain English, 1911.

In 1911, when much of New York City outside of commercial districts was still gaslit, an illuminating engineer found a way to use photography to measure "the relative amount of glare produced by the window lights and electric signs in various sections of a given street." In this case, the given street was Broadway, the time was shortly before midnight, and the camera, mounted on a moving trolley car and taking long exposures, was pointed sideways toward the building fronts as they swept by. The mounting intensity of Manhattan's nightlife as the viewer travels deeper into the entertainment district could not be more viscerally presented.

OPPOSITE

Matthew Leibowitz, Black and White Television. Color Television, from Fortune, February 1946.

Turning to frequencies of the electromagnetic spectrum outside of human vision, this diagram shows how the two television technologies, both in their infancy, transmit to the home screen. A year after this illustration was published, commercial black-and-white programming was launched; it would be twenty years before broadcasting switched predominantly color.

m. leibowitz

BLACK AND WHITE TELEVISION

COLOR TELEVISION

Light entering the camera strikes a mosaic of photoelectric cells at the back of the Iconoscope tube, creating tiny electrical charges in the cells. When the mosaic is bombarded by an electron gun, the charges flow as a current.

Light entering the camera is reflected by a mirror through a rotating color drum, which causes red, green, and blue images to fall in rapid succession on the photoelectric mosaic of an Orthicon tube — a very sensitive type of Iconoscope — thereby producing a color-modulated electrical current.

By cable, the current goes to the broadcast transmitter, usually located in a tall tower. (N.B.C.'s is atop the Empire State Building.) There the weak impulses, after being amplified electronically, are used to modulate an outgoing carrier wave.

Piped to C.B.S.'s transmitter in the tower of the Chrysler Building, the current is amplified, as in the black and white system, and used to modulate an ultra-high-frequency carrier wave, which radiates from the antenna.

When the carrier wave, eddying out into space, encounters a receiving antenna on top of a house, its radio-frequency signals are converted back into an electrical current, which flows down to the receiver.

The very short UHF waves radiating in all directions strike a highly directional parabolic receiving antenna (made of chicken wire) and are channeled to the receiver.

The current, vastly amplified, is fed onto the grid of a cathode-ray tube called a Kinescope. Thus controlled, the cathode-ray beam paints on the tube face 250,000 pin points of light, which vary in intensity as the current varies at the grid. The resulting picture may be viewed directly or magnified (as shown) by lenses and mirrors, then projected on a screen.

The image projected on the Kinescope face is in black and white. The illusion of color is created by viewing it through a revolving color disk that is automatically synchronized with the color drum in the studio camera by a radio pulse. One hundred and twenty separate red, green, and blue images are blended by the eye to produce twenty complete color frames a second.

- DR. PETER VENKMAN
- DR. RAYMOND STANTZ
- DR. EGON SPENGLER
- WINSTON ZEDDEMORE
- DANA BARRETT
- LOUIS TULLY
- JANINE MELNITZ
- WALTER PECK
- STAY PUFT MARSHMALLOW MAN

December, 1951   N.M.S.L. 7001

Andrew DeGraff, *Paths of the Ghostbusters*, 2014.

"There's no small films, only small illustrative mappers," illustrator
Andrew DeGraff proclaimed in an interview. He created diagrams
of characters' trajectories—through space or time—in a number of
iconic movies. This one indicates where the characters in *Ghostbusters*,
keyed individually to the color of each path, could be found in New
York. The movie's denouement, where the ghostbusters finally crossed
paths with their nemesis at the top of 55 Central Park West, unfolds
at the top of the map.

**Guide to the Statue, from *Statue of Liberty National
Monument, Liberty Island, New York*, by Benjamin Levine
and Isabelle Story, 1957.**

A simple and crisp cutaway with a coloring-book aesthetic visualizes
a guided tour of the city's most enduring symbol. "Anyone finding the
climb too arduous may cross over to the descending stair," suggests
the handbook about the two-way spiral at number seven.

TRISHA BROWN AND GROUP

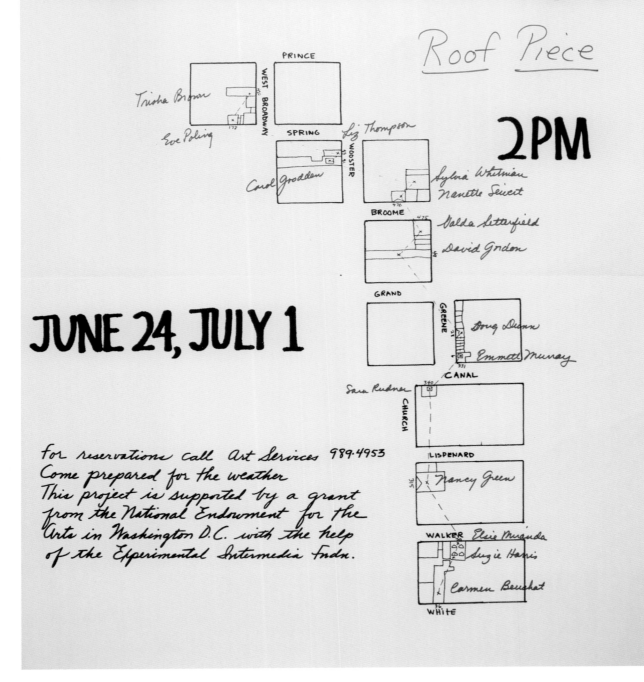

Roof Piece

2PM

JUNE 24, JULY 1

for reservations call Art Services 989·4953
Come prepared for the weather
This project is supported by a grant
from the National Endowment for the
Arts in Washington D.C. with the help
of the Experimental Intermedia Fndn.

PRINCE

Trisha Brown

Eve Poling

WEST BROADWAY

SPRING

Liz Thompson

Carol Gooddew

WOOSTER

Sylvia Whitman
Nanette Sievert

BROOME

Valda Setterfield

David Gordon

GRAND

GREENE

Doug Dunn

Emmett Murray

CANAL

Sara Rudner

CHURCH

LISPENARD

Nancy Green

WALKER Elsie Miranda

Suzie Harris

Carmen Beuchat

WHITE

Trisha Brown, poster for *Roof Piece*, 1973.

Dance notation can be fiendishly complex, but not this diagram for *Roof Piece*, where choreographer and dancer Trisha Brown deployed members of her group, named in red, on SoHo rooftops, with the sightlines between them indicated by dotted lines. Improvising on the first roof, Brown initiated a series of movements that were emulated along the chain, from one roof to the next. Even though the diagram contains very little information that would allow us to visualize the performance, it is surprisingly evocative.

Paula Scher, poster for *Ballet Tech*, 1999.

The type does the dancing in Scher's poster for Eliot Feld's Ballet Tech dance company, while the actual dancers in Lois Greenfield's photographs are there to give structure to the image. The background, a lighting design plan for the Joyce Theater where the performance will take place, connects the poster to a specific New York place and, more generally, to a sense of motion through the city.

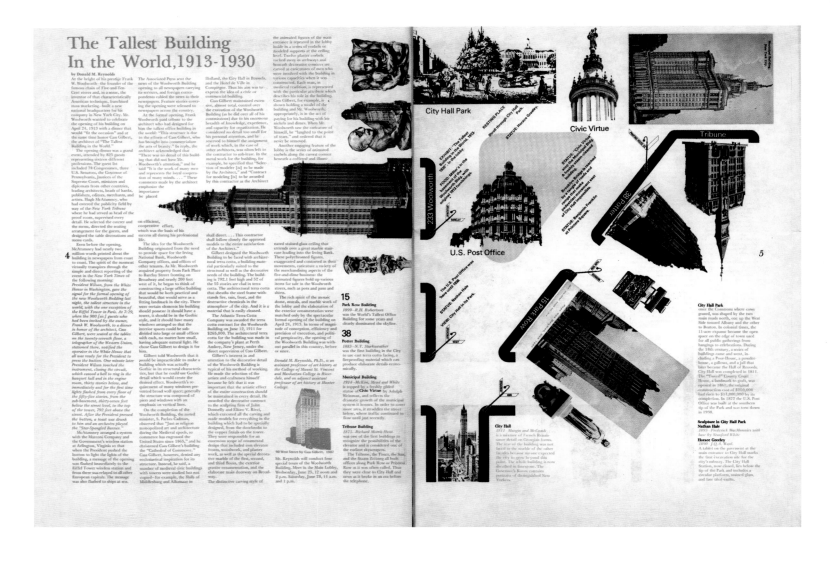

ABOVE AND OPPOSITE

Keith Godard, *Immovable Objects Walking Tour Route*, from *Immovable Objects: An Outdoor Exhibition about City Design on View throughout Lower Manhattan* by the Cooper Hewitt Museum, 1975.

Some objects can't be moved into a museum, so in 1975, the Cooper Hewitt sent the museum to the streets: The exhibition *Immovable Objects* focused on the design of Lower Manhattan by sending museum goers on a walking tour. The catalogue: a tabloid guide printed on newsprint sold at downtown newsstands for fifty cents.

FOLLOWING SPREAD

The UN Building, from *Popular Mechanics*, April 1953.

The United Nations Headquarters occasioned much press coverage when it opened in 1952. But only *Popular Mechanics* magazine took special interest in the organization's electronic communications system, which allowed for simultaneous translation and transmission of meetings throughout the complex in five languages; technology that promised to tame the babel of voices that doomed human cooperation through all of history.

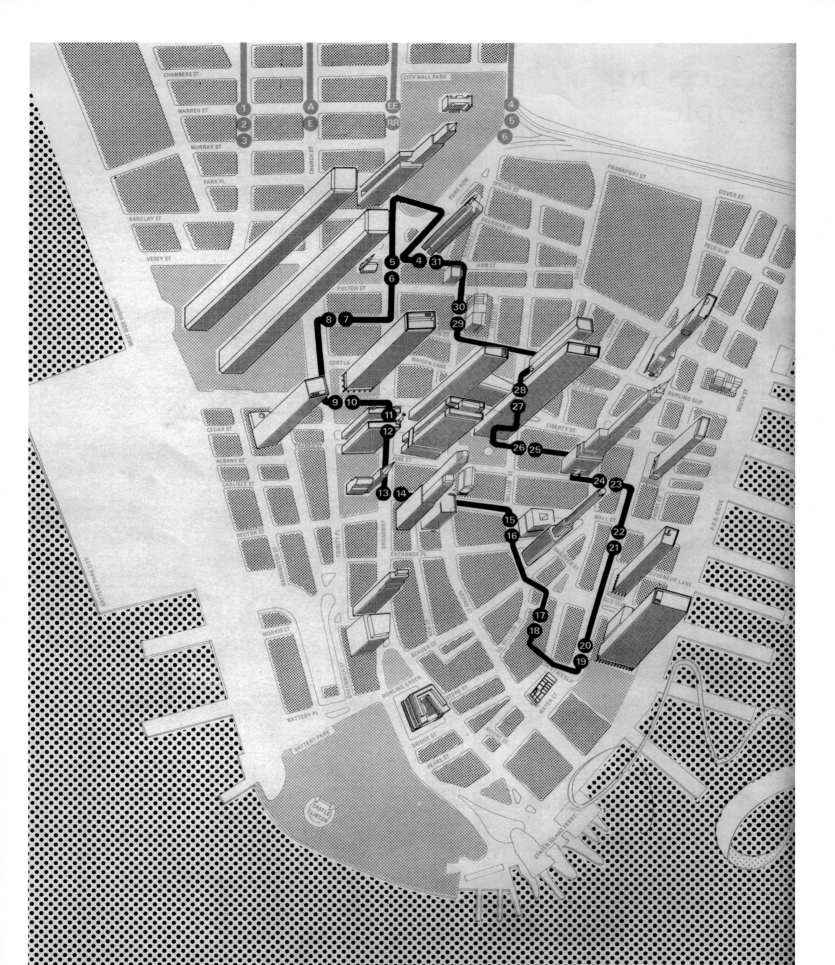

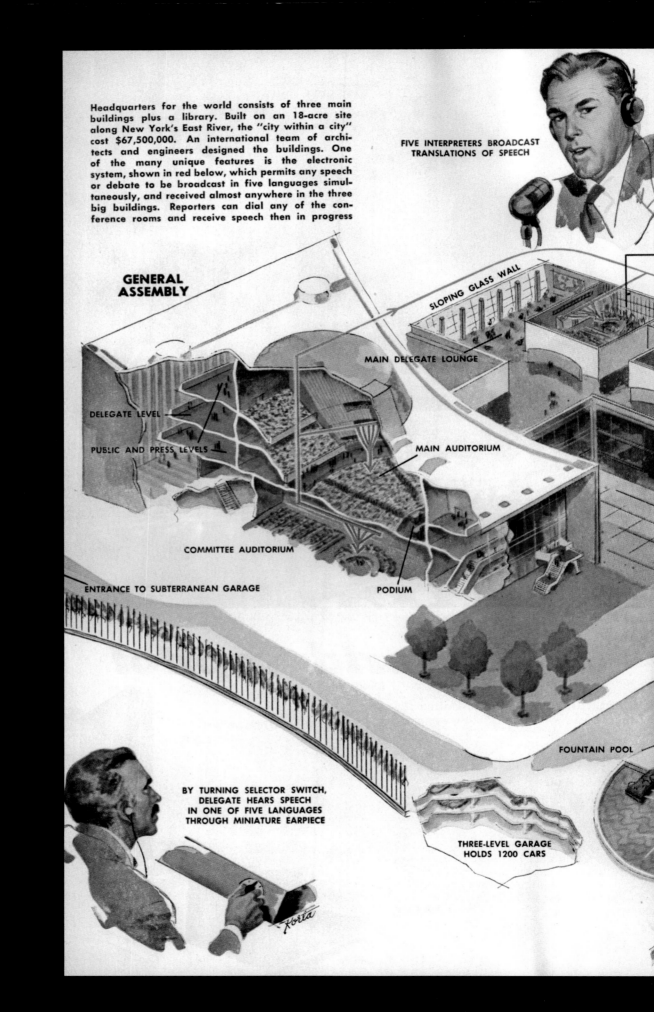

Headquarters for the world consists of three main buildings plus a library. Built on an 18-acre site along New York's East River, the "city within a city" cost $67,500,000. An international team of architects and engineers designed the buildings. One of the many unique features is the electronic system, shown in red below, which permits any speech or debate to be broadcast in five languages simultaneously, and received almost anywhere in the three big buildings. Reporters can dial any of the conference rooms and receive speech then in progress

FIVE INTERPRETERS BROADCAST TRANSLATIONS OF SPEECH

GENERAL ASSEMBLY

SLOPING GLASS WALL

MAIN DELEGATE LOUNGE

DELEGATE LEVEL

PUBLIC AND PRESS LEVELS

MAIN AUDITORIUM

COMMITTEE AUDITORIUM

ENTRANCE TO SUBTERRANEAN GARAGE

PODIUM

FOUNTAIN POOL

BY TURNING SELECTOR SWITCH, DELEGATE HEARS SPEECH IN ONE OF FIVE LANGUAGES THROUGH MINIATURE EARPIECE

THREE-LEVEL GARAGE HOLDS 1200 CARS

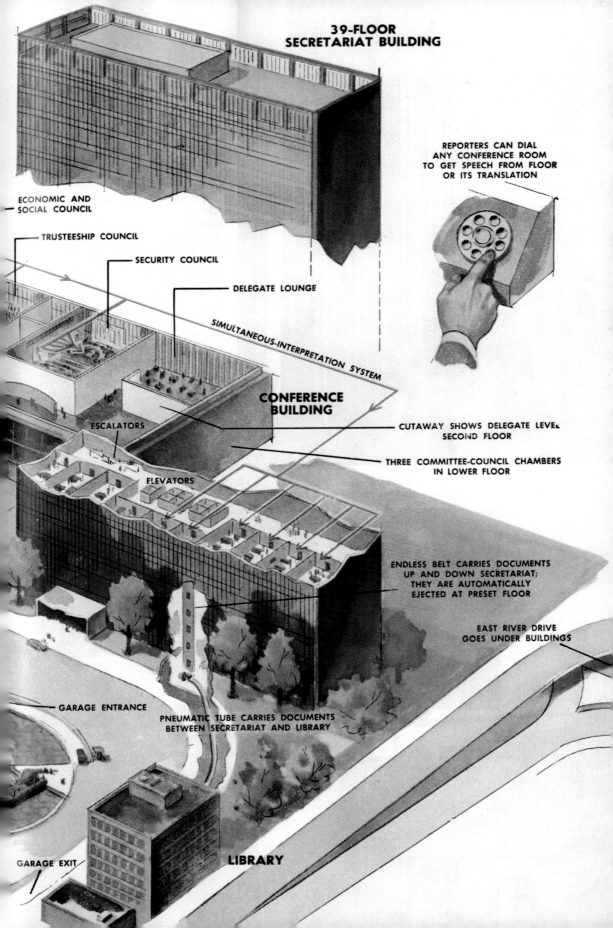

39-FLOOR SECRETARIAT BUILDING

REPORTERS CAN DIAL ANY CONFERENCE ROOM TO GET SPEECH FROM FLOOR OR ITS TRANSLATION

ECONOMIC AND SOCIAL COUNCIL

TRUSTEESHIP COUNCIL

SECURITY COUNCIL

DELEGATE LOUNGE

SIMULTANEOUS-INTERPRETATION SYSTEM

CONFERENCE BUILDING

CUTAWAY SHOWS DELEGATE LEVEL, SECOND FLOOR

ESCALATORS

THREE COMMITTEE-COUNCIL CHAMBERS IN LOWER FLOOR

ELEVATORS

ENDLESS BELT CARRIES DOCUMENTS UP AND DOWN SECRETARIAT; THEY ARE AUTOMATICALLY EJECTED AT PRESET FLOOR

EAST RIVER DRIVE GOES UNDER BUILDINGS

GARAGE ENTRANCE

PNEUMATIC TUBE CARRIES DOCUMENTS BETWEEN SECRETARIAT AND LIBRARY

GARAGE EXIT

LIBRARY

Candy Chan, *Project Subway NYC, X-Ray Area Maps*, 2017.

With *Project Subway NYC*, Candy Chan set out to map subway stations, those complex puzzle pieces that fit so seamlessly into the subterranean cityscape. She reported that as the project developed, "what set out to be a straightforward, mechanical exercise of surveying and drawing gradually turned into a journey of observation, discovery, and amusement."

TOP
Columbus Circle, New York City

MIDDLE
Times Square, New York City

BOTTOM
Union Square, New York City

PAGE 6
Herald Square, New York City

OPPOSITE
Renzo Picasso, *New York Subway—stazioni e vedute prospettiche—tav. 12*, 1929.

Picasso was fascinated by urban transportation systems. A virtuoso draftsman, here he visualizes in elegant diagrams the then-under-construction Broad Street and Fulton Street stations of BMT Nassau line extension, which opened in 1931. Today, these stations are served by J and Z trains.

FOLLOWING SPREAD, LEFT
Renzo Picasso, *New York—ponti e tunnel—tav. 14*, 1929.

Sections of bridges, tunnels, and ferries, showing the disposition of pedestrians, automobiles, and trains.

FOLLOWING SPREAD, RIGHT
Renzo Picasso, *Pulsazioni di Manhattan: Genova e New York a confront—tav.17*, 1929.

Picasso notates the pulses of Manhattan in the city's gridded veins and the traffic lights that regulate the flows and tempos (staggered stoplight systems that kept traffic moving along major arteries were implemented in the late 1920s). He contrasts the complex traffic patterns of Times Square with a sedate intersection on Genoa's Via XX Settembre.

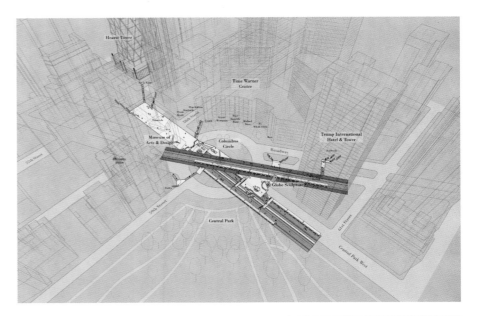

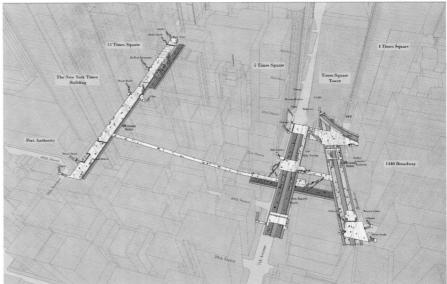

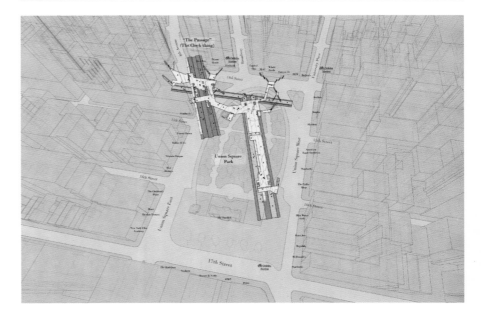

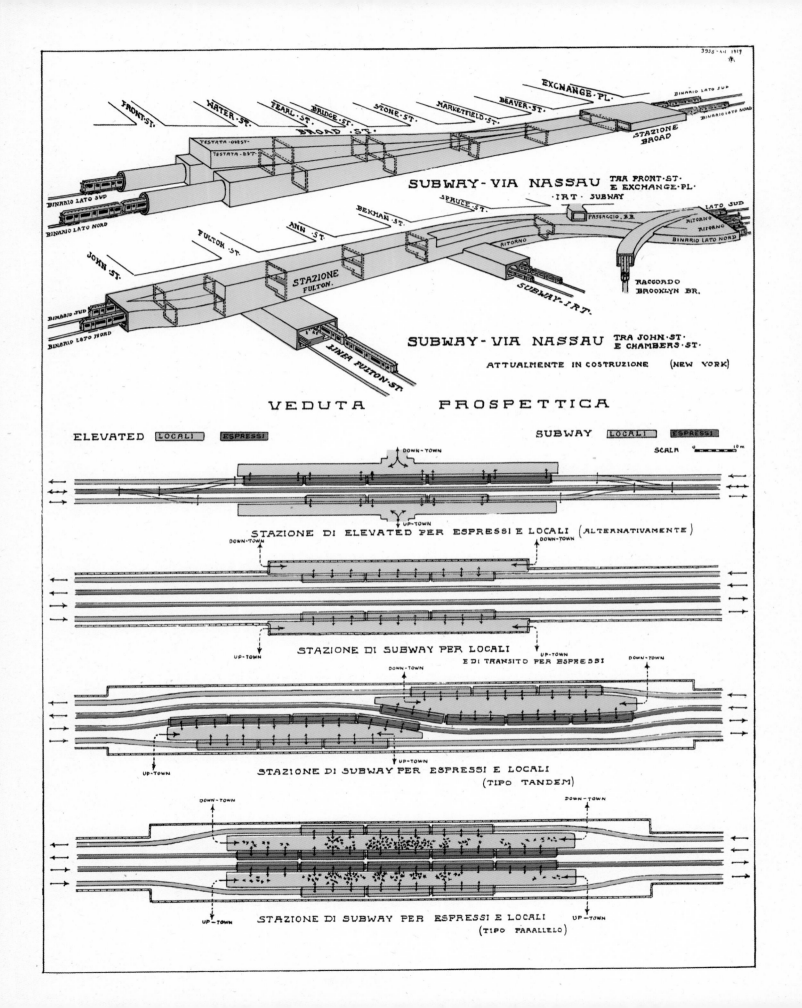

3935 · XII 1929

SUBWAY - VIA NASSAU TRA FRONT·ST· E EXCHANGE·PL·

IRT · SUBWAY

SUBWAY - VIA NASSAU TRA JOHN·ST· E CHAMBERS·ST·

ATTUALMENTE IN COSTRUZIONE (NEW YORK)

VEDUTA PROSPETTICA

ELEVATED LOCALI ESPRESSI   SUBWAY LOCALI ESPRESSI

SCALA 0 10 m

STAZIONE DI ELEVATED PER ESPRESSI E LOCALI (ALTERNATIVAMENTE)

STAZIONE DI SUBWAY PER LOCALI
E DI TRANSITO PER ESPRESSI

STAZIONE DI SUBWAY PER ESPRESSI E LOCALI
(TIPO TANDEM)

STAZIONE DI SUBWAY PER ESPRESSI E LOCALI
(TIPO PARALLELO)

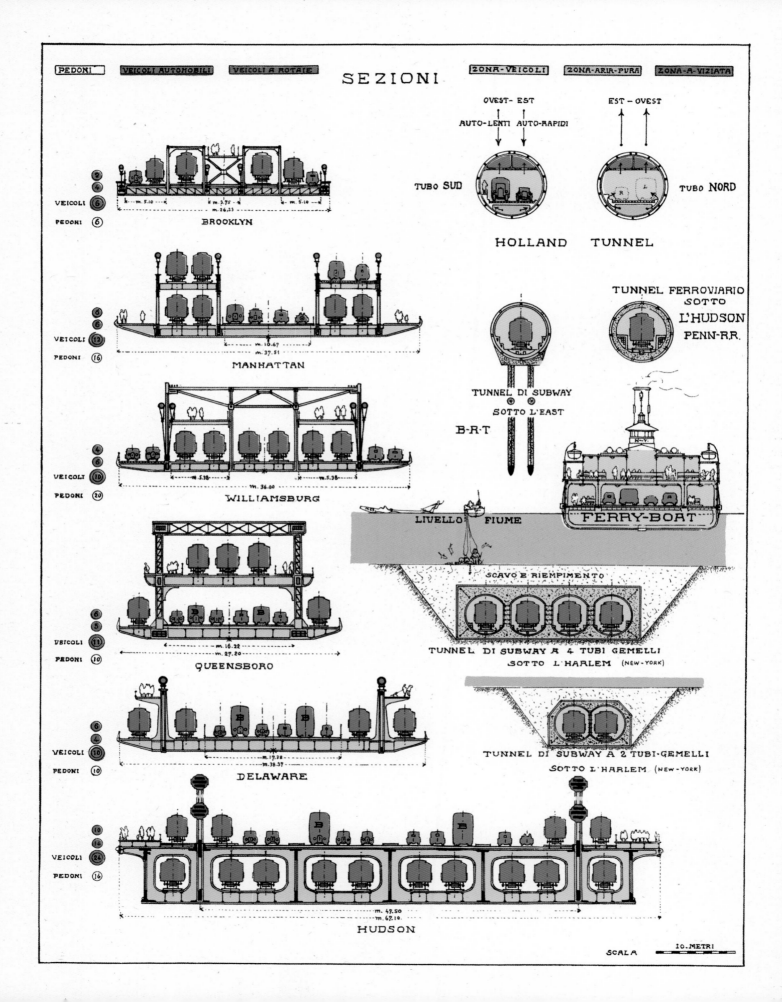

SEZIONI

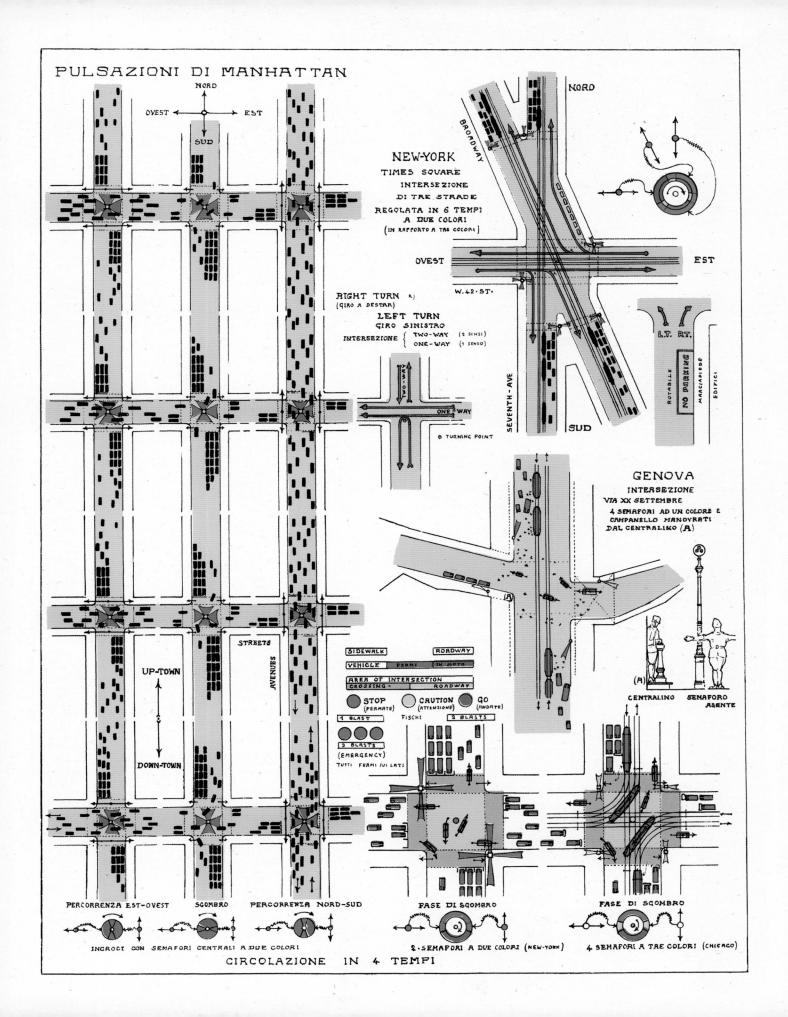

PULSAZIONI DI MANHATTAN

NORD
OVEST — EST
SUD

NEW-YORK
TIMES SQUARE
INTERSEZIONE
DI TRE STRADE
REGOLATA IN 6 TEMPI
A DUE COLORI
(IN RAPPORTO A TRE COLORI)

OVEST — EST

BROADWAY
NORD
W. 42· ST.
SEVENTH · AVE
SUD

RIGHT TURN (R.)
(GIRO A DESTRA)
LEFT TURN
GIRO SINISTRO
INTERSEZIONE { TWO-WAY (2 SENSI)
ONE-WAY (1 SENSO)

ONE-WAY
ONE-WAY
⊕ TURNING POINT

L.T. RT.
ROTABILE
NO PARKING
MARCIAPIEDE
EDIFICI

GENOVA
INTERSEZIONE
VIA XX SETTEMBRE
4 SEMAFORI AD UN COLORE E
CAMPANELLO MANOVRATI
DAL CENTRALINO (A)

STREETS
AVENUES

UP-TOWN
DOWN-TOWN

SIDEWALK   ROADWAY
VEHICLE   FERMI   IN MOTO
AREA OF INTERSECTION
CROSSING —   ROADWAY
STOP (FERMATE)   CAUTION (ATTENZIONE)   GO (ANDATE)
1 BLAST   FISCHI   2 BLASTS
3 BLASTS
(EMERGENCY)
TUTTI FERMI SUI LATI

(A)
CENTRALINO   SEMAFORO
AGENTE

PERCORRENZA EST-OVEST   SGOMBRO   PERCORRENZA NORD-SUD

INCROCI CON SEMAFORI CENTRALI A DUE COLORI

FASE DI SGOMBRO

2· SEMAFORI A DUE COLORI (NEW-YORK)

FASE DI SGOMBRO

4 SEMAFORI A TRE COLORI (CHICAGO)

CIRCOLAZIONE IN 4 TEMPI

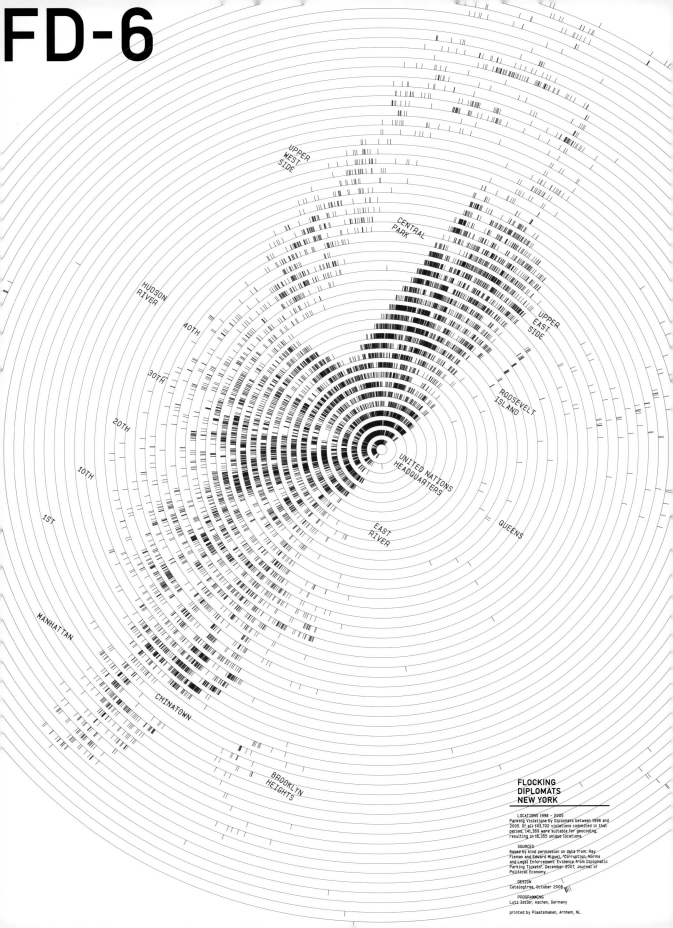

FD-6

FLOCKING
DIPLOMATS
NEW YORK

LOCATIONS 1998 – 2005
Parking Violations by Diplomats between 1998 and
2005. Of all 143,702 violations commited in that
period, 141,369 were suitable for geocoding,
resulting in 15,355 unique locations.

SOURCES
Based by kind permission on data from: Ray
Fisman and Edward Miguel, "Corruption, Norms
and Legal Enforcement: Evidence from Diplomatic
Parking Tickets", December 2007, Journal of
Political Economy.

DESIGN
Catalogtree, October 2008

PROGRAMMING
Lutz Issler, Aachen, Germany

printed by Plaatsmaken, Arnhem, NL

FD-3

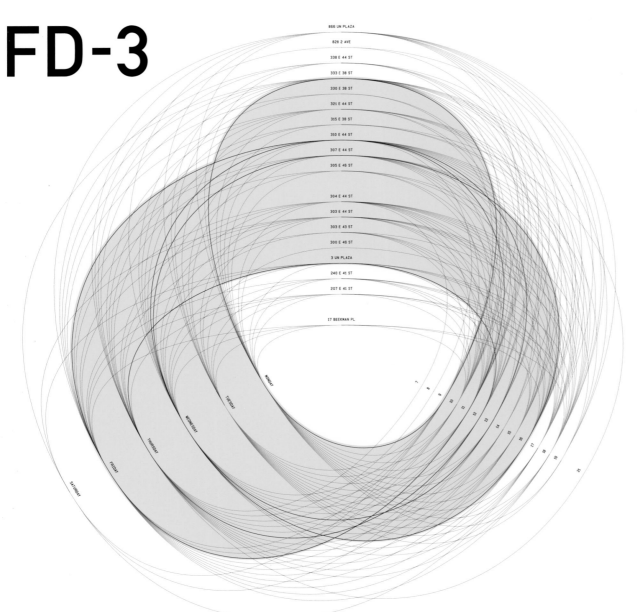

FLOCKING
DIPLOMATS
NEW YORK

SAME TIME, SAME PLACE
Parking Violations by Diplomats in 1999 shown as
polar graph. The Top 20 of addresses with most
violations is shown vertically. The lines connect
the address, time and day of week.
Dotted line: 3 to 6 diplomats meeting
Continuous line: 7 to 11 diplomats meeting

SOURCES
Based by kind permission on data from: Ray
Fisman and Edward Miguel, "Corruption, Norms
and Legal Enforcement: Evidence from Diplomatic
Parking Tickets", December 2007, Journal of
Political Economy.

DESIGN
Catalogtree, January 2008

printed by Plaatsmaken, Arnhem, NL.

Catalogtree (Daniel Gross and Joris Maltha), *Flocking Diplomats,*
2008. Data gathered by Ray Fisman and Edward Miguel.

It sometimes feels like New York City is besieged by diplomats, whose
reluctance to pay parking tickets can lead to outbreaks of public cen-
sure. In 2006, Catalogtree, a multidisciplinary design studio, got hold
of a portion of a large dataset that included unpaid parking tickets
issued to diplomats in New York. The material had been gathered
for research that investigated the role of cultural norms versus legal
enforcement in controlling corruption in different countries. Catalogtree used it to create vibrant visualizations of diplomatic parking
patterns in the city.

OPPOSITE
FD-6

Locations throughout New York City of parking violations by diplomats between 1998 and 2005. Of all 143,702 violations recorded in
that period, 141,369 were suitable for geocoding, resulting in 16,355
unique locations. Programming by Lutz Issler.

ABOVE
FD-3

Parking violations shown as polar graph. The lines connect the
address, time of day, and day of the week. Dotted line: three to six
diplomats meeting. Solid line: seven to eleven diplomats meeting.

PAGE 84
FD-2

Violation-frequency tracings of the top twenty violating diplomats
in 1999.

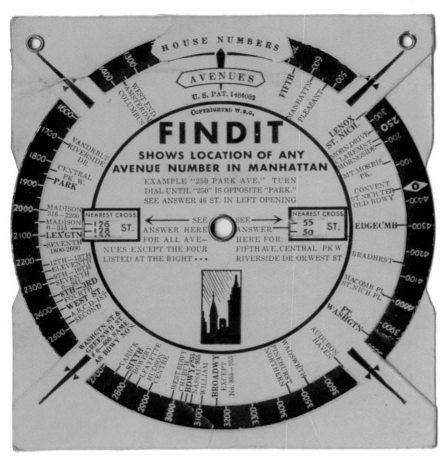

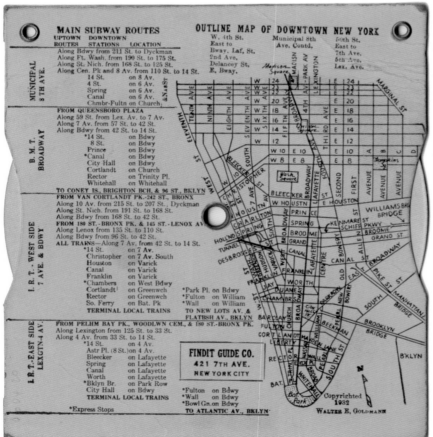

FINDIT GUIDE CO.
421 7TH AVE.
NEW YORK CITY

LEFT

FindIt Guide, 1932.

Rotating volvelles, also known as wheel charts, were very popular in the analog age for just about every need, including wayfinding. This one allows the user trying to locate a specific Manhattan avenue address (say, the Flatiron Building at 175 Fifth Avenue) to find its cross streets (between 22nd Street and 23rd Street).

OPPOSITE

Jason Logan, *Scents and the City*, from the *New York Times*, August 30, 2009.

For illustrator Jason Logan, summer in the city is an excellent time to follow one's nose. "As my nostrils led me from Manhattan's northernmost end to its southern tip, some prosaic scents recurred (cigarette butts; suntan lotion; fried foods); some were singular and sublime (a delicate trail of flowers mingling with Indian curry around 34th Street); while others proved revoltingly unique (the garbage outside a nail salon). Some smells reminded me of other places, and some will forever remind me of New York."

Op-Art

JASON LOGAN

Scents and the City

New York secretes its fullest range of smells in the summer; disgusting or enticing, delicate or overpowering, they are liberated by the heat. So one sweltering weekend, I set out to navigate the city by nose. As my nostrils led me from Manhattan's northern-most end to its southern tip, some prosaic scents recurred (cigarette butts; suntan lotion; fried foods); some were singular and sublime (a delicate trail of flowers mingling with Indian curry around 34th Street); while others proved revoltingly unique (the garbage outside a nail salon). Some smells reminded me of other places, and some will forever remind me of New York.
— JASON LOGAN, an illustrator and the author of "If We Ever Break Up, This Is My Book"

I NY

COMMON AND RECURRENT SUMMER SMELLS

THE PSEUDO-IRISH-PUB SCENT
Bar cloth; last night's party.

THE GALLERY SMELL
Ceiling paint (matte); cardboard; air conditioning and nothing else.

HARLEM, OUTSIDE CHURCH
Shellacked church pews; wintergreen gum; chips.

THE SMELL OF MONEY
Tangy; metallic-dusty; Play-Doh.

THE SUBWAY SCENT
Smells like the Industrial Revolution.

THE SUBWAY-GRATE SCENT
Rotting oranges.

THE PAY PHONE SCENT
Mostly urine.

THE GROCERY STORE SCENT
Floor polish; cardboard; packaging.

THE BOOKSTORE SCENT
Plastic wrap.

A.T.M. SCENT
Laser printer ink on receipt paper.

N.Y.U. CAMPUS
Slight smell of chicken soup (at night).

COLUMBIA CAMPUS
Parents.

CITY COLLEGE CAMPUS
No scent.

STRONG ALMOST EVERYWHERE
Pretzels; coffee chain garbage; cigarettes; fried stuff; tourists; urine.

FORT GEORGE, THE CLOISTERS
Spilled beer; mown grass; something sweet; something musky-and-woodsy that may or may not be deodorant; organic dog food; dog feces; dogs; spicy-mossy-fruity shrubbery; piney orange blossom; vanilla; faint roses; light perfume; subtle, incense-like burning cloves mixed with a dash of patchouli; Camphor Artemisia; fennel flowers; mint; pear; lemon balm; sweet bay leaf; fig ripening; Spanish lavender.

WASHINGTON HEIGHTS
Urine; diesel; chips; burgers; unventilated garbage; mashed potatoes and gravy (P.S. 28); cardboard; beer; rose soap; yucca; waxy deodorant; car air freshener; dog; bacon, egg and cheese sandwich; old fry grease; Popsicle; cannolis; fabric softener; fried noodles with MSG; window cleaner; silkscreened shirts; all-purpose cleaner; spicy salami; spicy-sweet perfume; onions and pizza; ketchup; cigarettes; macaroni; onion mixed with cough drops; cinnamon and roast pork; ripe plantains; overripe mangoes; decaying bananas; cigar and Creamsicle; roasting chickens; cabbage with beef broth; watermelon; cheese Danish; vinegar; burned-out motor; sour-metallic (George Washington Bridge Bus Station); cream soda; fish cakes.

HAMILTON HEIGHTS
Chicken; syrupy perfume; fried fish; grocery garbage; cardboard; soapy perfume; banana; faint sawdust; tar; shellacked church pews; wintergreen gum; rum or cologne; frying fish; pineapple Popsicle; stinky Laundromat; apple-y beer.

MORNINGSIDE HEIGHTS
Wood chips; damp tennis ball; general dog scent; cabbage; cocoa; simple floral perfume; paint; fountain; greenery; air conditioning; chlorine; lemon balm; Port-o-Potty; melon mixed with air conditioner; fruit salad; socks; urine.

CENTRAL PARK (NORTH END)
Canada geese; runners' sweat; spicy-lemony pink flowers; bark; pink blossoms; subtle sun-drenched lime; fertilizer (stinks); mulch; moss; rock; beer; dead leaves; mown grass; ripe blackberries (untouched); wildflower meadow; dewy grass; mown grass; sour gooseberry; silt; mud; pungent Chihuahua.

CENTRAL PARK (SOUTH END)
Horses; algae; ice cream; duck dander; shopping bags; sweat and hair conditioner; fragrant tree; burgers (on the Sheep Meadow); glossy magazines; dust; green acorns; very bright red Slurpee; ice cream sandwich; delicious curry; touch of pine; the lake; algae; oil paint (cheap).

MIDTOWN
New clothes; sporty perfume; new jeans; popcorn; sharp perfume; sundaes with nuts; horses; garbage; horse urine; salami; butter and white wine sautéing; citrus with leather; confusing scent from shopping bag; fries; exhaust; fries; ripening pineapple; ginger; soap; baby powder; nuts; pretzels; body odor; sweet perfume; cheap leather; tea-tree oil; knockoff handbags; gum; cigarettes; yoga sweat; New York cheesecake; wood; flip-flops; new jeans; plastic bags; homeless man with cats; tourists; salty Armani leather; cigar; lip gloss; tropical fruit; touch of vomit; jelly beans; butterscotch; artificial tropical fruit candy; citronella; sweet, rotten-oats horse breath.

MIDTOWN SOUTH
Perfect grilled cheese; sweet barbecue; tangy cologne mingled with beef broth and celery; a woman purposely wearing no scent; toasting Indian spices; rich curries; cigarettes; figs ripening; muffins; subtle but rank perfume.

THEATER DISTRICT
Pretzels; diesel; cigarettes; hot bus tires; pavement; close, thick scent; whiff of modeling clay, carried on the warm air from a vent; licorice-y bus toilet; old beer; green apple shampoo; nice smelling women.

HELL'S KITCHEN
Cops (soap); tomato sauce (metallic); freshly watered tomato plants; plum sauce; Dumpster under tarp; urine in mud puddle; glossy magazine; gin or vodka on sweat; lemon cleaner; car hood/engine; wet soil; fried popcorn shrimp; homeless man eating Chinese food; garage; suntan lotion; fake strawberry; spa garbage; roses mixing with rose perfume (at a church); cat urine or some kind of ripe flower; sweet-and-sour barbecue; luggage; strong gust of air freshener from taxi.

CHELSEA
Freesia; nachos; slice in a box; floor polish; cardboard; packaging; pizza; cilantro; clean sweat; dandruff shampoo; coffee grounds and sour milk; cologne; canvas; crates; spicy cologne; stinky subway grate; pet store.

WEST VILLAGE
Italian cologne; chaps; bourbon; vanilla air freshener; gasoline; drywall; ketchup and onions; horse; cilantro and butter; blood; meat; chocolate ice cream; calamari; fresh grass; leather vest; mouthwash; feet; spearmint gum; fertilizer; exotic-island flowering tree; floral; dog; parking garage; wood; beer; organic cigarettes; red wine in a plastic cup; candles.

GREENWICH VILLAGE
Strong urine becoming floral; toast becoming barbecue; watermelon; honeydew; onion; pineapple; roasting running shoes; wintergreen; drought-tolerant Russian sage; cedar chips; bitter Ethiopian coffee; burnt sugar undertones; black pepper; printed cotton; Indonesian silkscreen; bamboo; gladiolas wrapped in newspaper; waffles; cocoa butter; butcher's garbage; bleach; hair wax; sweat; falafel; burgers; chocolate crepes; black coffee.

TRIBECA
Deep-fried something; good cigar; bus; deep-dust-mineral smell of subway; fries; tar; diesel; warm bacon-y wind; tangy metal; toilet chemicals; fry grease; pretzel eaters; broken bricks; musky deodorant; onion rings; hot dogs; sauerkraut; blood; faux-leather fanny pack.

HARLEM
Aggressively (almost territorially) soapy cologne; rum; peanuts; hot sauce mixed with mayo; pizza mixed with fried chicken; crazy perfume; urine; cat litter; wet wool coat; wet charcoal; vodka mixed with pineapple juice; delicious shrimp grilling; spilled gas; laundry soap; black tea; Chinese food; laundry; cardboard; strawberry drink; ham.

EAST HARLEM
Buffalo-chicken nuggets; cigarettes; exhaust; cherry lip gloss; rotting tangerine; strong floor polish; dry grass; almond perfume; grapefruit rind; gas; diapers (unused); pink roses and Russian sage (very faint); white-Cheddar pop-corn (very strong); touch of urine; black locust blossoms; leafy bark; aftershave; fresh laundry; blossoms and grassy perfume; wet cigar; rancid apricot; Polish, Italian and German sausages cooking in water; deep-fried Oreos.

SPANISH HARLEM
Cigarettes; powdered cleanser; sweet fried dough; mildewing towels; car wax; roses; mole sauce; beans going sour, through exhaust fan; green peppers; dill and mint at tiny farmers' market; dog urine; human urine; freshly shaved men; orange drink; garbage.

YORKVILLE
Everything bagels.

TURTLE BAY
Cleaning products; "Elegant Lobster Pie"; doughnut; bananas.

UPPER EAST SIDE
Fragrant flowering bush (behind a statue of Samuel Morse); fresh plants; shampoo-y deodorant; soft strawberry ice cream; freshly watered ferns; medicinal-smelling person.

LENOX HILL
Musty, metallic phone booth; cookies mixed with bus exhaust; mildewy towels; soft ice cream; dust; fries; cardboard; garbage; coffee; baby's breath (the flower).

SUTTON PLACE
Tiramisu; dogs; celery salt; babies; Indian cologne; urine; beer; garbage; bland cheese; hot bagels in plastic bag.

BEEKMAN
Gladiolas.

MURRAY HILL
Watermelon; hair salon; doughnut; pizza; sesame seeds.

KIPS BAY
Long Island peaches; shower gel; uncooked pizza dough; zucchini; cinnamon bun; grocery scent; doughnuts.

GRAMERCY PARK
Dark; earthy; green.

STUYVESANT TOWN
Fried dough; pizza; hair spray; soap; dog feces.

NOLITA
Mildew; tacos; Moroccan spice; something tingly-youthful-citrus.

SOHO
Excessive farmers' market basil; suntan lotion; tortilla chips; Russian sage; mild urine; mineral brick; sewage; brunch; dryish fine cheese; soapy; cigarettes; patchouli; leather; frozen yogurt; soap; recycled paper; gallery; ketchup and potatoes; doughnut; hot nuts; deep-fried something; old cigar; bus; mayo; shawarma; onion; strong urine; indecipherable metal.

LITTLE ITALY
Garlic; lotion; cypress; rotting lettuce; dry concrete.

ALPHABET CITY
Laundry; beer; juniper; hair wax; soap; dog feces; frying chicken; tanning oil; possible human feces.

BOWERY
Packaging; brunch; nail polish; sweet meat; hard-to-place perfume; plywood; upscale perfume; knish; charcoal; garbage; suburban shampoo; calamari; ceviche; beeswax; falafel.

LOWER EAST SIDE
Barbecue chicken; teak; sugary nuts; a zingy flowery perfume with a powdery trail; packaging; confusing perfume; renovation; garbage; butter.

CHINATOWN
Green coconut milk; moldy newspapers; soap; muddy shellfish; lychee; fresh fish; clay; crabs; chicken; cigarettes; plastic; sharp, sweet pork; delicious Chinese lunch from trapdoor under restaurant; miniature orange tree in the sun; dried mushrooms; dried shrimp; still-breathing fish; tiny dried fish; unfresh snails; cigar; rum butter; something vanilla-coconut-sugary; soap; dog feces; garbage; floral sandalwood; pickled pavement.

WALL STREET
Onion bagel; hot dogs; ice cream sandwich; cheap suntan lotion; wet cigarette butts; gas.

CIVIC CENTER
Spray paint; garbage; vinegar.

WHITE HALL
Energy drink evaporating on sidewalk; waffles; sweat; nectarines; fresh oysters; zingy bathroom; air duct.

BATTERY PARK CITY
Soap; cologne; feet; hot dogs; welding; gum; shoe polish; cigarettes; tangerine candy; deodorant; cedar; bus clutch; spilled gas; wet wood; candied almonds; bathroom deodorizer.

Smell Stops

DAY
NIGHT

1. Hip wedding in the linden grove at Fort Tryon Park: scent of incense (like burning cloves mixed with patchouli); lightly perfumed guests.
2. Reconstruction of Alexander Hamilton's house (which has been relocated twice): whiff of sawdust.
3. Crawl space between the oft-used machines that recycle beer and wine bottles: fermentation; apples; fear. *
4. Baseball court covered in tiny white blossoms: a subtle smell like fresh linen (could be black locust).
5. Elegant lobster pie (East 45th Street): did not try it.
6. Apartment of a man I just met who lent me his bicycle after a very late-night discussion about the morality of poets and the writings of Guy de Maupassant and David Foster Wallace: Campari; cigarellos; undertone of Eastern European soup.
7. Fancy wedding on a deserted street: orange roses; unfriendly member of wedding party would not tell me which variety.
8. World Trade Center site: welding and tourists.
9. Breakfast: spaghetti carbonara; eggs and baked cod; fresh latte; hint of last night's rum and Campari; the waiter's fresh cologne.
10. On the sidewalk outside a trattoria on Ninth Avenue: freshly watered green tomato plants.
11. 33rd Street and Lexington Avenue: perfect-smelling grilled cheese.
12. Strawberry Fields, Central Park: someone eating a delicious curry.
13. The Wildflower Meadow, Central Park: milkweed; daisy; columbine; flocks of birds; toasted oats; wood; honey; my childhood; bark. **
14. The scent of Stoney, "E" and Bridget sitting on a stoop explaining to me the problems with the landlords, why food should be free and how the landlords and the rats are connected: vodka mixed with pineapple juice.
15. Delicious-smelling shrimp shish kebab ($5).
16. Columbia campus, beside the steps to Low Memorial Library: right after a heated argument with a young man, a young woman takes off a layer of clothing, sprays deodorant on; also a whiff of foundation; hair gel; background scents of greenery and the nearby fountain; very faint acrid smell of a new coat of black paint applied to the awning of the mathematics building.
17. Memorial to an Amiable Child: no scent.
18. A piñata store: not-so-fresh car air freshener.

* *Most vile.*

** *Most sublime.*

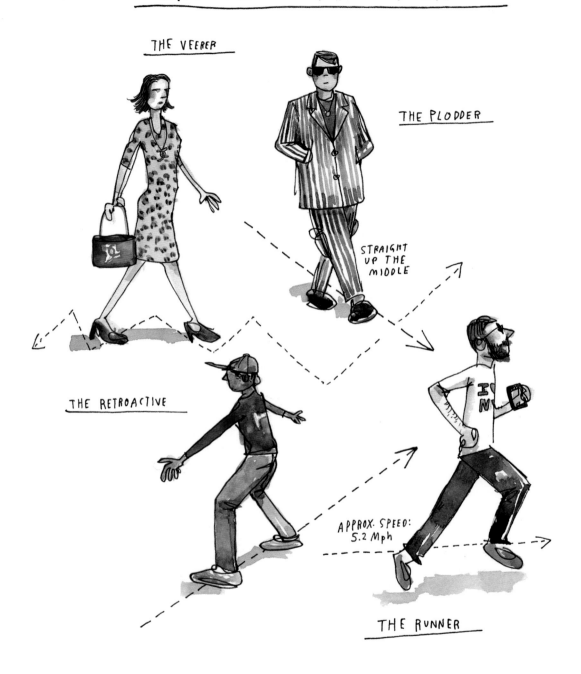

JAYWALKERS of NEW YORK

THE VEERER

THE PLODDER

STRAIGHT UP THE MIDDLE

THE RETROACTIVE

APPROX. SPEED: 5.2 Mph

THE RUNNER

ABOVE

Wendy MacNaughton and Maria Popova, *Jaywalkers of New York*, 2013.

The term "jaywalker," applied to someone who crosses the street against the stoplight or in midblock, was evidently first used by M. B. Levick in the *New York Times* in 1924. In 2013, writer Maria Popova read his piece, titled "The Confusion of Our Sidewalkers: And the Traffic Problem of the Future in the Erratic Pedestrian," and teamed up with illustrator Wendy MacNaughton to create contemporary avatars of the types described therein: the veerer, the plodder, the retroactive, and the runner.

OPPOSITE

Saul Steinberg, untitled drawing, 1984. Reproduced on the cover of *The New Yorker*, June 8, 1992.

There is nothing erratic in Steinberg's intimate schematic of his morning walk. Diligent street crossing "diagonally, never at the crosswalks" was a characteristic feature of his precise tour of his favorite store windows.

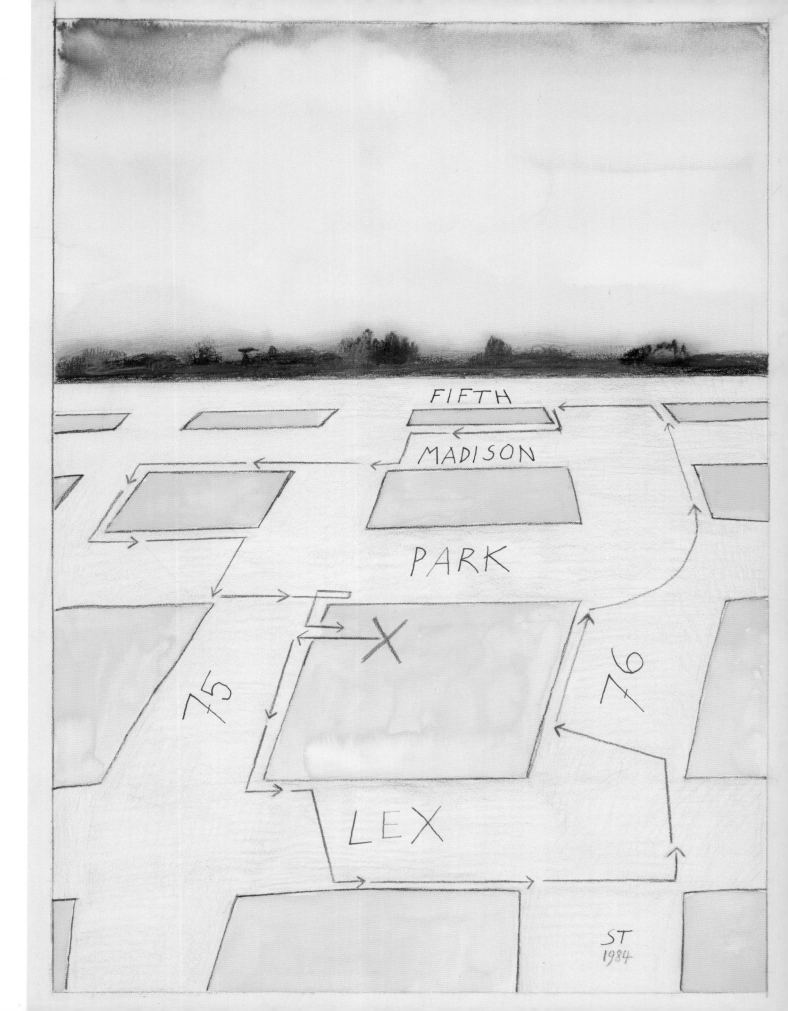

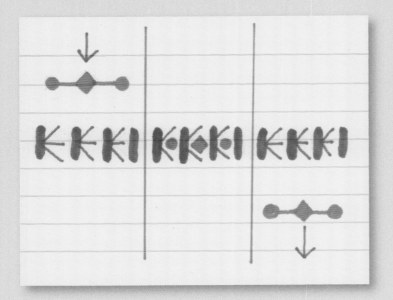

"Whenever I rode the subway with my two older boys, I tried to hold on to their hands at all times. In the process, I developed a special move. Anyone who saw it must have been impressed.

I would hold the boys' hands as we briskly made our way out of the station, then, just as we reached the turnstiles, I would let go. We would pass through the turnstiles simultaneously, and so smoothly that the boys' hands would still be up in the air when we got to the other side, where I would grab their little fingers again in one fluid motion. (Requires practice.)"

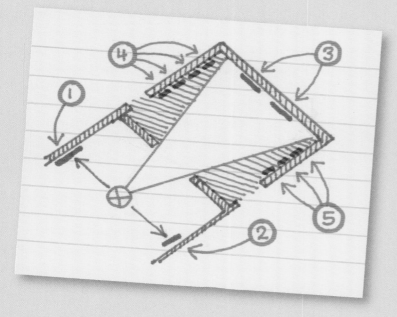

"It is always great to visit the Museum of Modern Art, but I have pretty strong likes and dislikes, especially when it comes to paintings from the nineteenth and twentieth centuries. And I have a hard time enjoying a beloved painting while being irritated by another, less beloved piece of art. If you happen to share my preferences, I suggest the following:

In room 1 on the fifth floor, stand exactly in between Gauguin's *Seed of the Areoi* (1) and *Braque's Landscape at La Ciotat* (2). Turn east, facing room 5, and you will be able to enjoy two wonderful Klimts (*Hope II* and *The Park*) (3) without being annoyed by the pointless Kandinskys (4), to the left, and Chagall's disturbing cow (5), to the right."

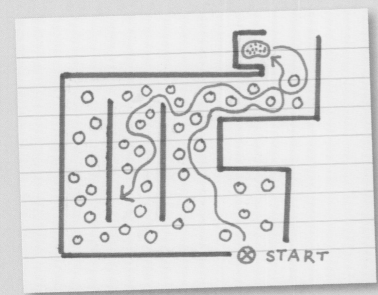

"Shopping at the crowded Fairway supermarket in Red Hook with an impatient toddler in your cart is not easy. (The first section—fruits and vegetables—is especially treacherous, as quick little hands can threaten the large pyramid of Fuji apples.)

The solution: Try to make it to the olive-oil-tasting station (opposite the cheese counter) and stock up on sliced baguette. This will keep the young shoppers happy, at least for a while. The only downside: going against the stream in the narrow soup aisle on your way back to the produce."

"Every parent knows that the surest way to get children to fall asleep is to roll them around in strollers on bumpy sidewalks. Since I spent a good chunk of the last several years pushing infants through New York, I have the following recommendations:

When our first son was born, we were living in Chelsea. Here you mostly find the standard four-by-four-foot concrete squares that result in roughly one bump per second. A perfectly fine starter surface for the new father.

With our second child, we graduated to the cobblestone streets of Dumbo, which have the bonus of being broken up by an occasional rail. Pushing a stroller here is physically challenging, but your little darling will be snoring within seconds.

With our third son, I discovered the Champs-Elysées for putting kids to sleep: the west sidewalk along Columbia Heights, in Brooklyn. Tree roots have rearranged the old granite slabs into a bizarre topography. Navigating a stroller through the jumps and jolts is not for the faint of heart, but to my amazement, I have never seen a baby fall asleep as peacefully."

"In the morning, I used to take the 2 or 3 train from Clark Street to get to my studio in Manhattan's Meatpacking District. Here's some advice, if you happen to make that commute, too: When you get off the elevator at the Clark Street station, go down the stairs to the left. On the platform, make a sharp left; this will position you directly behind a column (A). It's pretty close to the tracks, so there will be very few people around, thereby improving your chances of getting on, even at rush hour. If you happen to bring a newspaper, use one door farther up (B).

When you arrive at Fourteenth Street station and step off, you'll be near the Thirteenth Street exit, and the door will open right in front of the stairs (C). If you chose the newspaper option mentioned above, the door will open in front of a convenient trash can, where you can discard your paper (D) before leaving the subway system."

Christoph Niemann, _New York Cheat Sheets,_ from _Abstract City,_ the _New York Times_, October 13, 2008.
Christoph Niemann, known for his conceptual illustrations, published these deceptively meaningless Post-it Note diagrams of aspects of city life in his _New York Times_ column "Abstract City."

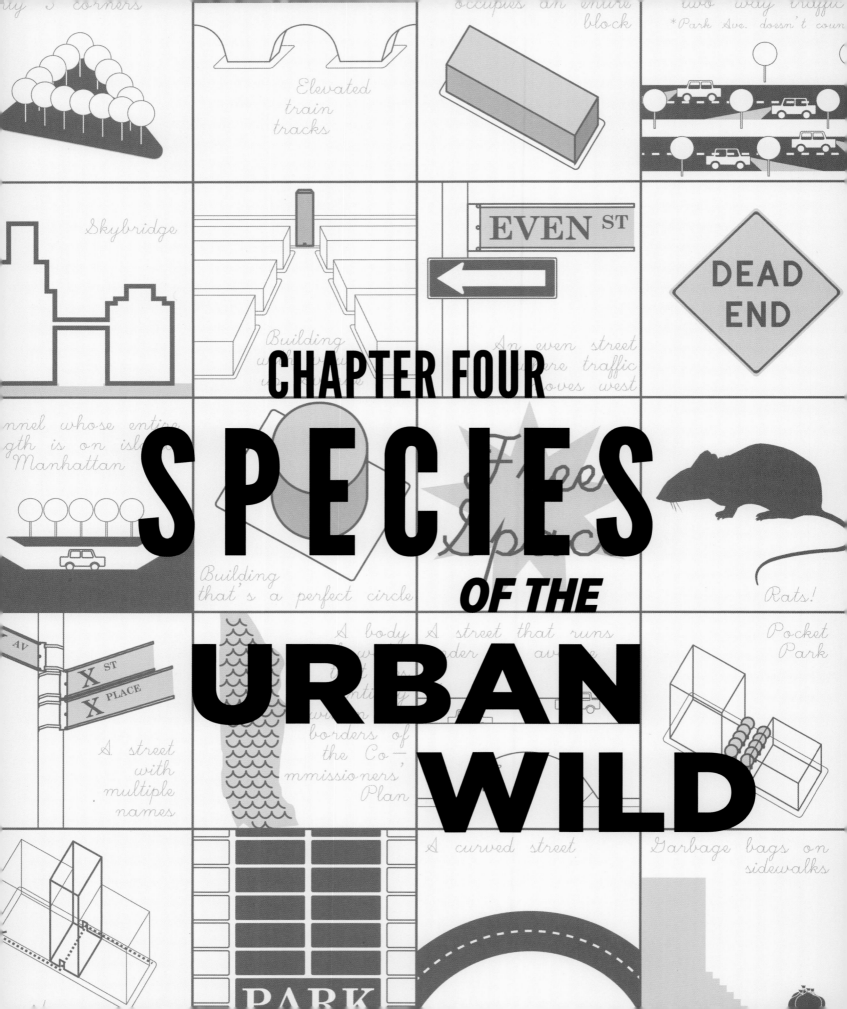

CHAPTER FOUR

SPECIES

OF THE

URBAN WILD

Jaywalkers

Central Park

Bike racks

Rail yard

4 AV

HARDLY A WILDERNESS, MANHATTAN IS NONETHELESS AN urban wild with a unique array of ecologies: diverse nationalities, cultural and sexual subcultures, aesthetic cliques, and social eccentrics. And add to ecologies, typologies of every conceivable variety of structure that mushroom out of the layers of cobblestone, asphalt, glassphalt, and concrete deposited by the endless Vesuvius of change.

Manhattan has its above-ground and underground worlds. Ever-higher, soaring buildings have long been a source of fascination, as in Nigel Holmes's *Rebuilding the World Trade Center (9 Years Later)* (page 128); so too the realms below, captured by Emil Lowenstein in *This Is What Lies Under the Surface*, a diagram for *Fortune* magazine in 1939 that pictures an intricate mélange of urban infrastructure that shows how fragile and complex Manhattan has become over the centuries (page 145).

To survive in Manhattan a species must adapt—for better and worse—or disappear. Take New York's building types, for example: We have already touched on Albert Berghaus's double-page cross section of tenement houses in 1865 (pages 114–115), which reveals the overcrowded conditions of the nineteenth-century urban poor (sadly not much has changed in some neighborhoods). Turn the page and juxtaposed are rows of neatly manicured, turn-of-the-century emporia, offices, and theaters (page 116) built for the better-off along Broadway. Many of those fell into disrepair and are gone. Below these, pictured about ninety years later in Steven Guarnaccia's intriguing *Walk on 53rd Street*, are the corporate flagships that uprooted the old for the new (pages 116–117). Two proud renderings of Pennsylvania Station in 1910 (pages 122–124) show the majesty of the structure that was replaced by the hackneyed one seen in the cutaway by Henry Comstock of Madison Square Garden (page 125).

Manhattan is famously an island of quirky and eccentric people and things. Maira Kalman's comic portrait of Manhattanites wrangles some of the local types (page 150). Peter Arkle and Kurt Soller's illustration, *Ten Types of People You See at Fashion Week* (page 148) spotlights the genus *Fashionista* that takes to the streets for this annual celebration of commerce and design.

Such diagrams help visitor and resident learn the city's singular specialties. One of the most informative is a detailed 2009 guide to humble street vendors by Candy Chan, Sean Basinski, Rosten Woo, and John Mangin (pages 152–153). Knowing about this Manhattan phenomenon is as important as knowing exactly what a bodega is (see *What Is a Bodega?* by Nathan W. Pyle, page 153) or learning the periodical table of the wildest of all of the city's invasive species—its garbage, seen here in a witty *Periodic Table of NYC Trash* by Molly Young and Teddy Blanks (pages 154–155).

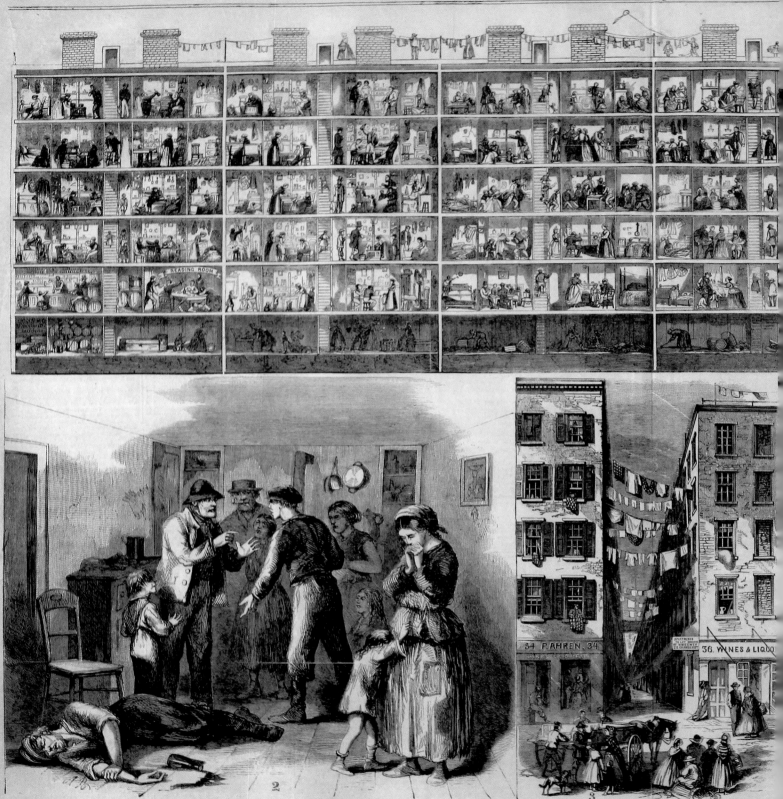

1. SIDE SECTIONAL VIEW OF TENEMENT HOUSE, 38 CHERRY STREET, N. Y.   2. AN ACTUAL SCENE IN ONE OF THE ROOMS, AS WITNESSED BY OUR ARTIST.   3. LOOKING UP WEST GOTHAM

THE TENEMENT HOUSES OF NEW YORK—HOW THE POOR LIVE IN CROWDED CITIES—HOW PESTILENCE IS GENERATED—HOW THE PARENTS ARE DEMORALIZED AND TH

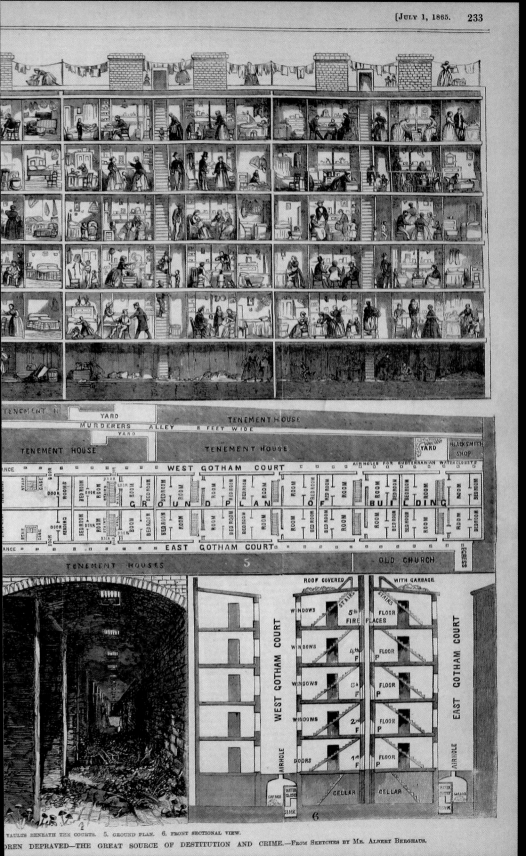

VAULTS BENEATH THE COURTS.   5. GROUND PLAN.   6. FRONT SECTIONAL VIEW.

DREN DEPRAVED—THE GREAT SOURCE OF DESTITUTION AND CRIME.—FROM SKETCHES BY MR. ALBERT BERGHAUS.

Albert Berghaus, *The Tenement Houses of New York*, from *Frank Leslie's Illustrated Newspaper*, July 1, 1865.

Here, for the middle-class readers of Frank Leslie's Illustrated Newspaper, is a somber vision of urban life: A warehouse packed with poor families, with the lack of light and air and the inadequate sanitary facilities carefully documented in diagrams. For all that, the rooms in this tenement are filled with life and incident, suggesting the combination of attraction and revulsion with which the establishment press viewed the immigrant city.

5-7-9 Union Sq.
CLUETT PEABODY & CO.,
Monarch Shir s, "Cluett," "Coon" and "Arrow" Brand
Collars.

16-18 E. 15th   19 Union Sq.

BROADWAY, WEST SIDE. 14TH TO 17TH ST

J. A. SCRIVEN COMPANY   MUSICAL COURIER.
Shirts & Patent Elastic Seam Drawers.

25 Union S

WHITE & MA,

Umbrellas and Pa

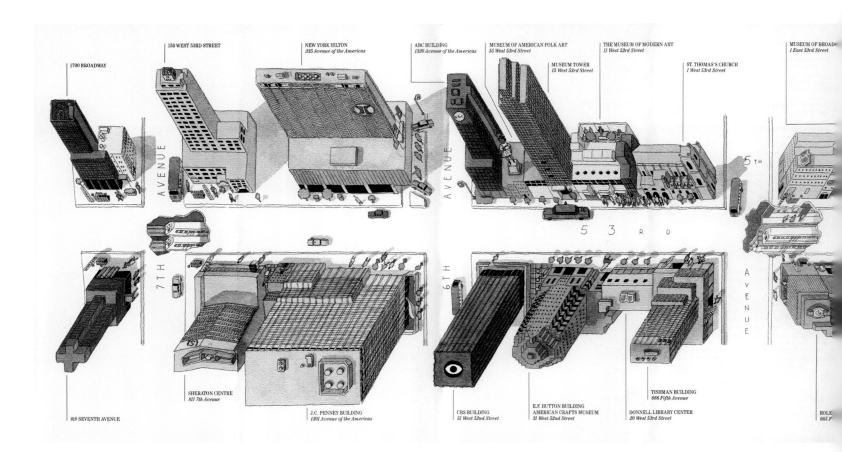

1700 BROADWAY

159 WEST 53RD STREET

NEW YORK HILTON
1335 Avenue of the Americas

ABC BUILDING
1330 Avenue of the Americas

MUSEUM OF AMERICAN FOLK ART
55 West 53rd Street

MUSEUM TOWER
15 West 53rd Street

THE MUSEUM OF MODERN ART
11 West 53rd Street

ST. THOMAS'S CHURCH
1 West 53rd Street

MUSEUM OF BROAD
1 East 53rd Street

5 TH

5 3 R D

7 TH

6 TH

AVENUE

810 SEVENTH AVENUE

SHERATON CENTRE
811 7th Avenue

J.C. PENNEY BUILDING
1301 Avenue of the Americas

CBS BUILDING
51 West 52nd Street

E.F. HUTTON BUILDING
AMERICAN CRAFTS MUSEUM
31 West 52nd Street

DONNELL LIBRARY CENTER
20 West 53rd Street

TISHMAN BUILDING
666 Fifth Avenue

ROLE
665 F

29 Union Sq. 16th St.
BANK OF THE METROPOLIS.

33 Union Sq.
JAMES M. MILLER,
Men's Jewelry.

37 Union Sq. 39 Union Sq. 41 Union Sq.
A. JAECKEL & CO., REED & BARTON,
Furriers. Silversmiths.
SPERRY & BEALE,
Mattings, Carpet Linings. Fibre Carpets, &c.
UNION CARPET LINING Co.

Pictorial description of Broadway, from the *New York Mail and Express*, 1899.

Block-by-block streetscapes of Broadway—the Google Street Views of their day—were always in demand in the nineteenth century. Toward the end of their popularity, the *New York Mail and Express* published a block-by-block visual directory of the street, from Bowling Green to Columbus Circle. Here we find novelty stores, purveyors of umbrellas and parasols, glaziers, and other emporia of the city's past. What doomed the format, besides changing tastes, was the arrival of skyscrapers, which put an end once and for all to a city of roughly uniform building heights.

Steven Guarnaccia and Pentagram New York, *A Walk on 53rd Street*, map for the 53rd Street Association, 1987.

Guarnaccia updates the traditional streetscape with an overhead view of the buildings along 53rd Street that captures a slice of Midtown with a large number of Manhattan's more recognizable postwar skyscrapers. The axonometric projections are ideal for capturing the large bulk and unusual forms of the buildings, just as the elevations used for the *New York Mail and Express* project almost a century earlier suited the architecture of that era.

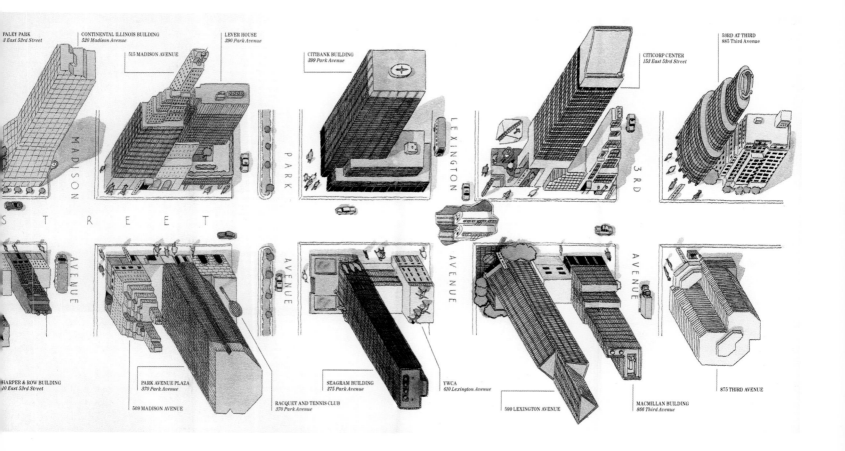

PALEY PARK
3 East 53rd Street

CONTINENTAL ILLINOIS BUILDING
520 Madison Avenue

515 MADISON AVENUE

LEVER HOUSE
390 Park Avenue

CITIBANK BUILDING
399 Park Avenue

CITICORP CENTER
153 East 53rd Street

53RD AT THIRD
885 Third Avenue

MADISON STREET

PARK AVENUE

LEXINGTON AVENUE

3RD AVENUE

HARPER & ROW BUILDING
10 East 53rd Street

PARK AVENUE PLAZA
370 Park Avenue

509 MADISON AVENUE

RACQUET AND TENNIS CLUB
370 Park Avenue

SEAGRAM BUILDING
375 Park Avenue

YWCA
610 Lexington Avenue

599 LEXINGTON AVENUE

MACMILLAN BUILDING
866 Third Avenue

875 THIRD AVENUE

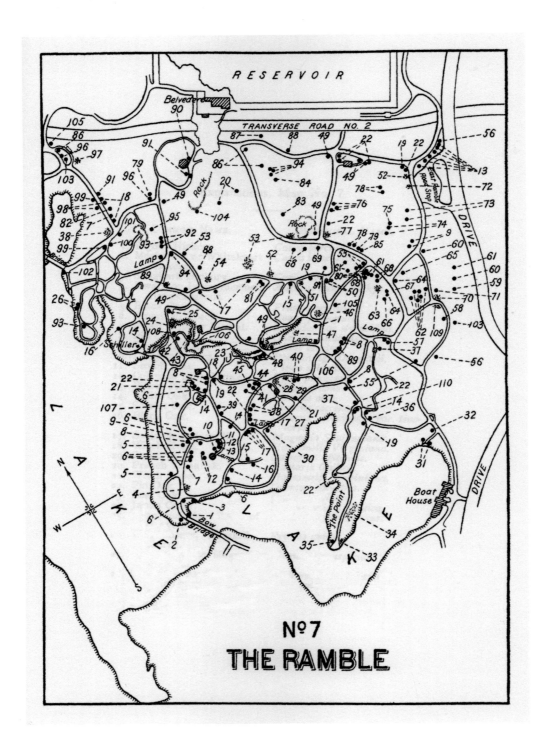

NO 7
THE RAMBLE

Louis Harman Peet, *Trees and Shrubs of Central Park*, 1903.

Central Park landscape designer Frederick Law Olmsted described the Ramble as his "wild garden." The Ramble is thoroughly domesticated in Louis Harman Peet's guide, which takes the mania for diagramming to the limit of comprehensibility: Hundreds of numbered points, keyed to lists of tree species, are situated in maps that could only sow confusion in the user confronted with the natural landscape.

Leslie Roberts, *New York City Approved Street Trees*, 2015.

Roberts transposes color-coded names of street trees into a lyrical grid via complex coding systems, with an element of randomness mixed in.

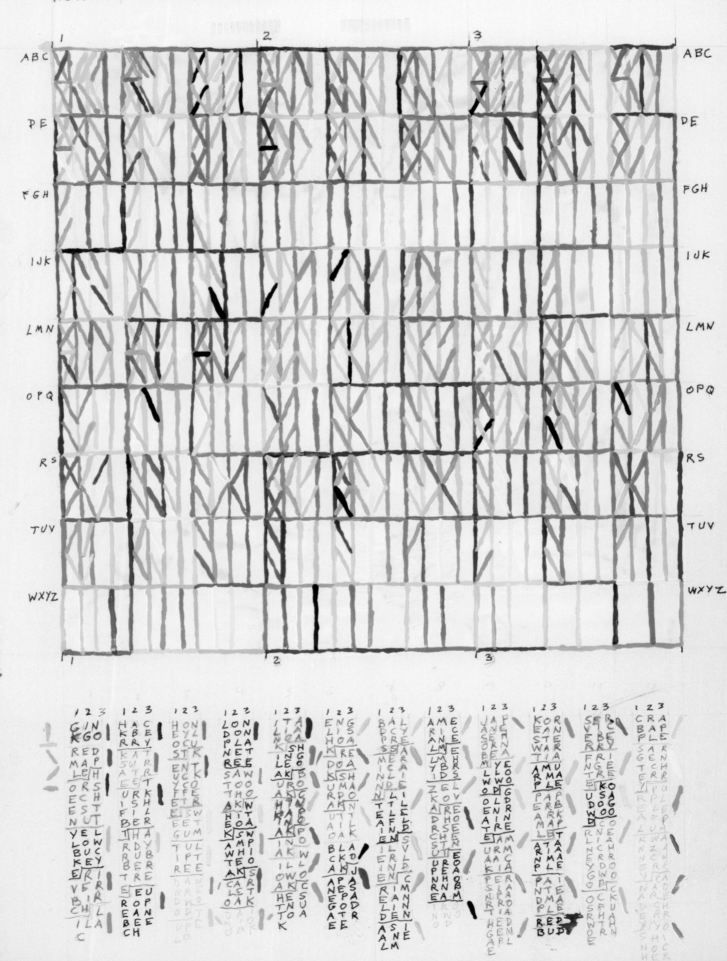

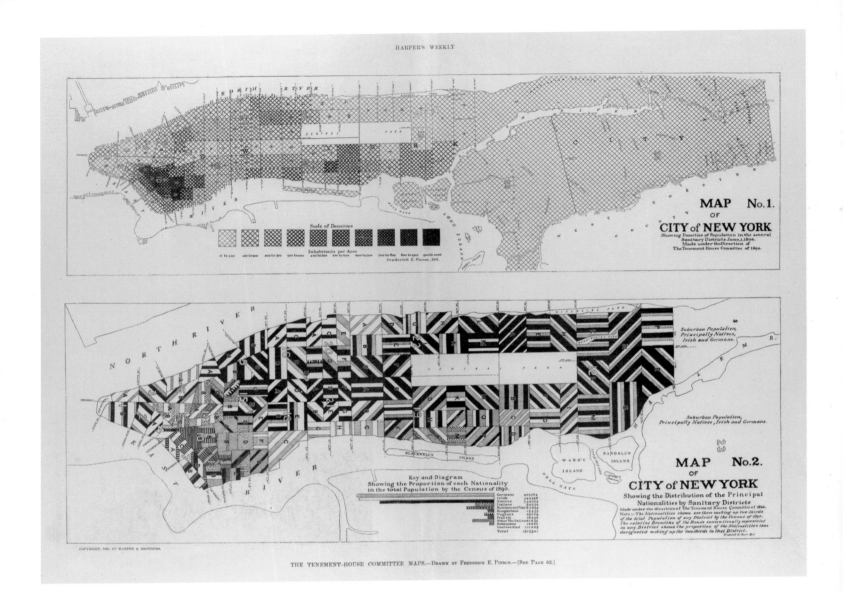

THE TENEMENT-HOUSE COMMITTEE MAPS.—DRAWN BY FREDERICK E. PIERCE.—[SEE PAGE 62.]

ABOVE

Frederick E. Pierce, *The Tenement House Committee Maps*, from *Harper's Weekly*, January 19, 1895.

In 1894, the New York State Legislature formed a Tenement House Committee to examine the living conditions of the poor in New York City. The committee's report, released a year later, included these two maps, which were published in *Harper's Weekly*. The upper one, showing population density in each of the city's sanitary districts, underscored the intense crowding on the Lower East Side. The lower one, showing a patchwork quilt of "the Distribution of the Principal Nationalities," divided the city between "Natives," shown in black bars, and "Negroes," and eight groups based on national origin, shown in variously patterned bars. As imprecise as the maps (and their terms) were, they could easily be read together to show that poverty and overcrowding in New York correlated with foreignness. If nothing else, these seemingly authoritative maps demonstrate the power of information graphics to shape popular perceptions.

OPPOSITE

Joseph R. Passonneau and Richard Saul Wurman, *New York West. Residential Population Density; Industrial, Commercial; Large Institutional, Park, Institutional, Airport, Cemetery*, from their *Urban Atlas: 20 American Cities. A Communication Study Notating Select Urban Data at a Scale of 1:48,000*, 1966.

This visually stimulating map uses two basic shapes, the circle and the square, in three colors, to describe residential population density in New York. An empty green square, for example, indicates parkland, while a solid red dot represents a density over 3,600—of course, these two never overlap. While trying to get familiar with these building blocks, one might be distracted by the map's Op-Art sensibility. Information graphics and art are rarely this intertwined.

RESIDENTIAL POPULATION DENSITY ○ 50 · 200 ⊙ 201 · 500 ◉ 501 · 1200 ◉ 1201 · 3600 ● over 3600

PENNSYLVANIA STATI

Seventh Avenue and 1

Looking toward

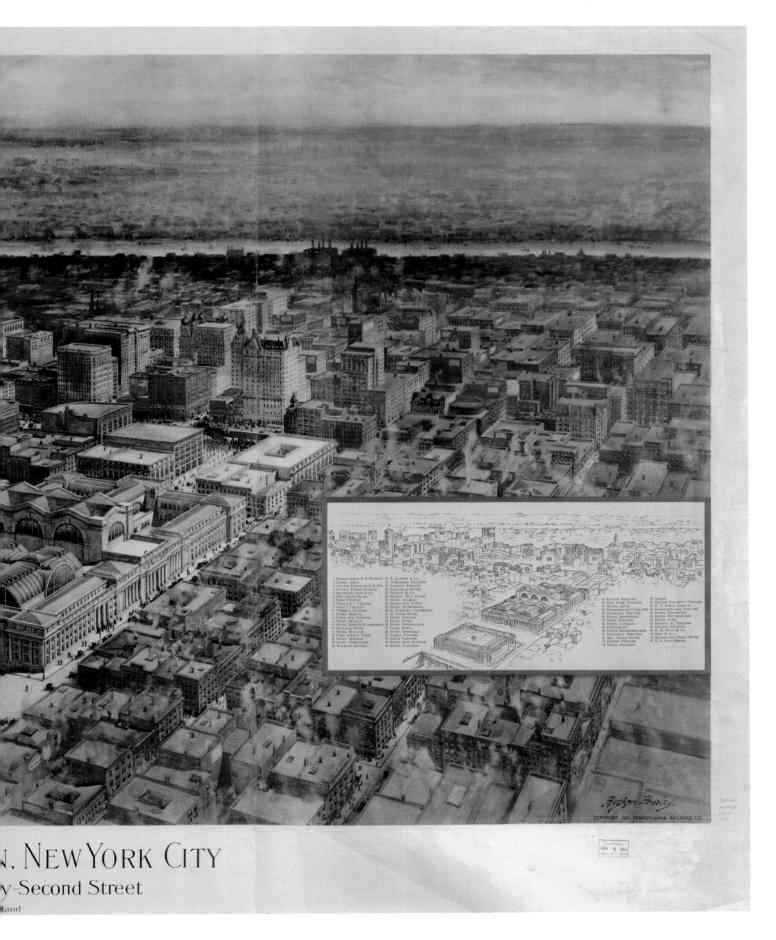

N. NEW YORK CITY

y-Second Street

and

PREVIOUS SPREAD
**Hughson Hawley, *Pennsylvania Railroad Station,
New York City: Seventh Avenue and Thirty-Second Street,
Looking Towards Long Island*, 1910.**

A shining Pennsylvania Station, highlighted in white, is envisioned
as a vast neoclassical gateway to the dark surrounding city. After the
station was demolished and replaced with a warren of underground
halls and corridors in the 1960s, the architectural historian Vincent
Scully spoke for many travelers when he wrote, "One entered the city
like a god. One scuttles in now like a rat."

ABOVE
**Interior View of the Magnificent Waiting Room Which Is
So Spacious That it Could Contain, Bodily, the New York City
Hall, from *Scientific American*, May 14, 1910.**

An elegant engraving of the interior of Pennsylvania Station brings
together two iconic New York City buildings, one now gone, one
still standing, and reveals the price that grandeur can impose on
human scale.

OPPOSITE
**Henry Comstock, *Madison Square Garden*, from *Popular
Mechanics*, November 1967.**

"Roundhouses used to hide behind railroad depots. Now one sits, like
a caramel-and-nut-frosted cake, on the site of New York City's razed
Pennsylvania Station. It's a seven-layered setting for sports gour-
mets—the new Madison Square Garden," proclaims the draftsman of
this exploded axonometric and cutaway of the polemical structure, the
city's fourth with that name. He continues his panegyric, listing the key
ingredients concocted by businessman/architect Charles Luckman:
money, accessibility, versatility, comfort, communications, and safety.
Yet he fails to warn of toxic reactions to the design of the most reviled
structure in Manhattan.

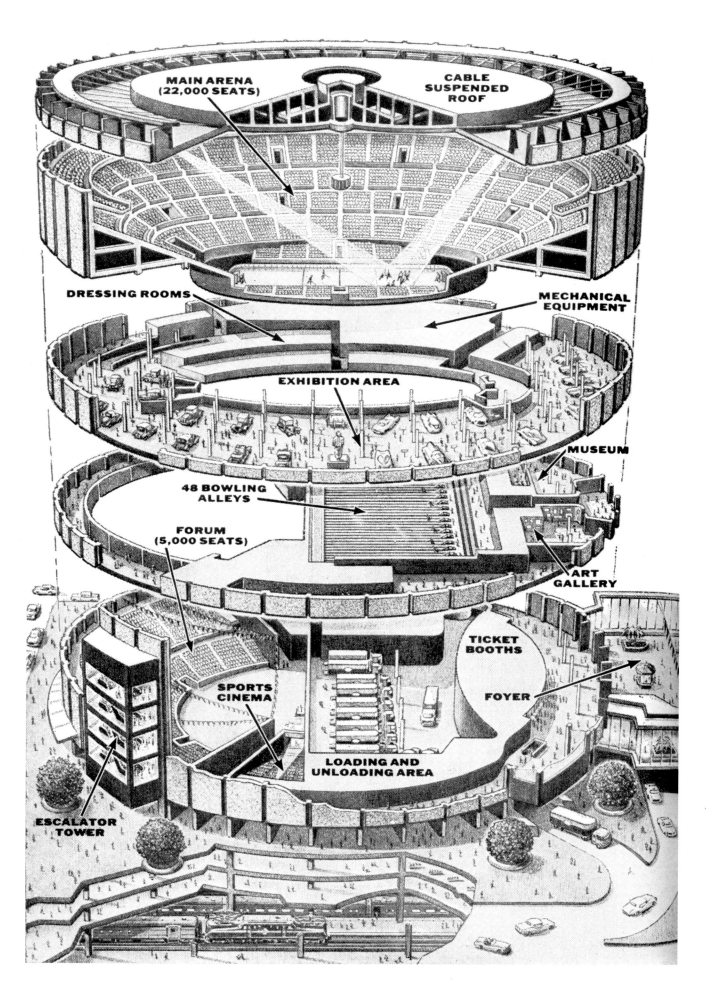

MAIN ARENA (22,000 SEATS)

CABLE SUSPENDED ROOF

DRESSING ROOMS

MECHANICAL EQUIPMENT

EXHIBITION AREA

MUSEUM

48 BOWLING ALLEYS

FORUM (5,000 SEATS)

ART GALLERY

TICKET BOOTHS

SPORTS CINEMA

FOYER

LOADING AND UNLOADING AREA

ESCALATOR TOWER

THE FUTURE OF TRINITY CHURCH.

ABOVE

**Albert Levering, *The Future of Trinity Church*,
from *Puck*, March 6, 1907.**

The skyscraper boom in Lower Manhattan around the turn of the century aroused conflicting sentiments in Manhattanites: If the dominant theme was pride in progress, there was also a distinct undercurrent of anxiety over the loss of the traditional cityscape, with its human scale. In 1905, the *New York Times* celebrated the survival of the venerable Trinity Church at the end of Wall Street, "in but not a part of the teeming world of dollars that surrounds it on every side." Here, in Levering's nightmare vision, the world of dollars has all but enveloped the old church: progress, finding an obstacle, flows around it.

OPPOSITE

**Dan Friedman and Anspach Grossman Portugal,
Citicorp Center 5, 1975.**

In 1957, Citicorp finally did wrap a skyscraper around a church. Faced with the requirement of rebuilding St. Peter's Church on the site of the bank's new headquarters, and capitalizing on zoning laws that permitted more height in exchange for public space, architect Hugh Stubbins and structural engineer William LeMessurier arrived at the daring idea of raising their skyscraper on a cruciform base and tucking the church, plazas, and a smaller building underneath it. Dan Friedman, a pioneer of postmodern "New Typography" in corporate identity design, made eight posters to promote the complex. Poster number five, with its axonometric perspective, clarifies this complex geometry in cheerful red, white, and blue.

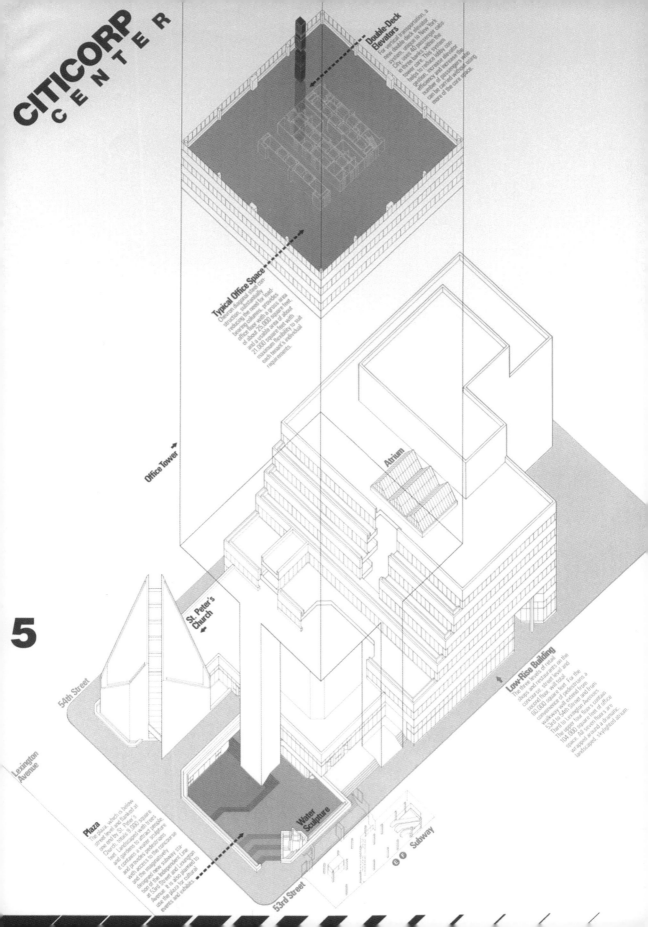

CITICORP CENTER

5

Double-Deck Elevators
For vertical transportation, a new double-deck elevator system, unique to New York City, uses 40 passenger cabs in three tiers within the tower core. This system helps to reduce lobby congestion, increase elevator efficiency and increase the number of passengers who can be carried without using more of the core space.

Typical Office Space
Chevron diagonal steel construction, substantially reducing the need for load-bearing columns, provides office space with gross area of about 25,000 square feet and a usable area of about 21,000 square feet with maximum flexibility to suit each tenant's individual requirements.

← Office Tower

Atrium

St. Peter's Church ←

Low-Rise Building
The three levels of retail shops and restaurants on the concourse, street level and second floor, will total 80,000 square feet. For the convenience of pedestrians, a walkway will extend from 53rd to 54th Street and from 3rd to Lexington Avenue. The upper four floors contain 104,000 square feet of office space. All seven floors are arranged around a dramatic, landscaped, skylighted atrium.

54th Street

Lexington Avenue

Plaza
The plaza, which is below street level, is flanked at one end by St. Peter's Church. Landscaped with trees, it contains a water sculpture and provides a pedestrian with access to the spacious, dramatically designed new subway station on the Independent Line at 53rd Street and Lexington Avenue. It is also planned to use the plaza for cultural events and exhibits.

Water Sculpture

🄵 🄶 **Subway**

53rd Street

Rebuilding the World Trade Center
(Nine years later)

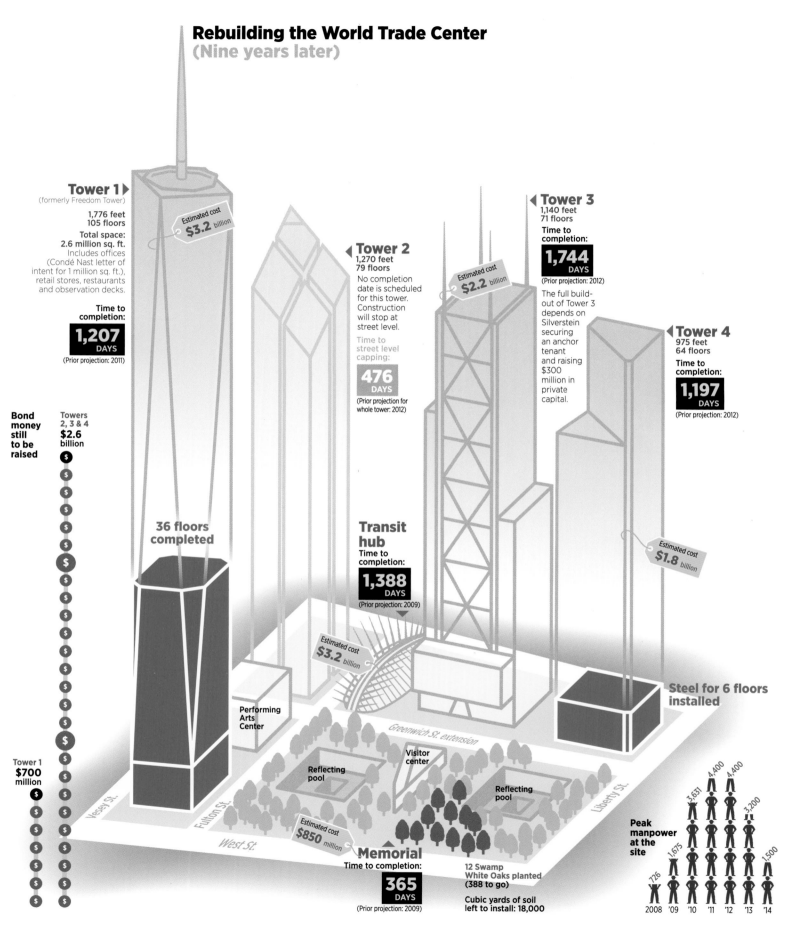

Tower 1 ▶
(formerly Freedom Tower)

1,776 feet
105 floors

Total space:
2.6 million sq. ft.
Includes offices
(Condé Nast letter of
intent for 1 million sq. ft.),
retail stores, restaurants
and observation decks.

**Time to
completion:**

1,207
DAYS

(Prior projection: 2011)

Estimated cost
$3.2 billion

◀ Tower 2
1,270 feet
79 floors

No completion
date is scheduled
for this tower.
Construction
will stop at
street level.

Time to
street level
capping:

476
DAYS

(Prior projection for
whole tower: 2012)

◀ Tower 3
1,140 feet
71 floors

**Time to
completion:**

1,744
DAYS

(Prior projection: 2012)

The full build-
out of Tower 3
depends on
Silverstein
securing
an anchor
tenant
and raising
$300
million in
private
capital.

Estimated cost
$2.2 billion

◀ Tower 4
975 feet
64 floors

**Time to
completion:**

1,197
DAYS

(Prior projection: 2012)

Estimated cost
$1.8 billion

**Bond
money
still
to be
raised**

**Towers
2, 3 & 4
$2.6
billion**

**Tower 1
$700
million**

**36 floors
completed**

**Transit
hub**
Time to
completion:

1,388
DAYS

(Prior projection: 2009)

Estimated cost
$3.2 billion

**Steel for 6 floors
installed**

Performing
Arts
Center

Greenwich St. extension

Visitor
center

Reflecting
pool

Reflecting
pool

Vesey St.

Fulton St.

Liberty St.

West St.

Estimated cost
$850 million

Memorial
Time to completion:

365
DAYS

(Prior projection: 2009)

**12 Swamp
White Oaks planted
(388 to go)**

**Cubic yards of soil
left to install: 18,000**

**Peak
manpower
at the
site**

726
1,675
3,631
4,400
4,400
3,200
1,500

2008 '09 '10 '11 '12 '13 '14

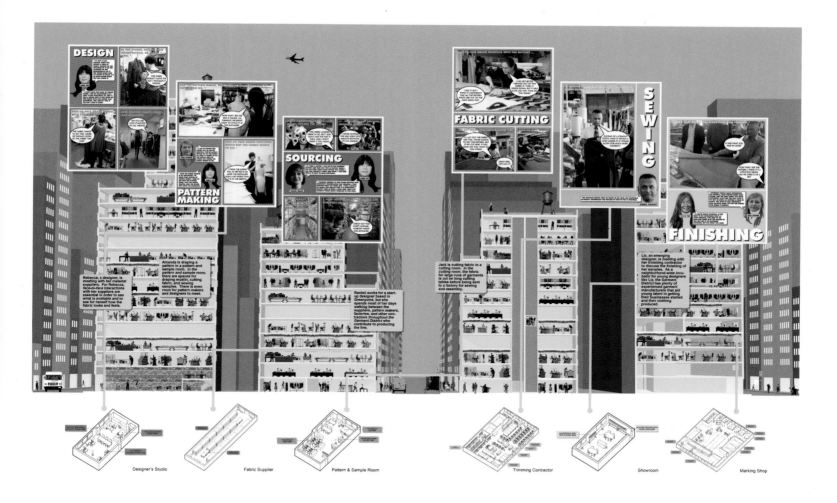

OPPOSITE

Nigel Holmes, *Rebuilding the World Trade Center (Nine Years Later)*, from *New York Observer*, 2010.

In 1977, Nigel Holmes was brought to New York from England to reinvigorate the information graphic department at *Time* magazine. Over time, he transformed the style of data visualization in newspapers and magazines through his precise simple line technique, which was influenced by Otto Neurath's prewar Isotype system of pictorial symbols for information graphics. This is a late example of Holmes's style.

ABOVE

Interboro Partners, *What's Going On in the Garment District?*, 2010. Project Team: Tobias Armborst, Daniel D'Oca, Georgeen Theodore, and Rebecca Beyer Winik.

In their portrayal of one block in the garment district, where clothing is designed, manufactured, and sold, Interboro Partners looked to French philosopher Bruno Latour's concept of the oligopticon, a site where a social structure is manufactured: "Our limited, situated knowledge of 'what's going on in the garment district' is compiled . . . from countless site visits and from dozens of interviews with designers, manufacturers, wholesalers, retailers, industry experts, and city officials. In Latourian fashion, we 'followed the actors' as best as we could, in the hope that we could tell an interesting story about this remarkable place."

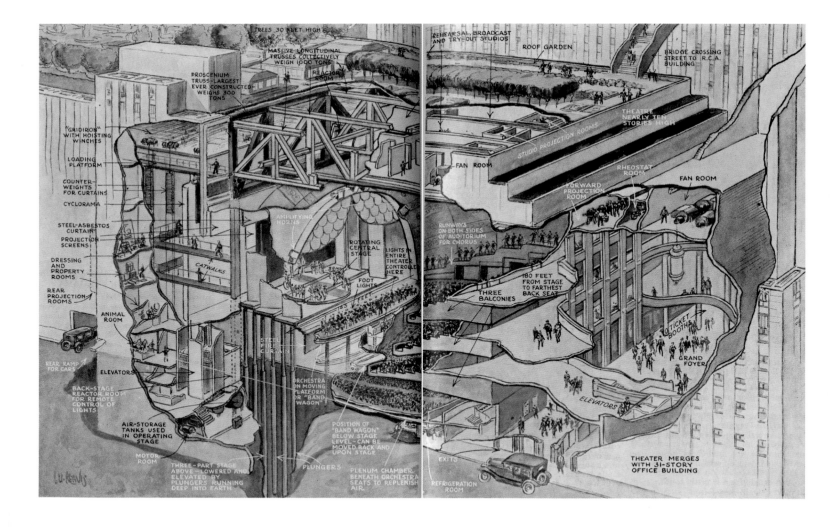

The image labels include:

TREES 30 FEET HIGH • MASSIVE LONGITUDINAL TRUSSES COLLECTIVELY WEIGH 1000 TONS • REACTOR ROOM • PROSCENIUM TRUSS—LARGEST EVER CONSTRUCTED—WEIGHS 300 TONS • "GRIDIRON" WITH HOISTING WINCHES • LOADING PLATFORM • COUNTER-WEIGHTS FOR CURTAINS • CYCLORAMA • STEEL-ASBESTOS CURTAIN • PROJECTION SCREENS • DRESSING AND PROPERTY ROOMS • REAR PROJECTION ROOMS • ANIMAL ROOM • CATWALKS • AMPLIFYING HORNS • ROTATING CENTRAL STAGE • LIGHTS IN ENTIRE THEATER CONTROLLED HERE • FOOT LIGHTS • 75 FEET • REAR RAMP FOR CARS • ELEVATORS • BACK-STAGE REACTOR ROOM FOR REMOTE CONTROL OF LIGHTS • AIR-STORAGE TANKS USED IN OPERATING STAGE • MOTOR ROOM • THREE-PART STAGE ABOVE—LOWERED AND ELEVATED BY PLUNGERS RUNNING DEEP INTO EARTH • PLUNGERS • ORCHESTRA ON MOVING PLATFORM OR "BAND WAGON" • POSITION OF "BAND WAGON" BELOW STAGE LEVEL—CAN BE MOVED BACK AND UPON STAGE • PLENUM CHAMBER BENEATH ORCHESTRA SEATS TO REPLENISH AIR • STEEL FIRE CURTAIN

REHEARSAL, BROADCAST AND TRY-OUT STUDIOS • ROOF GARDEN • BRIDGE CROSSING STREET TO R.C.A. BUILDING • THEATRE NEARLY TEN STORIES HIGH • STUDIO PROJECTION ROOMS • FAN ROOM • RHEOSTAT ROOM • FAN ROOM • FORWARD PROJECTION ROOM • RUNWAYS ON BOTH SIDES OF AUDITORIUM FOR CHORUS • 180 FEET FROM STAGE TO FARTHEST BACK SEAT • THREE BALCONIES • TICKET BOOTHS • GRAND FOYER • ELEVATORS • EXITS • REFRIGERATION ROOM • THEATER MERGES WITH 31-STORY OFFICE BUILDING

ABOVE

L. U. Reavis, *Radio City Music Hall*, from *Popular Mechanics*, August 1932.

Published just as Radio City Music Hall was topped out and four months before it opened, L. U. Reavis's diagram emphasizes the brawny construction of what was the world's largest auditorium at the time, but he also notes the animal room that so amused architect Rem Koolhaas in *Delirious New York,* his paean to the island: "Furthermore, there is a menagerie—horses, cows, goats and other animals. They live in ultramodern stables, artificially lit and ventilated; an animal elevator—dimensioned to carry even elephants—not only deposits them on the stage but also on a special grazing ground on Radio City's roof." The axonometric cutaway shows the interior of the building in sepia, with structural elements in gray.

OPPOSITE

The New York Tennis and Racquet Club, from *Scientific American*, April 15, 1893.

The *Scientific American* gushed over the second clubhouse of the New York Racquet and Tennis Club, at 27 West 43rd Street: "A luxurious home where the members may shut out the busy world, don their flannels, and after an hour or more of such form of active exercise as may please the individual fancy of the member, may, if tired and exhausted, enjoy the delightful lassitude of a Turkish bath, or, if his mind turns to a less enervating form of treatment, he may take a plunge in the capacious swimming tank." As portrayed here, the two courts on the top floor, "are all lighted from above and have no windows. They are painted black, and the lines or chases indicating where the players are to stand or play are painted orange or green in color. Black has been selected as the most desirable color, owing to the fact that the ball stands out from it distinctly and because there can be no delusive shadows."

1. Tennis court.　**2.** Fives court.　**3.** Sparring room.　**4.** Gymnasium.　**5.** Fencing room.　**6.** Card room.　**7.** Backgammon room.　**8.** Lounging room.　**9, 10, and 11.** Dressing and bath rooms.　**12.** Billiard room.　**13 and 14.** Reading rooms.　**15.** Hall.　**16.** Sitting room.　**17.** Dining room.　**18.** Bowling alleys and shooting galleries.　**19.** Hall.　**20, 21, 22.** Turkish, Roman, and plunge baths.　**23, 24, and 25.** Store rooms, etc.

THE NEW YORK TENNIS AND RACQUET CLUB.—[See page 232.]

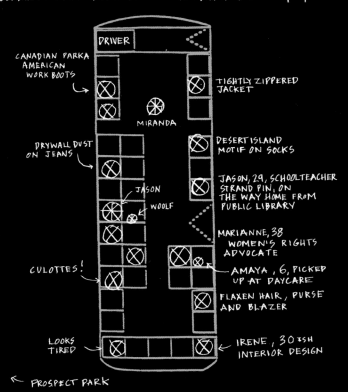
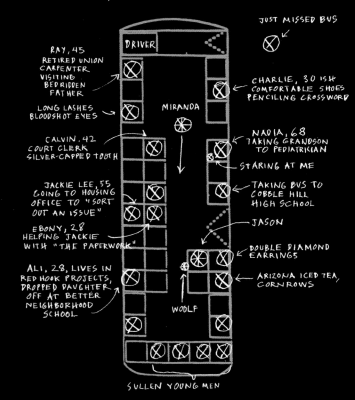
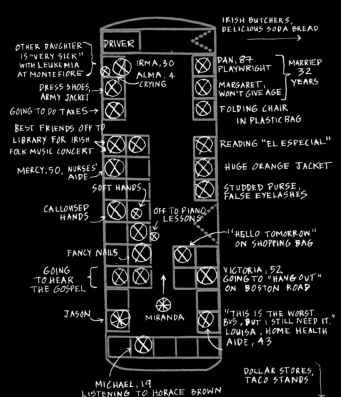
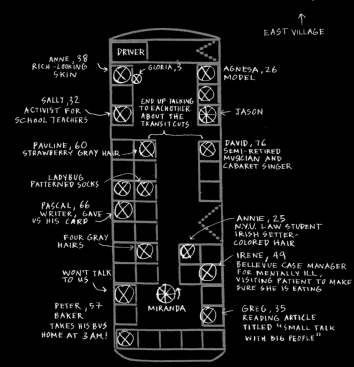

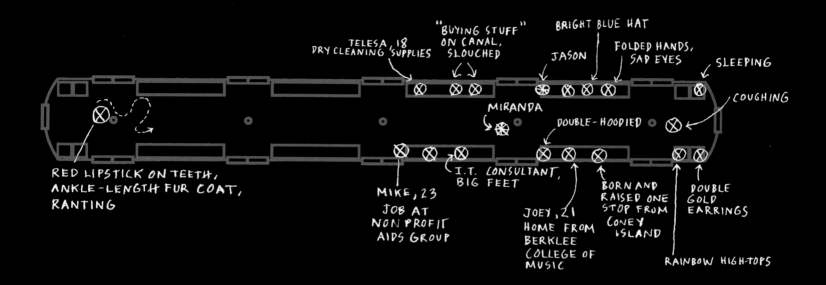

TRAIN: M LOCAL (BAY PARKWAY BOUND)
BOARDED: ATLANTIC / PACIFIC TIME: 6:25 P.M. DATE: 03/13/09

"BUYING STUFF" ON CANAL, SLOUCHED

BRIGHT BLUE HAT

TELESA, 18 DRY CLEANING 'SUPPLIES

JASON

FOLDED HANDS, SAD EYES

SLEEPING

COUGHING

MIRANDA

DOUBLE-HOODIED

RED LIPSTICK ON TEETH, ANKLE-LENGTH FUR COAT, RANTING

MIKE, 23
JOB AT NON PROFIT AIDS GROUP

I.T. CONSULTANT, BIG FEET

JOEY, 21 HOME FROM BERKLEE COLLEGE OF MUSIC

BORN AND RAISED ONE STOP FROM CONEY ISLAND

DOUBLE GOLD EARRINGS

RAINBOW HIGH-TOPS

Miranda Purves and Jason Logan, *The Last Bus Home*, from the *New York Times*, March 28, 2009.

"I take my 3-year-old son, Woolf, to preschool in the morning on the B75 bus, in Brooklyn—the 8:48 if we are firing on all cylinders, the 9:28 when the chaos wins out," wrote Miranda Purves in 2009. "Initially, I resented this routine: crabby bus drivers; occasionally menacing-seeming passengers; the excessive lurching. But slowly, I became familiar with the other regulars: the old woman with the bad knees en route to her quilting class, the drunk in a wheelchair who still maintains a cheerful independence. Woolfie and I made our 'doughnut friends,' a single mom and her son, who get on with a different doughnut every day, and now always sit behind us. The two boys both speak public transit. 'What's your favorite train?' Woolfie asks, running his toy N express train along the back of the seats. 'The G!' his friend says, referring to the one train that doesn't dip through Manhattan on its way from Queens to Brooklyn." When the M.T.A. threatened to reduce service across the city, including eliminating the B75, Purves became an activist. "'Our bus!' rang Woolfie's little voice in my head. . . . In the weeks before the M.T.A. vote, the artist Jason Logan and I spent a lot of time on the buses and subways that, unless the state steps in with a last-minute rescue package, will soon be gone or severely cut back." In the diagrams that they created to convey "the less tangible costs of service cuts and fare hikes," large X's indicated adults and small X's children. A year later, the B75 was gone.

Jim Flora, *A Room with Ghost $4 and Up*,
from *Life*, September 18, 1964.

Life in the Chelsea Hotel, New York's SRO landmark for artists, presided over by the ghosts of Mark Twain, Annie Russell, Thomas Wolfe, O. Henry, Dylan Thomas, and Brendan Behan. *Life*'s story failed to mention the astonishing roster of living talent making a go of it in "New York's most illustrious third-rate hotel" in the early 1960s.

Steven Guarnaccia, *The SPY Map of Who's Who at Lunch*
***at the Russian Tea Room*, from *SPY*, June 1987.**

SPY magazine offered a satiric, and sociologically precise, overview of New York life in the 1980s. This chart claims the food at a famous eatery on 57th Street is "so-so" but the sightings "of more-or-less glamorous, self-important people" are top notch. Many of the names invoked have faded with time. *Sic transit gloria mundi.*

"My Usual, Highly Visible Booth, Please, Ona"

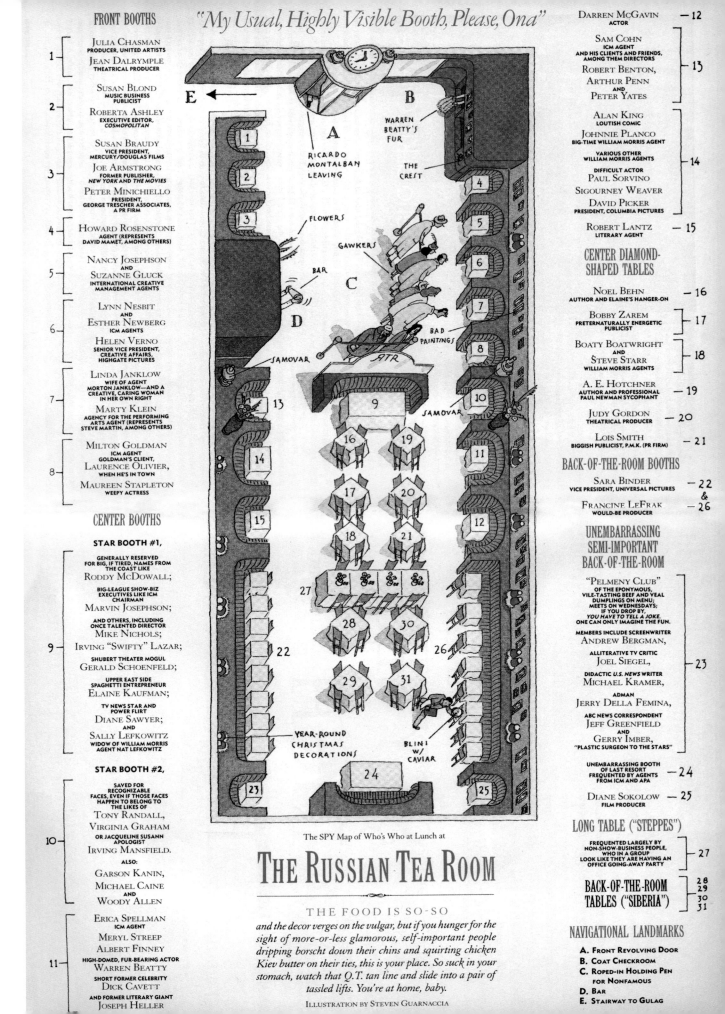

FRONT BOOTHS

1 — JULIA CHASMAN, PRODUCER, UNITED ARTISTS; JEAN DALRYMPLE, THEATRICAL PRODUCER

2 — SUSAN BLOND, MUSIC BUSINESS PUBLICIST; ROBERTA ASHLEY, EXECUTIVE EDITOR, COSMOPOLITAN

3 — SUSAN BRAUDY, VICE PRESIDENT, MERCURY/DOUGLAS FILMS; JOE ARMSTRONG, FORMER PUBLISHER, NEW YORK AND THE MOVIES; PETER MINICHIELLO, PRESIDENT, GEORGE TRESCHER ASSOCIATES, A PR FIRM

4 — HOWARD ROSENSTONE, AGENT (REPRESENTS DAVID MAMET, AMONG OTHERS)

5 — NANCY JOSEPHSON AND SUZANNE GLUCK, INTERNATIONAL CREATIVE MANAGEMENT AGENTS

6 — LYNN NESBIT AND ESTHER NEWBERG, ICM AGENTS; HELEN VERNO, SENIOR VICE PRESIDENT, CREATIVE AFFAIRS, HIGHGATE PICTURES

7 — LINDA JANKLOW, WIFE OF AGENT MORTON JANKLOW—AND A CREATIVE, CARING WOMAN IN HER OWN RIGHT; MARTY KLEIN, AGENCY FOR THE PERFORMING ARTS AGENT (REPRESENTS STEVE MARTIN, AMONG OTHERS)

8 — MILTON GOLDMAN, ICM AGENT; GOLDMAN'S CLIENT, LAURENCE OLIVIER, WHEN HE'S IN TOWN; MAUREEN STAPLETON, WEEPY ACTRESS

CENTER BOOTHS

9 — STAR BOOTH #1, GENERALLY RESERVED FOR BIG, IF TIRED, NAMES FROM THE COAST LIKE RODDY McDOWALL; BIG-LEAGUE SHOW-BIZ EXECUTIVES LIKE ICM CHAIRMAN MARVIN JOSEPHSON; AND OTHERS, INCLUDING ONCE TALENTED DIRECTOR MIKE NICHOLS; IRVING "SWIFTY" LAZAR; SHUBERT THEATER MOGUL GERALD SCHOENFELD; UPPER EAST SIDE SPAGHETTI ENTREPRENEUR ELAINE KAUFMAN; TV NEWS STAR AND POWER FLIRT DIANE SAWYER; AND SALLY LEFKOWITZ, WIDOW OF WILLIAM MORRIS AGENT NAT LEFKOWITZ

10 — STAR BOOTH #2, SAVED FOR RECOGNIZABLE FACES, EVEN IF THOSE FACES HAPPEN TO BELONG TO THE LIKES OF TONY RANDALL, VIRGINIA GRAHAM OR JACQUELINE SUSANN APOLOGIST IRVING MANSFIELD. ALSO: GARSON KANIN, MICHAEL CAINE AND WOODY ALLEN

11 — ERICA SPELLMAN, ICM AGENT; MERYL STREEP; ALBERT FINNEY; HIGH-DOMED, FUR-BEARING ACTOR WARREN BEATTY; SHORT FORMER CELEBRITY DICK CAVETT; AND FORMER LITERARY GIANT JOSEPH HELLER

Right side

12 — DARREN McGAVIN, ACTOR

13 — SAM COHN, ICM AGENT AND HIS CLIENTS AND FRIENDS, AMONG THEM DIRECTORS ROBERT BENTON, ARTHUR PENN AND PETER YATES

14 — ALAN KING, LOUTISH COMIC; JOHNNIE PLANCO, BIG-TIME WILLIAM MORRIS AGENT; VARIOUS OTHER WILLIAM MORRIS AGENTS; DIFFICULT ACTOR PAUL SORVINO; SIGOURNEY WEAVER; DAVID PICKER, PRESIDENT, COLUMBIA PICTURES

15 — ROBERT LANTZ, LITERARY AGENT

CENTER DIAMOND-SHAPED TABLES

16 — NOEL BEHN, AUTHOR AND ELAINE'S HANGER-ON

17 — BOBBY ZAREM, PRETERNATURALLY ENERGETIC PUBLICIST

18 — BOATY BOATWRIGHT AND STEVE STARR, WILLIAM MORRIS AGENTS

19 — A. E. HOTCHNER, AUTHOR AND PROFESSIONAL PAUL NEWMAN SYCOPHANT

20 — JUDY GORDON, THEATRICAL PRODUCER

21 — LOIS SMITH, BIGGISH PUBLICIST, P.M.K. (PR FIRM)

BACK-OF-THE-ROOM BOOTHS

22 & 26 — SARA BINDER, VICE PRESIDENT, UNIVERSAL PICTURES; FRANCINE LeFRAK, WOULD-BE PRODUCER

UNEMBARRASSING SEMI-IMPORTANT BACK-OF-THE-ROOM

23 — "PELMENY CLUB" OF THE EPONYMOUS, VILE-TASTING BEEF AND VEAL DUMPLINGS ON MENU; MEETS ON WEDNESDAYS; IF YOU DROP BY, YOU HAVE TO TELL A JOKE. ONE CAN ONLY IMAGINE THE FUN. MEMBERS INCLUDE SCREENWRITER ANDREW BERGMAN, ALLITERATIVE TV CRITIC JOEL SIEGEL, DIDACTIC U.S. NEWS WRITER MICHAEL KRAMER, ADMAN JERRY DELLA FEMINA, ABC NEWS CORRESPONDENT JEFF GREENFIELD AND GERRY IMBER, "PLASTIC SURGEON TO THE STARS"

24 — UNEMBARRASSING BOOTH OF LAST RESORT FREQUENTED BY AGENTS FROM ICM AND APA

25 — DIANE SOKOLOW, FILM PRODUCER

LONG TABLE ("STEPPES")

27 — FREQUENTED LARGELY BY NON-SHOW-BUSINESS PEOPLE, WHO IN A GROUP LOOK LIKE THEY ARE HAVING AN OFFICE GOING-AWAY PARTY

BACK-OF-THE-ROOM TABLES ("SIBERIA")

28, 29, 30, 31

NAVIGATIONAL LANDMARKS

A. FRONT REVOLVING DOOR
B. COAT CHECKROOM
C. ROPED-IN HOLDING PEN FOR NONFAMOUS
D. BAR
E. STAIRWAY TO GULAG

The SPY Map of Who's Who at Lunch at

THE RUSSIAN TEA ROOM

THE FOOD IS SO-SO

and the decor verges on the vulgar, but if you hunger for the sight of more-or-less glamorous, self-important people dripping borscht down their chins and squirting chicken Kiev butter on their ties, this is your place. So suck in your stomach, watch that O.T. tan line and slide into a pair of tassled lifts. You're at home, baby.

ILLUSTRATION BY STEVEN GUARNACCIA

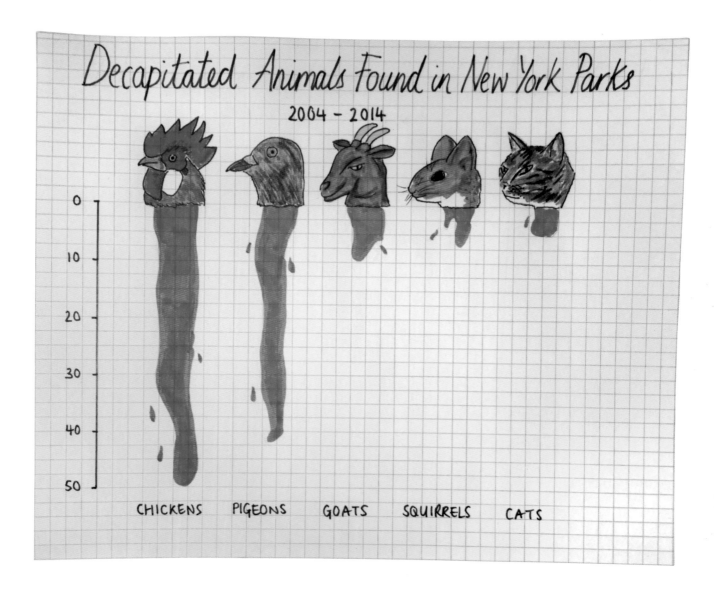

Decapitated Animals Found in New York Parks

2004 – 2014

CHICKENS   PIGEONS   GOATS   SQUIRRELS   CATS

Mona Chalabi, *Decapitated Animals Found in New York Parks 2004–2014*, 2016. Data compiled by Useless Press.

Mona Chalabi's explicit hand-drawn pictorial translations of data— she refers to them as data sketches—give a fresh immediacy to subjects ranging from race and gender politics to birthdays and nose picking. For this gruesome portrayal, she used reports filed to New York City Parks Department. "The animals weren't all found individually—in November 2009 five pigeons and a rooster were found in a children's playground. All were headless," she clarifies.

Gary Panter, *2 Months of Mayhem in Central Park*, from *SPY*, April 1987.

Central Park is viewed as a crime scene in the mid-1980s. Statistics comparing the first months of 1986 and 1987 are pictured in this vivid and unsettling cartoon map, a board game of violence, which ran in *SPY* magazine without commentary. Like the Tenement House Committee's maps that ran in *Harper's Weekly* approximately a century earlier (see page 120), this is a diagram with emotionally charged content based on data that is difficult to interpret and that may reinforce a received opinion.

January
1986

GRAND LARCENY
(basic mugging)

1
102nd Street cutoff

2
63rd Street and East Drive

ROBBERY
(mugging involving
use of force and/or fear)

3
110th Street and Lenox Avenue

4
106th Street and East Drive

5
106th Street and Fifth Avenue

6
97th Street tennis courts (2)

7
Loeb Boathouse

8
79th Street transverse
off Fifth Avenue

9
79th Street and Fifth Avenue

10
74th Street and West Drive

11
61st Street and East Drive

12
The Pond, 60th Street
and East Drive

13
Grand Army Plaza

FELONIOUS ASSAULT

14
Band shell

15
Concession on north
side of the Sheep Meadow

RAPE

16
104th Street and Fifth Avenue

BURGLARY

17
The Children's Zoo (2)

18
The Dairy (2)

GRAND LARCENY / AUTO
(car theft)

19
The old Police Athletic
League Center,
north of transverse at
97th Street

January
1987

GRAND LARCENY
(basic mugging)

1
The Great Lawn

2
Metropolitan Museum of Art area (2)

3
Tavern on the Green area (3)

4
67th Street and East Drive

5
67th Street and Central Park West

ROBBERY
(mugging involving
use of force and/or fear)

6
79th Street and Fifth Avenue

7
63rd Street and Park Drive

GRAND LARCENY / AUTO

8
In front of the
American Museum
of Natural History

2
MONTHS OF
MAYHEM
in
CENTRAL PARK

*How January's statistics
for the Central Park Police
Precinct compared with those
of a year earlier*

RESEARCH BY ANN C. MATHERS
ILLUSTRATION BY GARY PANTER

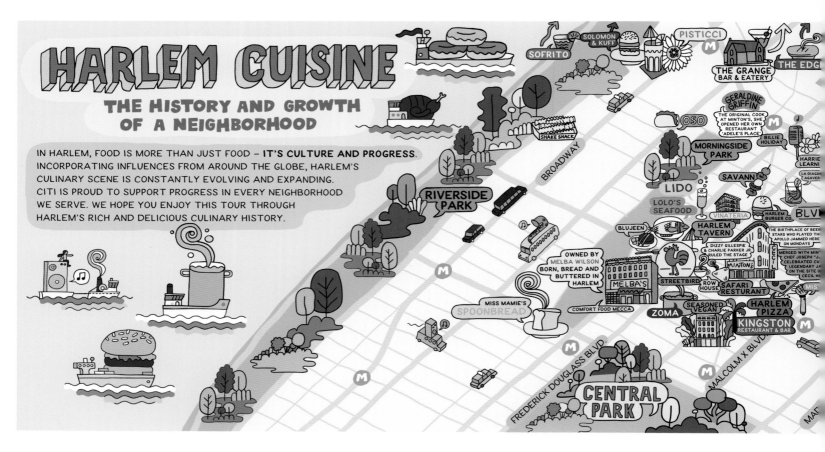

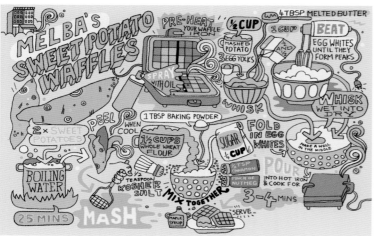

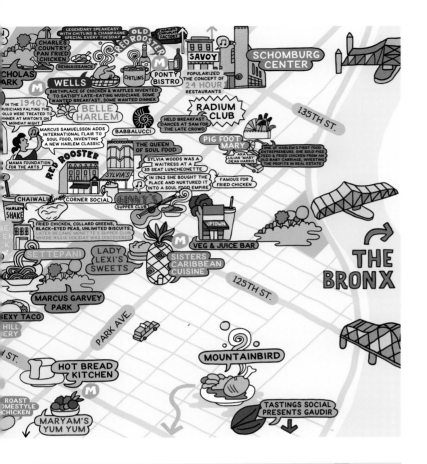

James Gulliver Hancock and Publicis North America, billboard-sized banners to postcards for Harlem EatUp!, 2018.

You could (almost) cook a meal from these visual recipes for classic dishes from Harlem restaurants, which capture the energetic culinary spirit of the neighborhood, created to promote the weeklong annual festival Harlem EatUp!, celebrating food, art, and culture.

LEFT

Harlem Cuisine: The History and Growth of a Neighborhood

BELOW, CLOCKWISE FROM TOP LEFT

Melba's Sweet Potato Waffles

Red Rooster Harlem Cornbread

Agaveria La Diagonal Empanadas Vegetarianas

Lolo's Corn on the Cob

Vinatería Pollo Milanese

Renaissance Harlem Chef Cisse's Red Wine Braised Short Rib Sliders

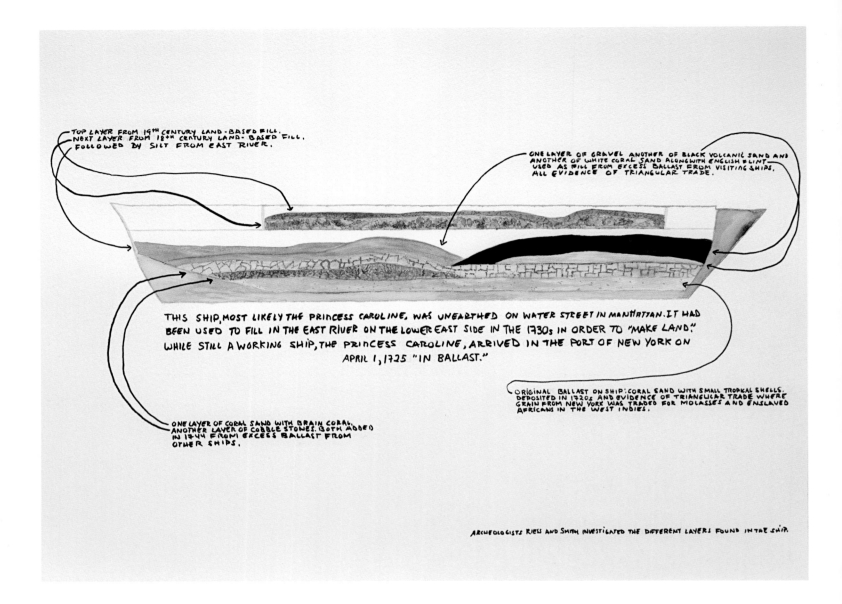

The handwritten notations on the diagram read:

TOP LAYER FROM 19TH CENTURY LAND-BASED FILL.
NEXT LAYER FROM 18TH CENTURY LAND-BASED FILL.
FOLLOWED BY SILT FROM EAST RIVER.

ONE LAYER OF GRAVEL ANOTHER OF BLACK VOLCANIC SAND AND ANOTHER OF WHITE CORAL SAND ALONGWITH ENGLISH FLINT USED AS FILL FROM EXCESS BALLAST FROM VISITING SHIPS, ALL EVIDENCE OF TRIANGULAR TRADE.

THIS SHIP, MOST LIKELY THE PRINCESS CAROLINE, WAS UNEARTHED ON WATER STREET IN MANHATTAN. IT HAD BEEN USED TO FILL IN THE EAST RIVER ON THE LOWER EAST SIDE IN THE 1730s IN ORDER TO "MAKE LAND." WHILE STILL A WORKING SHIP, THE PRINCESS CAROLINE, ARRIVED IN THE PORT OF NEW YORK ON APRIL 1, 1725 "IN BALLAST."

ORIGINAL BALLAST ON SHIP: CORAL SAND WITH SMALL TROPICAL SHELLS. DEPOSITED IN 1720s AND EVIDENCE OF TRIANGULAR TRADE WHERE GRAIN FROM NEW YORK WAS TRADED FOR MOLASSES AND ENSLAVED AFRICANS IN THE WEST INDIES.

ONE LAYER OF CORAL SAND WITH BRAIN CORAL, ANOTHER LAYER OF COBBLE STONES. BOTH ADDED IN 1744 FROM EXCESS BALLAST FROM OTHER SHIPS.

ARCHEOLOGISTS RIESS AND SMITH INVESTIGATED THE DIFFERENT LAYERS FOUND IN THE SHIP.

ABOVE

Maria Thereza Alves, *Caribbean Coral Sand in Manhattan*, 2017.

Brazilian artist Maria Thereza Alves documents non-native plant species that were carried to their new habitats in ship ballast, traveling companions to humans also uprooted from their homes. Here, she diagrams the layers of material found inside the hull of an eighteenth-century merchant ship discovered in 1982 during excavation on Water Street in Lower Manhattan, with notations detailing the origin and historical associations of each stratum. For a careful "reader," the buried vessel tells a story about the notorious triangle trade, which enriched New Yorkers and helped to finance the slave trade.

OPPOSITE

Max Neuhaus, *Aural Topography of Times Square Sound Work*, 1977.

Percussionist and "sound sculptor" Max Neuhaus's sound work *Times Square* enveloped pedestrians who stepped on a grating at the intersection of Broadway and Seventh Avenue in a heavy blanket of sound. Writers have used words like "organlike drone," "chimes," "church bells," and "hum" to describe the experience. In a diagram of the approximately 150-square-foot area where the sound was audible, Neuhaus mapped its changing frequency, showing why it would undulate as a person moved through it.

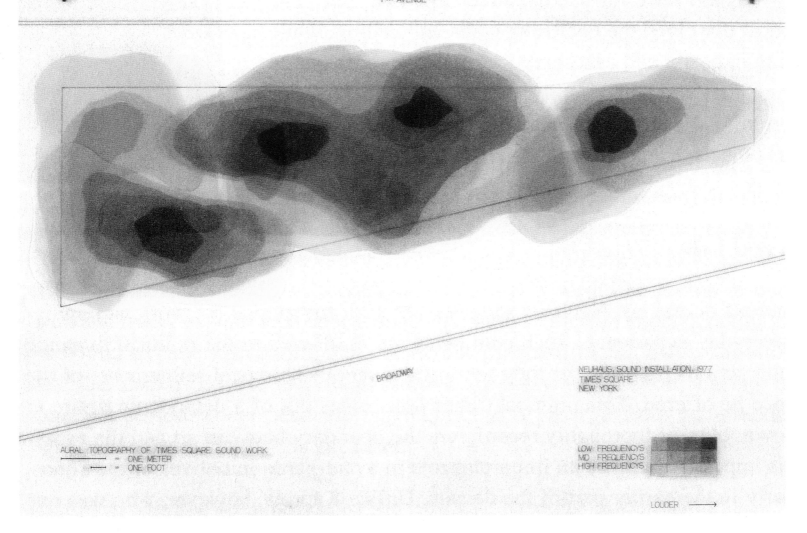

7TH AVENUE

BROADWAY

NEUHAUS, SOUND INSTALLATION, 1977
TIMES SQUARE
NEW YORK

AURAL TOPOGRAPHY OF TIMES SQUARE SOUND WORK
= ONE METER
= ONE FOOT

LOW FREQUENCYS
MID FREQUENCYS
HIGH FREQUENCYS

LOUDER ⟶

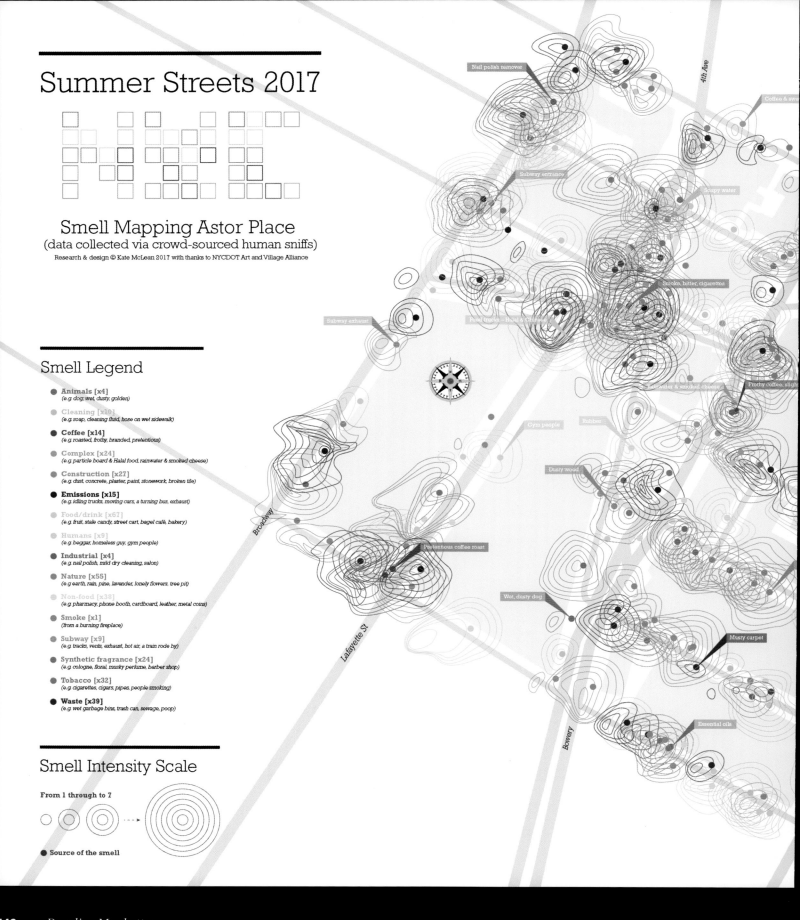

Summer Streets 2017

Smell Mapping Astor Place
(data collected via crowd-sourced human sniffs)

Research & design © Kate McLean 2017 with thanks to NYCDOT Art and Village Alliance

Smell Legend

- **Animals [x4]**
  (e.g. dog, wet, dusty, golden)
- **Cleaning [x10]**
  (e.g. soap, cleaning fluid, hose on wet sidewalk)
- **Coffee [x14]**
  (e.g. roasted, frothy, branded, pretentious)
- **Complex [x24]**
  (e.g. particle board & Halal food, rainwater & smoked cheese)
- **Construction [x27]**
  (e.g. dust, concrete, plaster, paint, stonework, broken tile)
- **Emissions [x15]**
  (e.g. idling trucks, moving cars, a turning bus, exhaust)
- **Food/drink [x67]**
  (e.g. fruit, stale candy, street cart, bagel café, bakery)
- **Humans [x9]**
  (e.g. beggar, homeless guy, gym people)
- **Industrial [x4]**
  (e.g. nail polish, mild dry cleaning, salon)
- **Nature [x55]**
  (e.g. earth, rain, pine, lavender, lonely flowers, tree pit)
- **Non-food [x38]**
  (e.g. pharmacy, phone booth, cardboard, leather, metal coins)
- **Smoke [x1]**
  (from a burning fireplace)
- **Subway [x9]**
  (e.g. tracks, vents, exhaust, hot air, a train rode by)
- **Synthetic fragrance [x24]**
  (e.g. cologne, floral, musky perfume, barber shop)
- **Tobacco [x32]**
  (e.g. cigarettes, cigars, pipes, people smoking)
- **Waste [x39]**
  (e.g. wet garbage bins, trash can, sewage, poop)

Smell Intensity Scale

From 1 through to 7

● Source of the smell

Map labels: Nail polish remover, Coffee & sweet, Subway entrance, Soapy water, Smoke, bitter, cigarettes, Subway exhaust, Food trucks – Halal & Chinese, Rainwater & smoked cheese, Frothy coffee, slight, Gym people, Rubber, Dusty wood, Pretentious coffee roast, Wet, dusty dog, Musty carpet, Essential oils, 4th Ave, Broadway, Lafayette St, Bowery

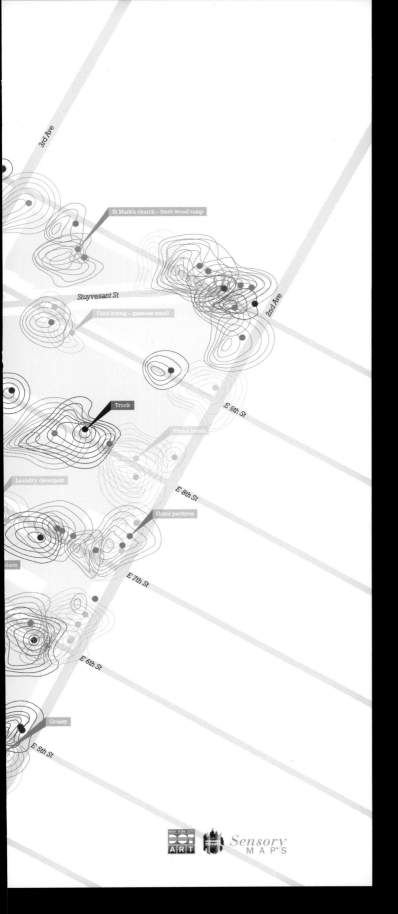

Kate McLean, *Summer Streets 2017, Smell Mapping Astor Place*, 2017.

English artist and designer Kate McLean specializes in sensory mapping—the presentation of "eye-invisible" data. For this project, commissioned by the NYC Department of Transportation, she crowd sourced smells in Astor Place from April to June, 2017. The results mapped suggestively to typical New York locations: "subway exhaust," "food frying," "laundry detergent," "floral perfume," and "pretentious coffee roast," among others.

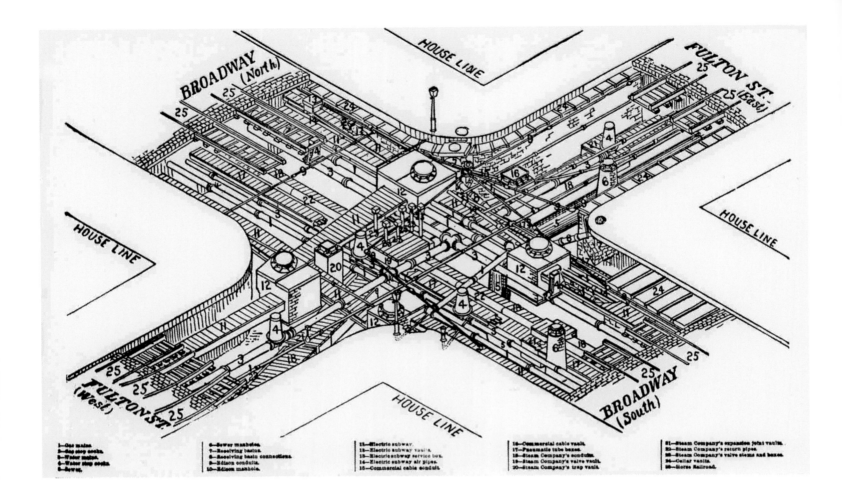

The Street Ideal. Marvels Present and Future About Metropolitan Road Building, from the Sun, November 2, 1890.

BROADWAY (North)

HOUSE LINE

FULTON ST. (East)

HOUSE LINE

HOUSE LINE

FULTON ST. (West)

HOUSE LINE

BROADWAY (South)

1—Gas mains.
2—Gas stop cocks.
3—Water mains.
4—Water stop cocks.
5—Sewer.

6—Sewer manholes.
7—Receiving basins.
8—Receiving basin connections.
9—Edison conduits.
10—Edison manhole.

11—Electric subway.
12—Electric subway vaults.
13—Electric subway service box.
14—Electric subway air pipes.
15—Commercial cable conduit.

16—Commercial cable vault.
17—Pneumatic tube boxes.
18—Steam Company's conduits.
19—Steam Company's valve vault.
20—Steam Company's trap vault.

21—Steam Company's expansion joint vaults.
22—Steam Company's return pipes.
23—Steam Company's valve stems and boxes.
24—Cellar vaults.
25—Horse Railroad.

ABOVE

The Street Ideal. Marvels Present and Future About Metropolitan Road Building, from the Sun, November 2, 1890.

A cutaway view of the infrastructure—including gas mains, water lines, sewers, electrical conduits, "commercial cable" conduits, pneumatic tubes, and steam pipes—beneath the intersection of Broadway and Fulton Street in 1890 suggests the controlled chaos that lies beneath the surface of modern life. Within twenty years of this diagram, Broadway would be dug up and the subway added to the mix.

OPPOSITE

Emil Lowenstein, *This Is What Lies Under the Surface*, from *Fortune*, July 1939.

A color-coded cutaway, based on official city blueprints, reveals the innards of the urban machine at Sixth Avenue and 50th Street, "not an especially complex intersection," with the same elements as the previous diagram, except that telegraph and telephone lines have replaced pneumatic tubes for communication and the subway has been added.

At the very bottom of the illustration, two hundred feet below street level, is the water main called City Tunnel No. 1, twelve feet in diameter.

FOLLOWING SPREAD

The Map of Wall Street, from *Fortune*, March 1930.

Wall Street, New York's financial dynamo, was entering the doldrums of the Great Depression when this cheerful map was published—hence, perhaps, its droll subtitle. By then, the street's western end had been populated with stately office buildings occupying some of the world's most expensive real estate. The vestiges of old New York visible in this map at its eastern end—small counting houses dating from the days of sailing ships—disappeared in a wave of new skyscraper construction after World War II.

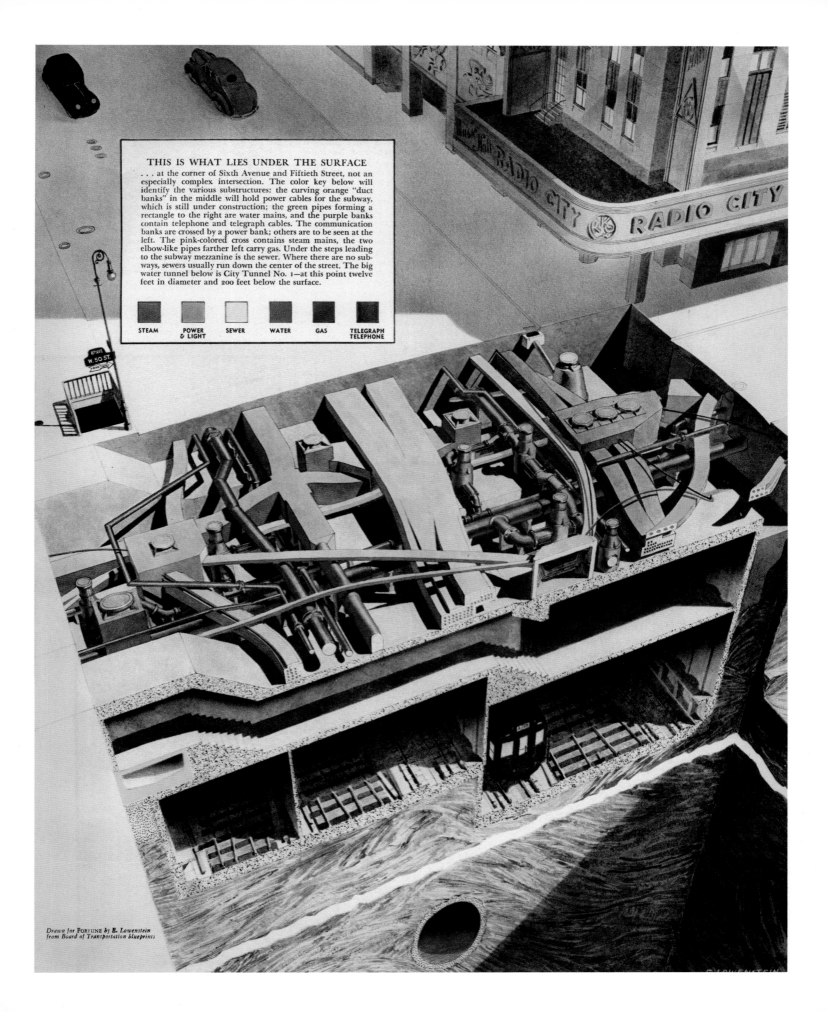

THIS IS WHAT LIES UNDER THE SURFACE

... at the corner of Sixth Avenue and Fiftieth Street, not an especially complex intersection. The color key below will identify the various substructures: the curving orange "duct banks" in the middle will hold power cables for the subway, which is still under construction; the green pipes forming a rectangle to the right are water mains, and the purple banks contain telephone and telegraph cables. The communication banks are crossed by a power bank; others are to be seen at the left. The pink-colored cross contains steam mains, the two elbow-like pipes farther left carry gas. Under the steps leading to the subway mezzanine is the sewer. Where there are no subways, sewers usually run down the center of the street. The big water tunnel below is City Tunnel No. 1—at this point twelve feet in diameter and 200 feet below the surface.

STEAM   POWER & LIGHT   SEWER   WATER   GAS   TELEGRAPH TELEPHONE

*Drawn for FORTUNE by B. Lowenstein
from Board of Transportation blueprints*

THE MAP OF WALL STREET

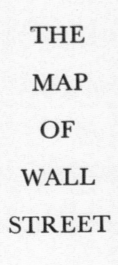

Trinity Church is large Manhattan landowner, with properties whose book value is $15,022,236. Rentals total over $1,000,000 annually. Bishop Manning was rector (1908-21).

Vestrymen: John Erskine (Helen of Troy); Thomas C.T.Crain (District Attorney); William Barclay Parsons. Office of Trinity Church Corp. at 72 Wall St.

THE STREET

WITH A

GRAVEYARD

AT ONE END

AND AT THE

OTHER END

THE RIVER

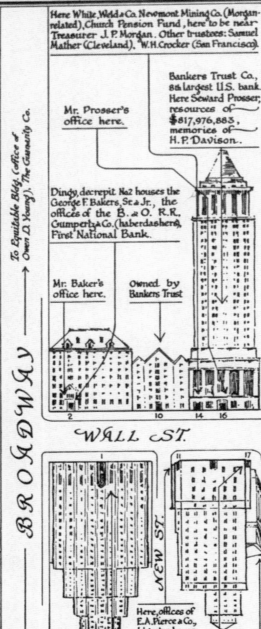

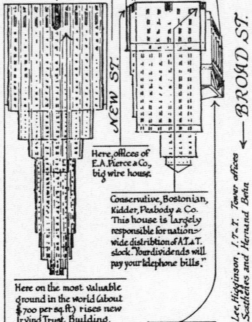

To Equitable Bldg. (office of Owen D. Young). The Guaranty Co. →

BROADWAY →

To No. 26 Broadway, office of John D. Rockefeller →

Here White, Weld & Co. Nevemont Mining Co. (Morgan-related), Church Pension Fund, here to be near Treasurer J. P. Morgan. Other trustees: Samuel Mather (Cleveland), W. H. Crocker (San Francisco).

Mr. Prosser's office here.

Bankers Trust Co., 8th largest U.S. bank. Here Seward Prosser, resources of $817,976,883, memories of H. P. Davison.

Dingy, decrepit No. 2 houses the George F. Baker, Sr. & Jr., the offices of the B. & O. R.R., Gumpertz & Co. (haberdashers), First National Bank.

Mr. Baker's office here.

Owned by Bankers Trust

WALL ST.

THE CORNER

NASSAU ST. →

To Otis & Co., Chase Bank, Bonbright & Co, Dillon, Read & Co., Federal Reserve →

Bank of the Manhattan Co. Second highest N.Y. bldg., beaten by Chrysler's Tower in architects' battle. Prospective tenants: Cadwalader, Wickersham (George W.) & Taft (Henry W.); Phelps, Dodge Corp. (Arthur Curtiss James); E.A. Pierce & Co; A. Iselin & Co; Aldred & Co. (bankers for Gillette Safety Razor Co.); Field, Glore & Co. (Marshall Field, Charles Glore). Bank founded by Aaron Burr in 1799.

U.S. Assay Office. Here is stored more gold than anywhere else on earth. Here come refiners, burglars, pawnbrokers, dentists to turn in gold. U.S. cannot ask questions, must buy all gold which is one-fifth pure.

Old Subtreasury. New York has had no subtreasury since 1920. Building now used for minor gov't. offices: Passports, Prohibition, Radio, Etc.

Bank of America Bldg. Giannini's N.Y. headquarters, also office of Cerro de Pasco Copper Corp.

To Harris, Forbes → Kuhn, Loeb. →

WILLIAM ST. →

Bomb concealed in wagon exploded here Sept. 16, 1920

NEW ST. →

Here, offices of E.A. Pierce & Co., big wire house.

Conservative, Bostonian, Kidder, Peabody & Co. This house is largely responsible for nation-wide distribution of A.T.&T. stock. "Your dividends will pay your telephone bills."

Here on the most valuable ground in the world (about $700 per sq. ft.) rises new Irving Trust Building. Tenants: Willis H. Booth, C. Ledyard Blair; Cornelius H. Bliss. Only 3 buildings ever before erected on site, the first about 1650, known as The house in the Heerewegh (highway) by the Land Gate.

STOCK EXCHANGE In 1919 paper worth $90,000,000,000 changed hands in this room.

BROAD ST. →

To Lee, Higginson, I.T.&T. Tower offices of Seatheists and Herrand Beha →

Office of Mr. Morgan.

Office of Mr. Lamont. Here bankers met daily during market panic

Equitable Trust Co. Here many law firms: 1) Davis (John W.), Polk, Wardwell, Gardiner & Reed; 2) Cravath (Paul D.), de Gersdorff, Swaine & Wood; 3) Murray, Aldrich (W.W. president of the Equitable Trust & Rockefeller representative) & Webb. ~ Other tenants: Ivy Ledbetter Lee; Wm. Hale Harkness; Hemphill, Noyes & Co; Broad St. Club.

WILLIAM ST. →

Atlantic Building. St. Paul's School Alumni Ass'n. President: Bernon S. Prentice (Dominick & Dominick)

U.S. Trust Co. Has no branches, Chairman John A. Stewart died in 1926, aged 104.

Interstate Trust Co. Directors include Herbert C. Lakin (sugar), Carleton H. Palmer (Squibb).

J.P. Morgan & Co. Realtors consider this most extravagant N.Y. business bldg. Standing on property worth $600 or $700 per sq. ft., it has no tenant rental, rises only about 100 feet. Letterheads read, simply, 23 Wall St; hence it has become the most famous banking address in the world.

To Lehman Bros. →

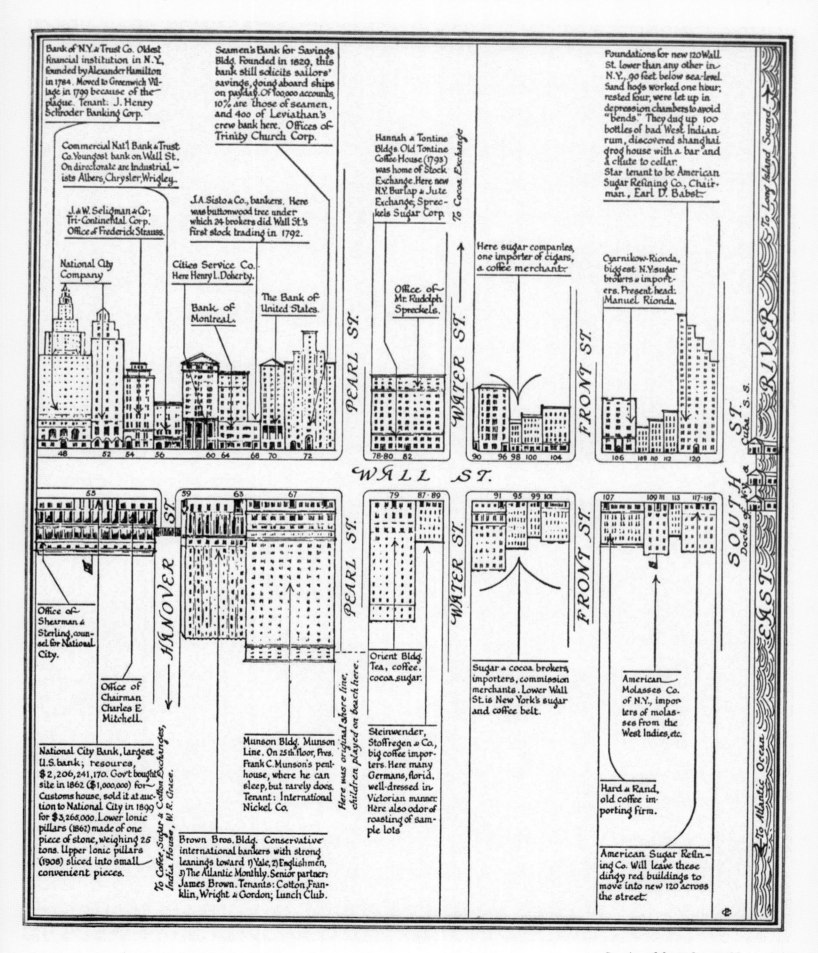

THE MENSWEAR PRE-1976 HERITAGE TUMBLR-BLOGGER/ MODEL

THE VETERAN EDITOR WITH CHILDREN-AS-ACCESSORIES (SATURDAYS ONLY)

THE NIGHTLIFE HEIRESS/ DJ/COKEHEAD/SHOE DESIGNER/ INSTAGRAM STAR

THE SEAT-STEALING JUNIOR BUYER IN A FASCINATOR

THE TOTALLY BLACK-CLAD POWER TRIPPING P.R. INTERN

THE TWENTYSOMETHING FASHION BLOGGER WHO ONLY CHANGES IN FRONT OF HER DRIVER

THE SHIVERING MODEL WITH HER LEATHER JACKET AND CHANEL 2.55

THE DANDY FREELANCE JOURNALIST WHOSE BYLINE YOU'VE NEVER SEEN

THE PACK OF RICH RUSSIANS IN FUR

THE STREET STYLE PHOTOGRAPHER WHO STANDS POSING, NOT SHOOTING

ABOVE

Peter Arkle (illustrations) and Kurt Soller (text), *Ten Types of People You See at Fashion Week*, **from** *New York Magazine*, **February 6, 2013.**

Twice a year, members of an exclusive tribe of urban power brokers flex their muscles during fashion week. Don't be deceived by the foibles of this squadron of wannabes—their ilk drives an industry.

OPPOSITE

Pop Chart Lab, *The Wondrous Towers of New York City*, **2014.**

Water towers have a style of their own. Most of New York's are made by two companies, Rosenwach Tank Co. and Isseks Brothers Inc. They're always described with words like "anachronistic" or "old-fashioned," but they're actually as efficient at doing their job as a skyscraper—or, for that matter, a fashionista.

NEW YORK CITY

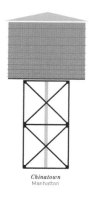
Chinatown
Manhattan

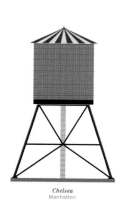
Upper West Side
Manhattan

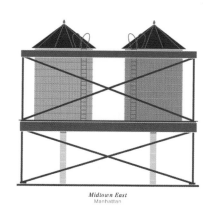
Chelsea
Manhattan

Midtown East
Manhattan

DUMBO
Brooklyn

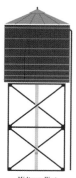
Midtown West
Manhattan

Chelsea
Manhattan

DUMBO
Brooklyn

Chelsea
Manhattan

Greenpoint
Brooklyn

Williamsburg
Brooklyn

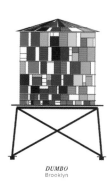
DUMBO
Brooklyn

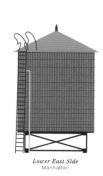
Lower East Side
Manhattan

Williamsburg
Brooklyn

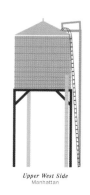
Upper West Side
Manhattan

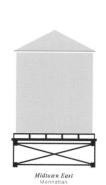
Midtown East
Manhattan

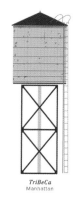
TriBeCa
Manhattan

Harlem
Manhattan

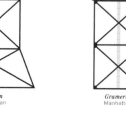
Gramercy
Manhattan

Financial District
Manhattan

SoHo
Manhattan

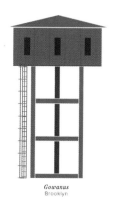
Gowanus
Brooklyn

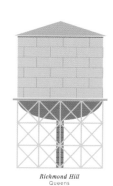
Richmond Hill
Queens

OPPOSITE
Maira Kalman, *Crosstown Boogie Woogie*, 1995. Reproduced on the cover of *The New Yorker*, December 4, 1995.
Artist Maira Kalman celebrates the diversity of the city, uptown and down, with glancing associations between its inhabitants and their habitats.

ABOVE
Ed Piskor, *Epic Battles!*, from his *Hip Hop Family Tree Vol. 1*, December 2013.
Urban legends have their urban myths, and so New York's hip-hop artists look to Marvel superheroes, with their outsize ids and out-of-control egos. Pittsburgh comics artist Ed Piskor tells their stories in his *Hip Hop Family Tree*.

Species of the Urban Wild   **151**

আইনকে জানুন 认识法律 اعرف القانون | Conozca la Ley

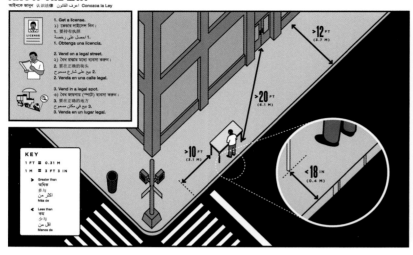

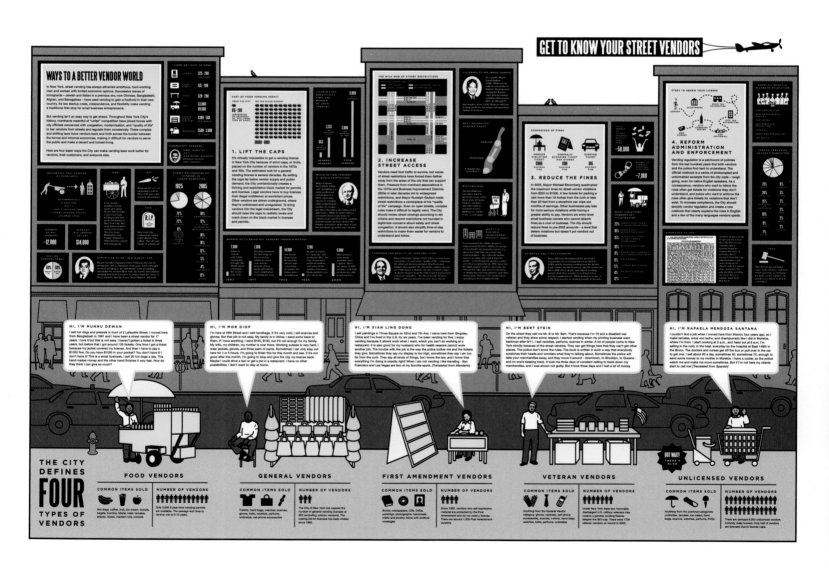

OPPOSITE

OPPOSITE

Center for Urban Pedagogy, *Vendor Power!: A Guide to Street Vending in New York City*, 2009. Project team: Candy Chan (designer), Sean Basinski (Street Vendor Project), and John Mangin and Rosten Woo (CUP).

For street vendors, the city's regulations can be incomprehensible. This guide, a fold-out poster produced for the Street Vendor Project, a vendor advocacy group, offers an accessible pictorial rendition of the law in diagrams and multilingual texts. It was distributed for free to vendors to help educate, empower, and protect them.

RIGHT, TOP AND PAGE 112

Interboro Partners, *Manhattan Grid Bingo*, from *The Guide to the Grid*, 2012. Project team: Tobias Armborst, Daniel D'Oca, and Georgeen Theodore, with Rebecca Beyer Winik, Ingrid Burrington, Kathleen Cahill, Adrian Garcia, Willy Mann, and Pedro Torres.

The grid has its mysteries and curiosities. With Grid Bingo, kids of all ages become urban explorers. No cheating on the Internet!

RIGHT, BOTTOM

Nathan W. Pyle, *What Is a Bodega?*, from his *NYC Basic Tips and Etiquette*, 2014.

Good question. There are more than ten thousand of these small convenience stores scattered through New York's five boroughs. Many are owned and run by Caribbean immigrants to the city or their children. Ohio native Pyle's visual solution to the problem is as good an answer as any—unless you feel that the addition of "magic" begs the question.

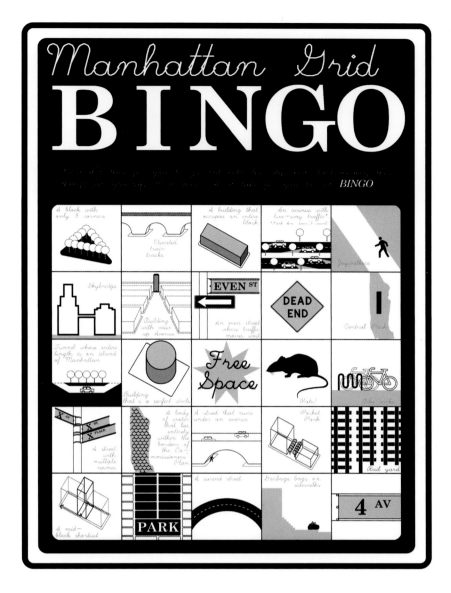

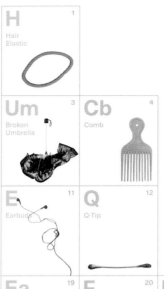

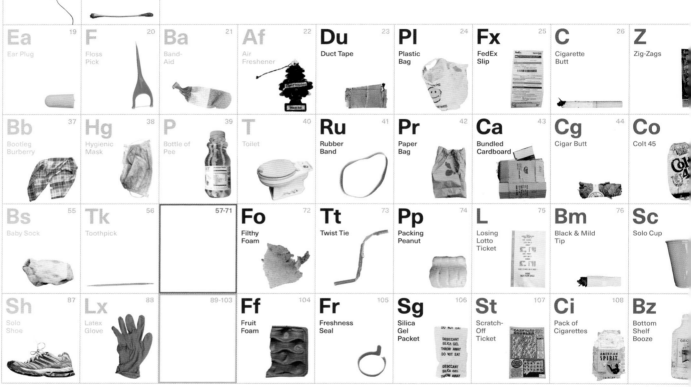

H 1 — Hair Elastic		
Um 3 — Broken Umbrella	**Cb** 4 — Comb	
E 11 — Earbuds	**Q** 12 — Q-Tip	

Ea 19 Ear Plug	F 20 Floss Pick	Ba 21 Band-Aid	Af 22 Air Freshener	**Du** 23 Duct Tape	**Pl** 24 Plastic Bag	**Fx** 25 FedEx Slip	**C** 26 Cigarette Butt	**Z** Zig-Zags
Bb 37 Bootleg Burberry	Hg 38 Hygienic Mask	P 39 Bottle of Pee	T 40 Toilet	**Ru** 41 Rubber Band	**Pr** 42 Paper Bag	**Ca** 43 Bundled Cardboard	**Cg** 44 Cigar Butt	**Co** Colt 45
Bs 55 Baby Sock	Tk 56 Toothpick	57-71	**Fo** 72 Filthy Foam	**Tt** 73 Twist Tie	**Pp** 74 Packing Peanut	L 75 Losing Lotto Ticket	**Bm** 76 Black & Mild Tip	**Sc** Solo Cup
Sh 87 Solo Shoe	Lx 88 Latex Glove	89-103	**Ff** 104 Fruit Foam	**Fr** 105 Freshness Seal	**Sg** 106 Silica Gel Packet	**St** 107 Scratch-Off Ticket	**Ci** 108 Pack of Cigarettes	**Bz** Bottom Shelf Booze

Apparel *Hygiene*   *Packing*   *Vices*

Household

Lifestyle

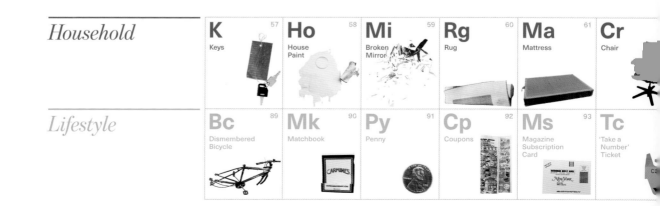

| K 57 Keys | Ho 58 House Paint | Mi 59 Broken Mirror | Rg 60 Rug | Ma 61 Mattress | Cr Chair |
| Bc 89 Dismembered Bicycle | Mk 90 Matchbook | Py 91 Penny | Cp 92 Coupons | Ms 93 Magazine Subscription Card | Tc 'Take a Number' Ticket |

BLE
SH

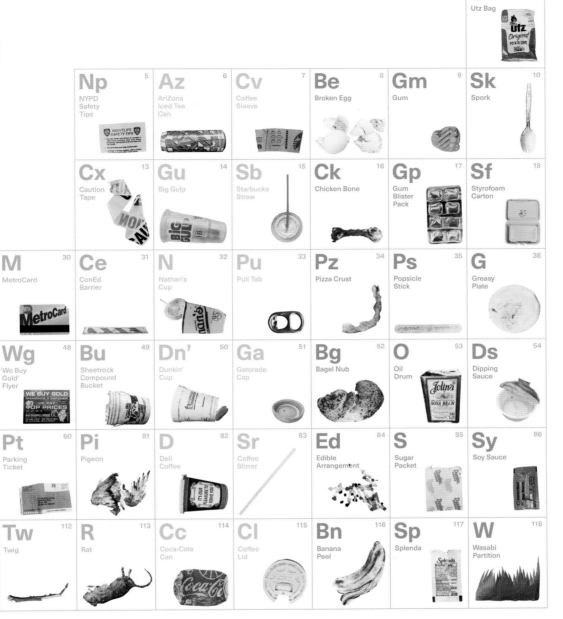

						U 2 — Utz Bag
Np 5 — NYPD Safety Tips	Az 6 — AriZona Iced Tea Can	Cv 7 — Coffee Sleeve	Be 8 — Broken Egg	Gm 9 — Gum	Sk 10 — Spork	
Cx 13 — Caution Tape	Gu 14 — Big Gulp	Sb 15 — Starbucks Straw	Ck 16 — Chicken Bone	Gp 17 — Gum Blister Pack	Sf 18 — Styrofoam Carton	

Mc 28 — McDonald's	Am 29 — AM New York	M 30 — MetroCard	Ce 31 — ConEd Barrier	N 32 — Nathan's Cup	Pu 33 — Pull Tab	Pz 34 — Pizza Crust	Ps 35 — Popsicle Stick	G 36 — Greasy Plate
Cm 46 — Condoms	Ny 47 — New York Post	Wg 48 — 'We Buy Gold' Flyer	Bu 49 — Sheetrock Compound Bucket	Dn' 50 — Dunkin' Cup	Ga 51 — Gatorade Cap	Bg 52 — Bagel Nub	O 53 — Oil Drum	Ds 54 — Dipping Sauce
Dg 78 — Drug Bag	Pb 79 — Playbill	Pt 80 — Parking Ticket	Pi 81 — Pigeon	D 82 — Deli Coffee	Sr 83 — Coffee Stirrer	Ed 84 — Edible Arrangement	S 85 — Sugar Packet	Sy 86 — Soy Sauce
Re 110 — Reese's	Wp 111 — 'Wet Paint' Sign	Tw 112 — Twig	R 113 — Rat	Cc 114 — Coca-Cola Can	Cl 115 — Coffee Lid	Bn 116 — Banana Peel	Sp 117 — Splenda	W 118 — Wasabi Partition

Municipal   *Beverage*   *Food*

i 63 — die air	Bd 64 — Baby Doll	Cn 65 — Clothespin	Wi 66 — Wire Hanger	B 67 — Button	Hp 68 — Halloween Pumpkin	Ac 69 — Air Conditioner	Tv 70 — Television	Pn 71 — Printer
h 95 — t Check m	Cf 96 — Pacifier	Ty 97 — Solo Tylenol	Mo 98 — Movie Stub	Su 99 — Plastic Sushi	Li 100 — Lint Wad	Bl 101 — Deflated Balloon	Pc 102 — Paper Clip	Px 103 — Canister of Poison

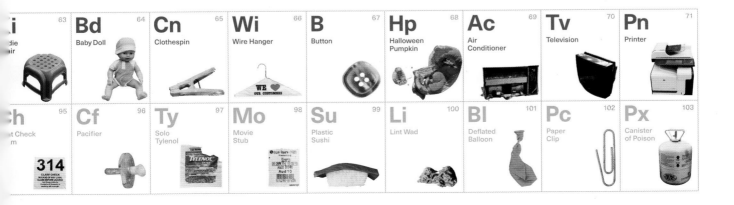

ANT LIFE – PAINTED BY ALAJÁLOV

Description on page 122

PREVIOUS SPREAD

Molly Young and Teddy Blanks,
***The Periodic Table of NYC Trash*, 2016.**
Writer Young and graphic designer Blanks
created this poster that sorts 118 "naturally
occurring" trash items into nine groups:
Apparel, Beverage, Food, Hygiene, Household, Lifestyle, Municipal, Packing, and Vices.

LEFT

**Constantin Alajálov, *The Museum of
Modern Art—A Cross-Section of Its
Exuberant Life*, from *Vogue*, July 1945.**
New Yorkers love to complain that successive
renovations of the Museum of Modern Art
have moved it further and further away from
the charm and intimacy of its first incar-
nation on West 53rd Street, which opened
in 1939, but who really remembers? This
illustration by Russian-born Constantin Alajálov, a popular editorial illustrator for major
American magazines, takes us back. But were
there really potted plants in the galleries?

woman in knee-high high heel boots, jeans and a white fur cape with high collar

white woman walking up and down talking on the phone seems aggravated!

"okay, enjoy, goodbye"

"Ma'am?"
no answer
"Miss! Miss! Miss!"

smell of cologne

Asian woman wearing a surgical mask

Man meets woman who is sitting on a security bollard
"You've literally been shopping all day!?" He says incredulously

wearing fedora

Black woman, long hair wearing brown fur hat and dark brown coat

leather baseball cap eye lashes puffy coat fur-lined hood

Girl with jean jacket with a rainbow on the back

"I am very sheltered"

woman with leopard faux fur coat, white fur bag 2 giant fur earmuffs

"You smell!" 3 men start laughing

3 police officers

young man seems impressed the 3 girls seem totally unimpressed and continue to ignore him

3 girls sit beside a boy standing beside them

Pigeon with 2 pi his shoulder back over group.
Pigeon showing bird's fe flies in a back

Man squeezing eyedrops into his eyes
Several full bags of shopping at his feet

"What's up?" Man yells to woman
"How are you?" She says smiling
"Tired! How are you?"
woman laughs, "the same!"

Big, tall white man, 50ish
fist bumps and high-fives with another man
The 2 men are laughing

ching

The smaller man almost jumping up and down

Man with a walking stick wearing an NYPD baseball cap

29

He falls to his knees

she drags steps

Taller man

Mother yanks boy to cross

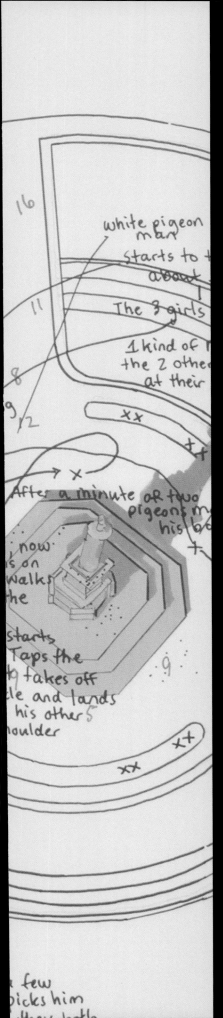

MANHATTAN THROBS WITH TYPOGRAPHIC MESSAGES. IN THIS chapter, type, typography, typefaces, and lettering serve both an informational and performative role in the diagrams of Manhattan. Maps are the most common genre of all-text diagrams. Paula Scher fills her maps with minute details arduously painted: *Manhattan at Night* of 2007 is composed of thousands of points of light that coalesce into pulsating words (page 174 and frontispiece). Sarah King uses a post-psyche-delic space-filling lettering style in her 2018 *Hip Hop Map of New York* (page 185). Jonathon Green and Adam Dant's *New York Tawk* of 2018 maps language, pinpointing neighborhoods associated with words like "groovy" (the East Village) and "bahfungoo" (Little Italy) (page 187).

There will always be diagrams where words threaten to upstage images. When, in 1904, the cartoonist Winsor McCay imagined the subway over-whelmed by a rising tide of advertising, he packed words onto every surface (page 170). In 2011, Frank Viva filled a cityscape with words evoking the *Mental Landscape* (page 175), the urban environment as a menu of different locales. In the work of Fortunato Depero, who briefly resided in Manhattan in the late 1920s, language joyously broke free of linear constraint: His iconic cityscape, titled *24th Street* (page 170), was constructed entirely from words forming not only streets and buildings but a text that evokes the kaleidoscopic density of objects and associations encountered on a walk through Midtown.

Some explicators abandon the image entirely. Ironically, text-only diagrams pop up frequently in descriptions of New York's art world. Fluxus, a loosely knit alternative art group led by George Maciunas had an affinity for using words alone and with pictures as a way to push social and aesthetic messages into the world. Maciunas generated a bracing black-and-white flowchart of the movement's historical antecedents in c. 1966 (page 176). Loren Munk's (a.k.a. James Kalm's) recent diagrammatic maps of art districts and artists deploy a more engaging color palette (pages 178–179) to similar ends: He traces histories, movements, and people in the art world.

Text is also indispenable for mapping ideas, another product of the big city. Take a look at Rachel Schragis's 2011 *Flowchart of the Declaration of Occupa-tion of NYC* (page 171), a crowd-sourced manifesto of the leaderless Occupy Wall Street movement, which united people of many political persuasions, races, and genders against the greed of the 1 percent. Her web of words, con-tributed by the Zuccotti Park demonstrators and rendered entirely in hand-writing, shows how a series of facts about corporate America, filling bubbles that encircle its center, result in the social harms listed in the outermost ring. Hundreds of people contributed to this image, and it was often distributed as an outreach tool to answer questions like, "What is this movement about?"

Texting, it predates cell phones by many centuries.

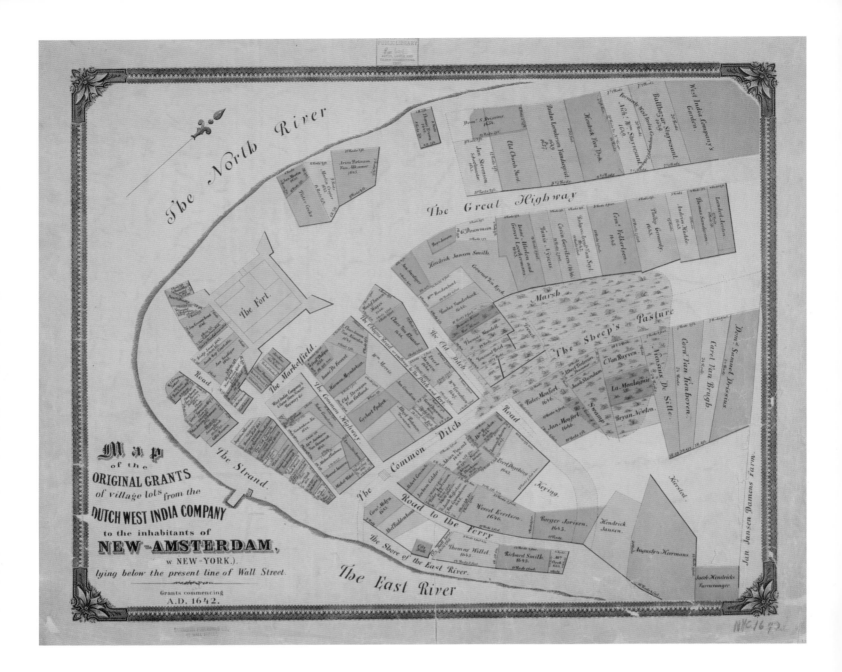

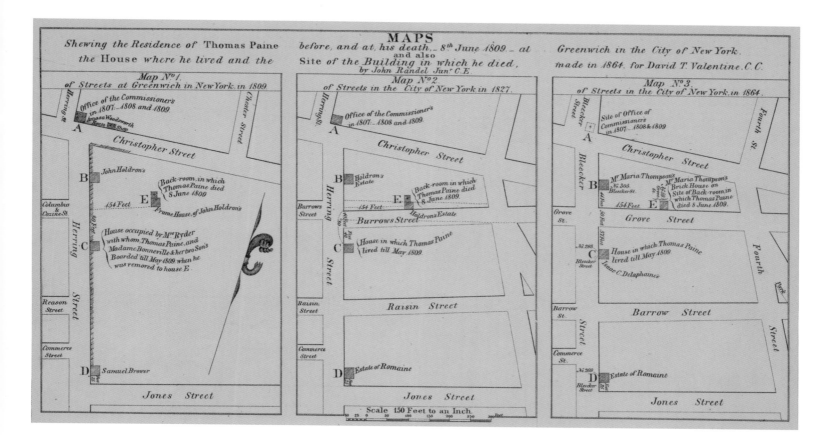

OPPOSITE AND PAGE 8

Henry Dunreath Tyler, *Map of the Original Grants of Village Lots from the Dutch West India Company to the Inhabitants of New-Amsterdam (Now New-York) Lying Below the Present Line of Wall Street: Grants Commencing A.D. 1642*, 1897.

This jigsaw puzzle of a map of New Amsterdam shows the original division of land into private lots by the Dutch West India Company, including owner names, lot dimensions, and year of grants. A small number of the names—Van Cortlandt and Stuyvesant, for example—have been woven into the geography of the city, but all of these old Dutch family names would have been of interest to the gatekeepers of New York society in the 1890s, when this map was drawn.

ABOVE

John Randel, Jr., *Maps Shewing the Residence of Thomas Paine before, and at, His Death, 8th June 1809, at Greenwich in the City of New York: and Also the House Where He Lived and the Site of the Building in Which He Died*, 1864.

Dancing typography animates a beautifully drawn section of Greenwich Village, repeated for three different dates, that is freighted with personal meaning. Many New Yorkers were touched that the Revolutionary War hero Thomas Paine ended his life in their midst in 1809. John Randel, Jr., famous as the surveyor and draftsman of the Manhattan grid plan (and a dissenter from Paine's deism), as a young man would often pass by Paine's house ("E" on this map) on the way to his office ("A"). Here, the precise Randel chronicles more than half a century of small changes in the street plan around the fixed points of the landmarks of his youth. Randel would pass away a year after this map was published.

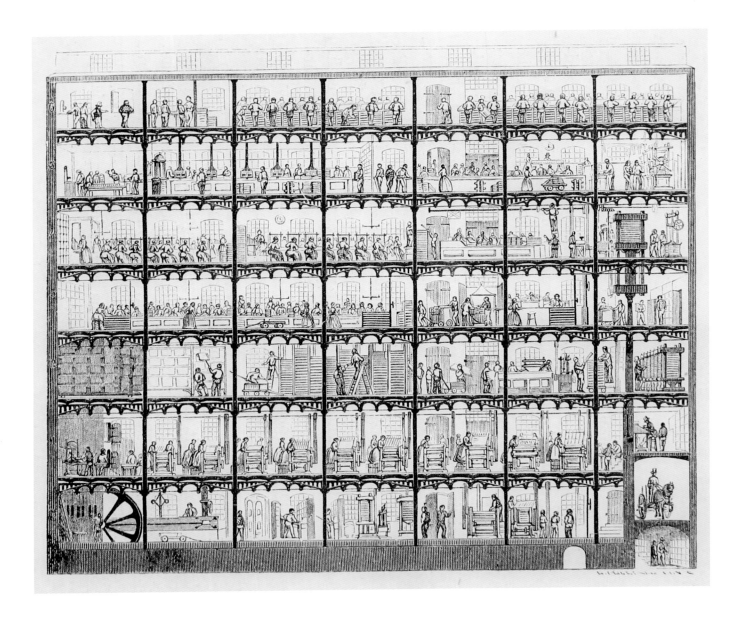

ABOVE

Sectional View of the Cliff Street Building, from the Harper Establishment; or How the Story Books Are Made by Jacob Abbott, **1855.**

Harper & Brothers was the largest publisher in antebellum New York, printing its own books at its state-of-the-art, cast-iron office and factory in Lower Manhattan, which is portrayed in this stylized illustration for a children's book by an unknown illustrator the year the company moved into its new headquarters. In this view, men compose type on the top floor, while women operate the presses on the second floor.

OPPOSITE, TOP

Piet Schreuders, _Manhattan, New York: Paperback Publishers' Offices, 1939–1959_, from his _Paperbacks, U.S.A.: A Graphic History_, 1981.

By the middle of the twentieth century, paperback publishers were scattered around Midtown. The lettering style of this map was inspired by Ruth Belew's scene-of-the-crime Mapback illustrations for paperback mysteries published by Dell in the 1940s and 1950s.

OPPOSITE, BOTTOM

Ken Fitzgerald, _New York Newspaper Buildings_, from Discover New York with Henry Hope Reed, Jr., _New York Herald Tribune_, 1964.

Henry Hope Reed's walking-tour columns, accompanied by diagrams with pleasantly awkward typography, for the _New York Herald Tribune_ in 1962–63 included one on Newspaper Row, whose legendary tenants had all abandoned their handsome headquarters buildings by the 1920s. The Tribune Building came down shortly after Reed's column was published, joining its ghostly neighbor to the north.

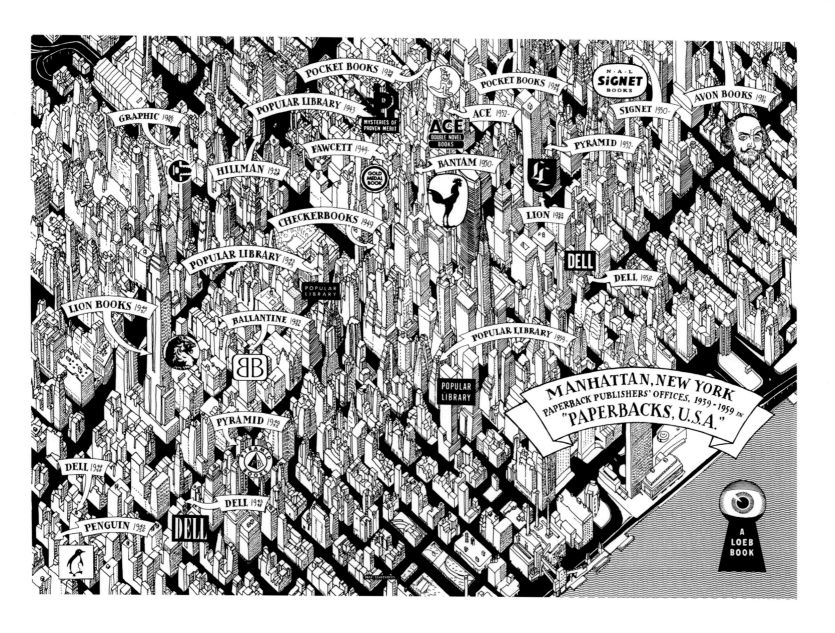

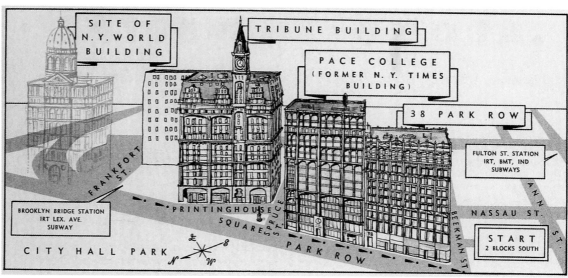

The year the New York Public Library's main branch at Fifth Avenue and 42nd Street was due to open, the city's major publications hyped the event with elaborate cutaways. The *New York Tribune* and the *New York Times* must have been working from a drawing provided by the architects, which the *Times* described as a new sort of "sectional perspective of the inside of the great structure, from which an excellent idea may be gained of its vastness and the amazing lengths to which its architects have gone in their endeavor to do everything possible for the comfort and satisfaction of bookworms." *Scientific American* zoomed in on the stacks, where clerks would later famously retrieve books on roller skates, to portray a very white male–dominated scene.

RIGHT, TOP

H. M. Pettit, *Sectional View of New York's New Public Library*, from the *New York Times*, May 14, 1911.

RIGHT, BOTTOM

***Sectional View of the Interior of the Library*, from the *New-York Tribune*, January 1, 1911.**

OPPOSITE

***A Sectional View of the New York Public Library*, from *Scientific American*, May 27, 1911.**

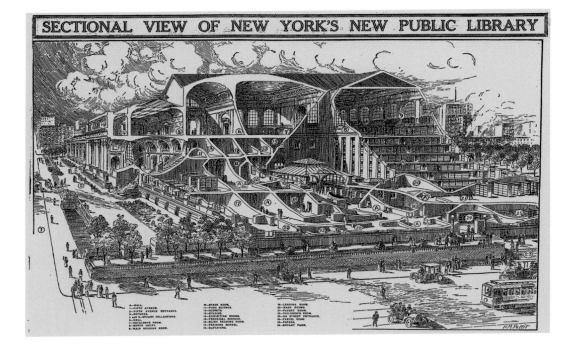

Anthony Velonis, *Better Housing the Solution to Infant Mortality in the Slums*, poster for Federal Art Project, c. 1936–1938.

Time has not been kind to the housing project, viewed idealistically in this poster from the vantage point of the 1930s. Most New Yorkers today, faced with the blank fortress that represents the happy future in master silkscreen printer Anthony Velonis's poster promoting better housing, would probably prefer to live in the X'ed-out small-scale residential neighborhood that he used to evoke the troubled past.

Muller, *Keep Your Fire Escapes Clear*, poster for Federal Art Project, c. 1936–1937.

As far as iconic urban architectural add-ons go, the tenement fire escapes are undisputed stars. This stylized poster, part of a campaign by the Tenement House Department to promote fire safety, presents a quaint isometric view carefully composed with domestic objects, as if for the stage set of a Broadway musical. An inviting setting that makes the advice a tough sell.

Vera Bock, *History of Civic Services in the City of New York: Fire Department and Water Supply*, posters for the Federal Art Project, 1936.

The Federal Art Project, which put artists to work during the Great Depression, produced results that celebrated civic life in many different visual idioms. From her charming series of posters on the "history" of the city's fire department and water supply, it should come as no surprise that the Russian-born Vera Bock was best known as a children's book illustrator.

HISTORY · OF CIVIC · SERVICES IN THE CITY · OF NEW · YORK
WATER SUPPLY — No. 1

New Amsterdam

1658
The water was drawn by the ancient method of bucket and balanced pole

The First Public well was dug opposite the Fort

HISTORY · OF CIVIC · SERVICES IN THE·CITY·OF NEW·YORK
WATER SUPPLY — No. 4

Almost one half of all the water used in New York City is supplied by the Catskill Mountains Water Supply System. It contains, among other things, an artificial lake twelve miles long for storing water & an underground aqueduct through which water flows unceasingly from the Catskill Mts. to Staten Island, 120 miles, at the rate of 500 million gallons daily 200ft. below street level.

1936

An Average of 950,000,000 Gallons is Consumed Daily

HISTORY · OF CIVIC · SERVICES IN THE·CITY·OF·NEW·YORK
FIRE DEPARTMENT — No. 1

..Therefore have we, with approbation of the Director-general and Councillors of New Netherland, appointed Fire Wardens..... ..to perform their duties according to the custom of our fatherland

Done this 26th day of Feb. 1656

FIRE DEPARTMENT FOUNDED BY PETRUS STUYVESANT

HISTORY · OF CIVIC · SERVICES IN·THE·CITY·OF·NEW·YORK
FIRE DEPARTMENT — No. 4

1936

Modern fire fighting equipment effectually prevents the spread of fires. But today the prevention of fires is especially emphasized by strict regulations enforced by rigid inspection by the Fire Department.

UP-TO-DATE MACHINERY · EFFICIENCY · SPEED

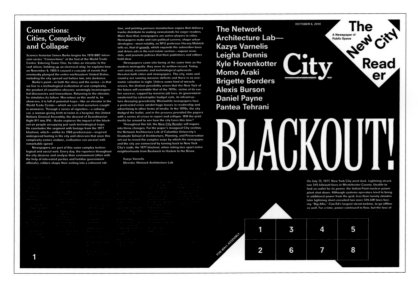

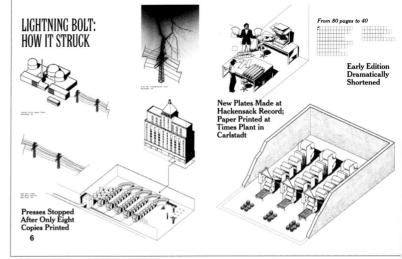

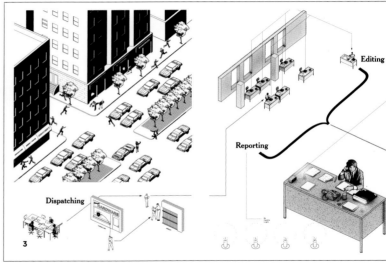

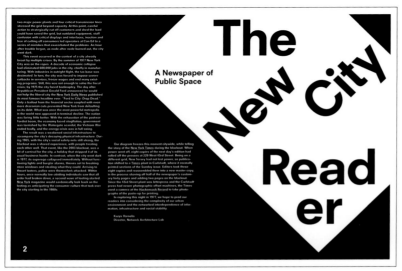

ABOVE

Network Architecture Lab, *City Blackout!*, from the *New City Reader*, October 6, 2010.

Using a format inspired by Chinese *dazibao*, the large-scale handwritten posters wall-mounted in public spaces for collective communication, *City Blackout!* tells how the *New York Times* got the paper out on the night of July 13, 1977, when a lightning strike caused a citywide blackout. The *New City Reader*, with fourteen weekly editions guest-edited by a contributing network of architects, theorists, and research groups, explored possible outcomes at a time when both cities and newspapers face serious challenges.

OPPOSITE

Richard Giovine and Ad Reinhardt, *The "Atom" of Big Business—or Why Struck Firms Stick Together*, from *PM*, 1946.

PM was a left-leaning, mostly advertising-free, daily newspaper published from 1940 to 1948 with some heavyweight talent. Here, in a deft bit of data visualization, five of America's largest corporations are linked to four leading New York banks through their boards of directors, using an atomic form that conveys both power and mutual attraction, with the help of the brilliant diagram maker (and leading abstract painter) Ad Reinhardt.

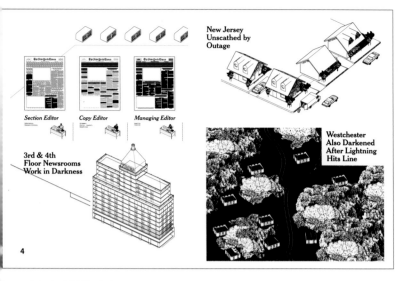

Section Editor

Copy Editor

Managing Editor

3rd & 4th
Floor Newsrooms
Work in Darkness

New Jersey
Unscathed by
Outage

Westchester
Also Darkened
After Lightning
Hits Line

4

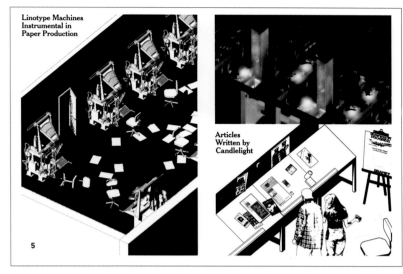

Linotype Machines
Instrumental in
Paper Production

Articles
Written by
Candlelight

5

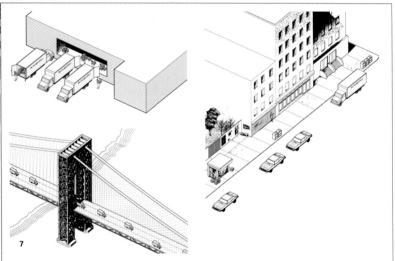

7

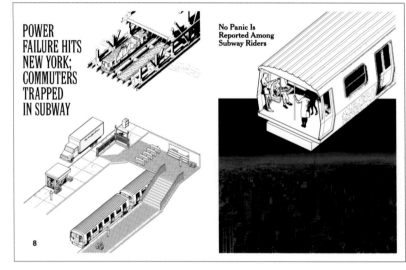

POWER
FAILURE HITS
NEW YORK;
COMMUTERS
TRAPPED
IN SUBWAY

No Panic Is
Reported Among
Subway Riders

8

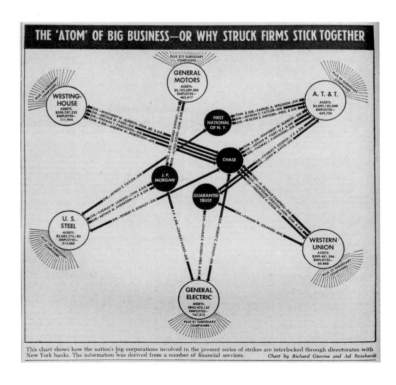

Text and the City   **169**

SUBWAY ADVERTISING IN 1907
As Foreseen Through THE SPECTROPHONE

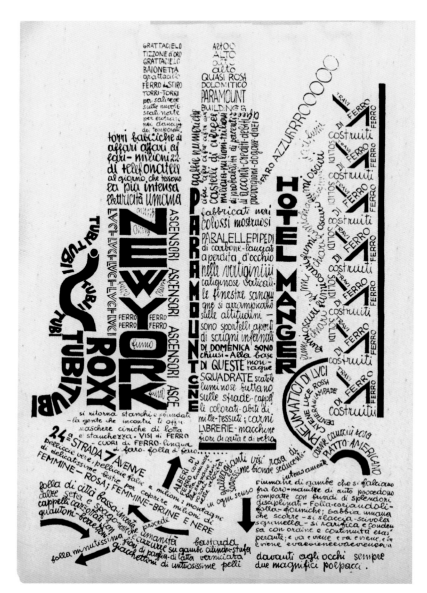

ABOVE

Winsor McCay, *Subway Advertising in 1907*, from the *New York Herald*, December 25, 1904.

McCay enters a subway station in 1904, the year the system opened to the public, encounters subway advertising for the first time, and imagines a day in the near future when he will drown in hype. A tour de force of hand lettering ensues. McCay's Spectrophone, which forecast the future in a series of cartoons, failed to predict another sort of phone: A century in the future, all of the advertising that tormented McCay, personalized for the recipient, would be compressible into a small, ubiquitous handheld device.

RIGHT

Fortunato Depero, *24th Street*, 1929.

Depero lived in Manhattan from 1928 to 1930, absorbing its intense rhythms and turning them into concrete poetry, as in this diagram of a walk near his house and workshop on West 23rd Street.

Rachel Schragis, *Flowchart of the Declaration of the Occupation of Wall Street*, 2011.

How does a leaderless movement find a unified voice? One possible solution is found in this crowd-sourced visual manifesto. Rachel Schragis scrupulously collected the ideas of the many activists who occupied Zuccotti Park in the fall of 2011, to protest against economic inequality, and organized them into an argument for social change.

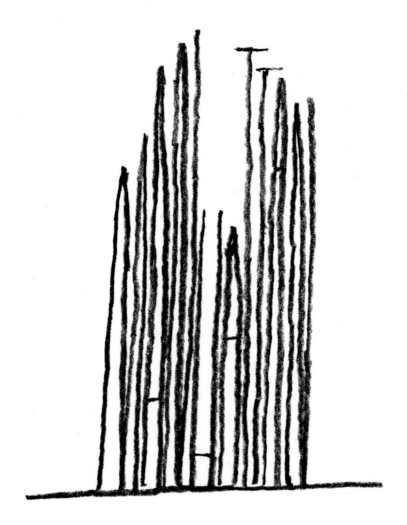

view driving in from the Triboro bridge

Alan Fletcher, *Manhattan*, undated.
"At rush hour, commuting New Yorkers drive out of Manhattan at sixty miles an hour," marveled English designer and artist Alan Fletcher in 1957. Here, in an iconic drawing, is his "view driving in from the Triboro Bridge." Designers and artists from Fortunato Depero (page 170) to Ivan Chermayeff (opposite) have used the skyline as a typographical metaphor.

Ivan Chermayeff, *AIGA/NY at Thirty Years*, 2012.
Designer Ivan Chermayeff's poster stands out for packing many essential Manhattan characteristics, like the subway, the grid, and density, into a muscular graphic.

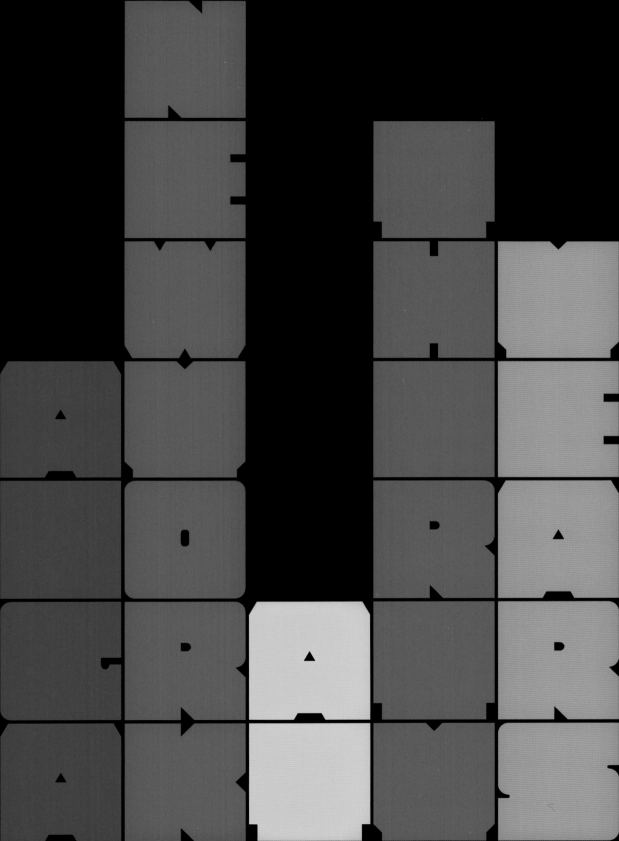

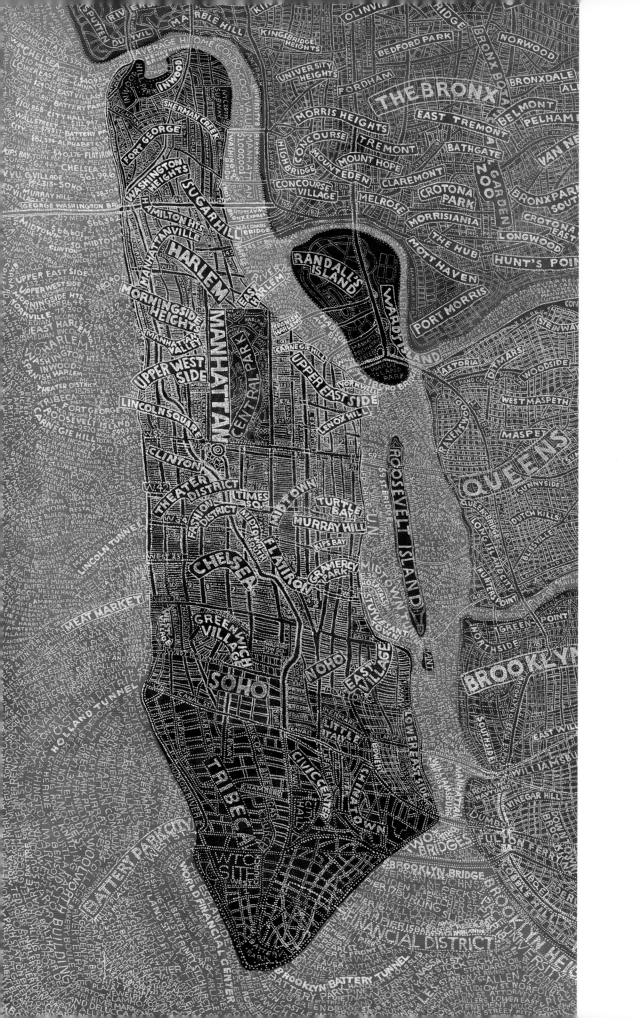

Paula Scher, *Manhattan at Night*, 2007.

Reality lurks within Scher's iridescent nightscape of Manhattan. Sobering statistics, flowing among the dense typographic currents of the island's waterways, show the population and median income of the city's neighborhoods. The contrast between, for example, Spanish Harlem (median income $17,370) and the Upper East Side (median income $80,405) reveals a glowing city marked by blistering inequalities.

Frank Viva, *Mental Landscape*, cover for *The New Yorker*, January 31, 2011.

Each Manhattanite reads the city differently. We each assign names to places based on our experience and lifestyle. In Frank Viva's vision, a beautiful glowing jumble of forms and type makes perfect sense of one person's mental landscape.

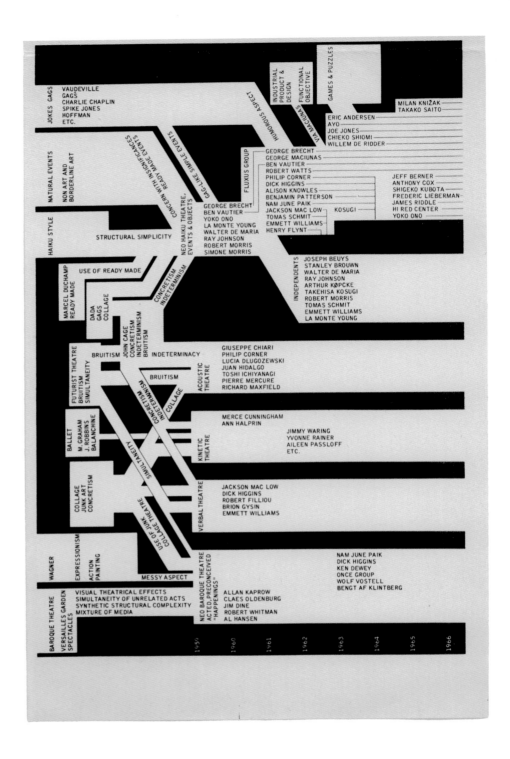

George Maciunas, *Fluxus (Its Historical Development and Relationship to Avant-Garde Movements)*, c. 1966.

The systematizing mind has always found plenty of material to work with in the history of avant-garde movements, of which Manhattan has had more than its share. Fluxus was the name adopted by an interdisciplinary, loosely knit group of artists, composers, designers, and poets, many of whom were based in New York, during the 1960s and 1970s. Here, the leading Fluxus artist George Maciunas diagrammed the group's sources of inspiration, with the thickness of the links indicating the strength of the influence.

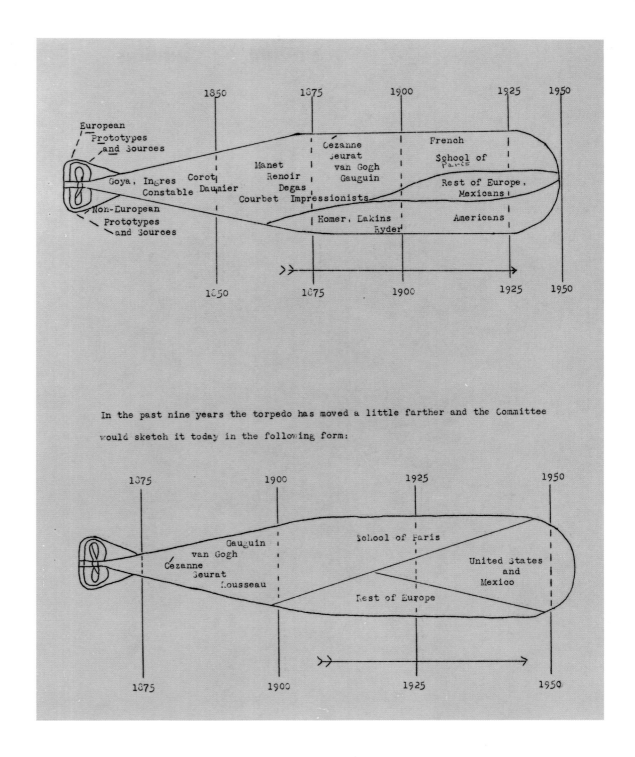

In the past nine years the torpedo has moved a little farther and the Committee would sketch it today in the following form:

Alfred H. Barr, Jr., diagrams of the ideal permanent collection of the Museum of Modern Art, 1933 and 1941.

Alfred H. Barr, Jr., the founding director of the Museum of Modern Art, made torpedo-shaped diagrams to communicate his vision for building the museum's permanent collection to his colleagues. This was a telling image for the power of modern art: Torpedoes are sinister machines that travel beneath the surface of the waves until they hit and destroy their target. By 1941 (lower torpedo), Barr was able to forecast the postwar triumph of American art, although his passion for the modern art of Mexico was not borne out by the museum's collecting priorities.

9. 1957, The Judson Memorial Church begins offering artists space for gallery presentations. In 1962, the Church founds the Judson Dance Theater featuring works with: Steve Paxton, Yvonne Rainer, Meredith Monk and Simone Forti at 55 Washington Square South.

10. In October 1959, artist and Rutgers professor Allan Kaprow presented 18 Happenings in 6 Parts in the Reuben Gallery at 61 Fourth Avenue, in New York's East Village.

11. 1959, Frank Stella takes a studio loft over a diner, and invites Carl Andre to share it. He paints the black stripe paintings here that were featured in "16 Americans" at MoMA, at 366 West Broadway

8. 1953, Next door was the first East 10th Street co-op gallery founded by Angelo Ippolito, William King and Fred Mitchell with Irving Sandler as Director. They show: Philip Pearlstein, Tom Wesselmann, Alex Katz, Sally Hazelet et al. at 90 East 10th Street.

1. 1932, While teaching in California, Hans Hofmann is warned by his wife not to return to Germany. He moves to New York and opens an art school. In 1938 it relocates to 52 West Eighth Street. He influences and educates hundreds of young artists.

2. 1942, Lee Krasner, a former Hofmann student, introduces Hans to Jackson Pollock, who lives around the corner at 48 East 8th Street, where he (Pollock) painted the Guggenheim mural

3. Late 1940s, Jackson Pollock, Mark Rothko, Willem de Kooning, Franz Kline, Landes Lewitin, Michael Goldberg, and Mercedes Matter all begin patronizing the Cedar Tavern at 24 University Place.

12. 1964, Kaymar Gallery is founded by Houston Peterson, shows works by FLUXUS and Minimal artists, including Robert Morris, and Dan Flavin who'd both worked with the Judson Dance Theater. At 548 West Broadway

7. 1952, Willem de Kooning moves his studio from 85 4th Avenue (where he's shared the space with Jack Tworkov) around the corner to 88 East 10th Street.

18. 1989, Larry Gagosian opens a gallery in partnership with Leo Castelli. He exhibits: Georg Baselitz, Ellen Gallagher, Andreas Gursky, Jeff Koons, Takashi Murakami, Richard Prince, Anselm Kiefer, Ed Ruscha, Damien Hirst, Rachel Whiteread, et al. He moves the gallery to Chelsea in 1999, at 65 Thomson Street

6. 1951, With Leo Castelli as curator and financial backer, members of the Artists' Club organize the Ninth Street Show, the first exhibition in which the New York School is featured including: Joan Mitchell, Robert Motherwell, Jackson Pollock, Lee Krasner, Grace Hartigan, Fairfield Porter, Richard Pousette-Dart, Ad Reinhardt, Milton Resnick, Robert Rauschenberg, Elaine de Kooning, Willem de Kooning, Hans Hofmann, Philip Guston et al. at 60 East 9th Street

17. 1977, After working as a secretary at the influential Bykert Gallery, Mary Boone opens her own gallery in SoHo. She shows: Julian Schnabel, Jean-Michel Basquiat, Eric Fischl, Ross Bleckner, and David Salle at 420 West Broadway.

16. 1971, 420 West Broadway opens with the galleries of Leo Castelli, his former wife Ileana Sonnabend and André Emmerich. This building becomes a major nexus of contemporary art for the next fifteen years.

15. 1968, Paula Cooper opens her own gallery, the first commercial venue in SoHo. She represents: Jennifer Bartlett, Donald Judd, Robert Ryman, Carl Andre, Jo Baer, Dan Flavin, Lynda Benglis, Jonathan Borofsky, Elizabeth Murray, Sol LeWitt and others at 96 Prince Street

5. 1948, Organized as an association to discuss Modern Art, and other cultural issues, the "Artists' Club" is founded by Willem de Kooning, Philip Pavia, Ad Reinhardt, Milton Resnick, Landis Lewitin, Jack Tworkov, et al. at 39 East 8th Street

4. 1948-9, The Subject of the Artist School is founded. The faculty includes: William Baziotes, David Hare, Robert Motherwell, Barnett Newman, and Mark Rothko. at 35 East 8th Street

13. 1965, As Director of Park Place Gallery, Paula Cooper relocates next door to Kaymar, calling it Art Research Inc. representing: Mark di Suvero, Peter Forakis, Forrest (Frosty) Myers, Ed Ruda, Robert Grosvenor, David Novros, Gay Glading and et al. at 542 West Broadway

14. 1968, having opened the FLUXUS Center two years earlier at 359 Canal Street, George Maciunas, with support from the J. M. Kaplan Foundation, and the National Foundation for the Arts, begins buying disused industrial buildings in SoHo and converting them into artists lofts.

Map labels: WEST 10TH STREET, WEST 9TH STREET, WEST 8TH STREET, WEAVERLY PLACE, WASHINGTON SQUARE PARK, WEST 3RD STREET, BLEECKER STREET, WEST HOUSTON STREET, PRINCE STREET, SPRING STREET, WEST BROADWAY, WOOSTER STREET, GREENE STREET, MERCER STREET, BROADWAY, CROSBY STREET, LAFAYETTE STREET, BOWERY, BROOME STREET, GRAND STREET, HOWARD STREET, CANAL STREET, AVENUE OF THE AMERICAS

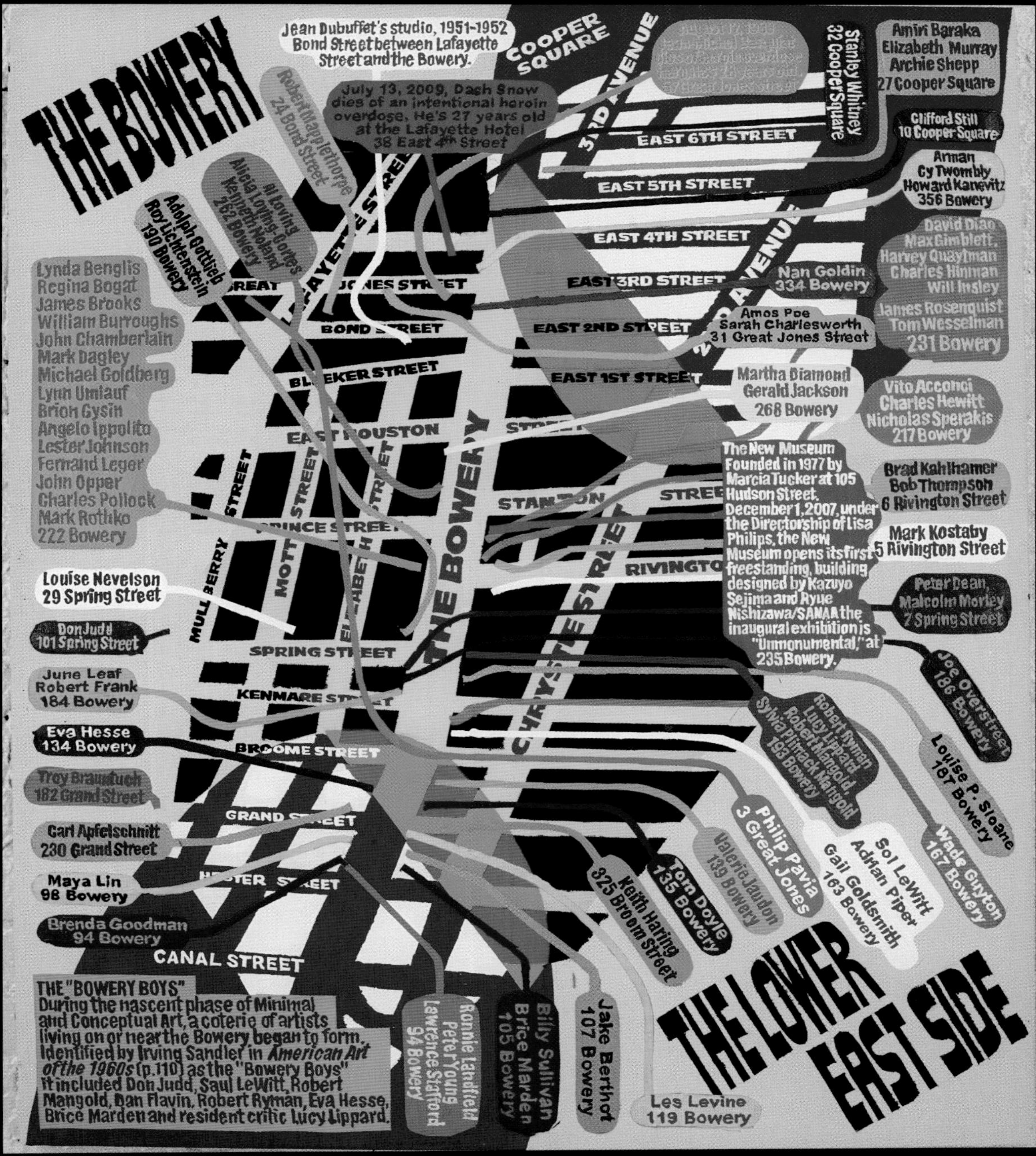
THE BOWERY
Jean Dubuffet's studio, 1951-1952
Bond Street between Lafayette
Street and the Bowery.
COOPER SQUARE
3RD AVENUE
Stanley Whitney
32 Cooper Square
Amiri Baraka
Elizabeth Murray
Archie Shepp
27 Cooper Square
Robert Mapplethorpe
24 Bond Street
July 13, 2009, Dash Snow
dies of an intentional heroin
overdose. He's 27 years old
at the Lafayette Hotel
38 East 4th Street
EAST 6TH STREET
Clifford Still
10 Cooper Square
EAST 5TH STREET
Arman
Cy Twombly
Howard Kanevitz
356 Bowery
Al Loving
Alicia Loving Gorres
Kenneth Noland
262 Bowery
Adolph Gottlieb
Roy Lichtenstein
190 Bowery
LAFAYETTE STREET
EAST 4TH STREET
David Diao
Max Gimblett
Harvey Quaytman
Charles Hinman
Will Insley
James Rosenquist
Tom Wesselman
231 Bowery
Lynda Benglis
Regina Bogat
James Brooks
William Burroughs
John Chamberlain
Mark Dagley
Michael Goldberg
Lynn Umlauf
Brion Gysin
Angelo Ippolito
Lester Johnson
Fernand Leger
John Opper
Charles Pollock
Mark Rothko
222 Bowery
GREAT JONES STREET
EAST 3RD STREET
Nan Goldin
334 Bowery
2ND AVENUE
Amos Poe
Sarah Charlesworth
31 Great Jones Street
BOND STREET
EAST 2ND STREET
BLEEKER STREET
EAST 1ST STREET
Martha Diamond
Gerald Jackson
268 Bowery
Vito Acconci
Charles Hewitt
Nicholas Sperakis
217 Bowery
EAST HOUSTON STREET
The New Museum
Founded in 1977 by
Marcia Tucker at 105
Hudson Street.
December 1, 2007, under
the Directorship of Lisa
Philips, the New
Museum opens its first
freestanding, building
designed by Kazuyo
Sejima and Ryue
Nishizawa/SANAA the
inaugural exhibition is
"Unmonumental," at
235 Bowery.
Brad Kahlhamer
Bob Thompson
6 Rivington Street
STANTON STREET
Mark Kostaby
5 Rivington Street
MULBERRY STREET
MOTT STREET
ELIZABETH STREET
PRINCE STREET
THE BOWERY
CHRYSTIE STREET
RIVINGTON
Louise Nevelson
29 Spring Street
Peter Dean
Malcolm Morley
7 Spring Street
Don Judd
101 Spring Street
SPRING STREET
Joe Overstreet
186 Bowery
June Leaf
Robert Frank
184 Bowery
KENMARE STREET
Robert Ryman
Lucy Lippard
Robert Mangold
Sylvia Plimack Mangold
193 Bowery
Louise P. Sloane
187 Bowery
Eva Hesse
134 Bowery
BROOME STREET
Troy Brauntuch
182 Grand Street
Philip Pavia
3 Great Jones
Sol LeWitt
Adrian Piper
Gail Goldsmith
163 Bowery
Wade Guyton
167 Bowery
GRAND STREET
Carl Apfelschnitt
230 Grand Street
Valerie Jaudon
139 Bowery
Tom Doyle
135 Bowery
Keith Haring
325 Broom Street
HESTER STREET
Maya Lin
98 Bowery
Brenda Goodman
94 Bowery
CANAL STREET
THE "BOWERY BOYS"
During the nascent phase of Minimal
and Conceptual Art, a coterie of artists
living on or near the Bowery began to form.
Identified by Irving Sandler in American Art
of the 1960s (p.110) as the "Bowery Boys"
It included Don Judd, Saul LeWitt, Robert
Mangold, Dan Flavin, Robert Ryman, Eva Hesse,
Brice Marden and resident critic Lucy Lippard.
Ronnie Landfield
Peter Young
Lawrence Stafford
94 Bowery
Billy Sullivan
Brice Marden
105 Bowery
Jake Berthot
107 Bowery
Les Levine
119 Bowery
THE LOWER EAST SIDE

Loren Munk is the New York art world's most passionate and versatile cartographer. As his alter ego, James Kalm, he uses the written word for essays and reviews. He switches to a handheld camera to give guided tours of art shows, published on YouTube as "The Kalm Report." Finally, and most importantly, he paints. Munk's geographies and subjects can vary significantly in scale and detail: Artists and art world figures, streets, neighborhoods, studios, galleries, museums, art movements—all are charted in time and space.

OPPOSITE

Loren Munk, *18 Situations over 6 Decades (Hofmann to SoHo to Chelsea)*, 2016.

ABOVE

Loren Munk, *The Bowery—The Lower East Side (study 1)*, 2017–18.

Mark Kostabi (text by Carlo McCormick in collaboration with Walter Robinson and Paul Benney), *Artropoly*, 1985.

The East Village art scene of the 1980s was the inspiration for this cheeky board-game poster to promote photographer Roland Hagenberg's book *East Village '85*. It's a hazardous dog-eat-dog microcosm ("48. You are featured in the East Village Eye, NY-TALK, The Paper and Details in the same month, but they all misspell your name. Lose a turn or change your name and roll again"), where victory for the player/aspiring artist comes at a price ("68. You become a major success and lose all your friends"). Artist Mark Kostabi had skin in this game: In 1984, the *East Village Eye* awarded him a tongue-in-cheek prize for appearing in the most exhibitions.

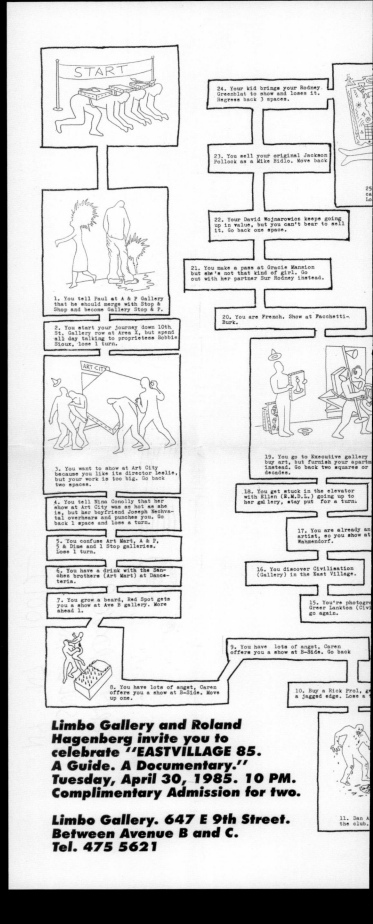

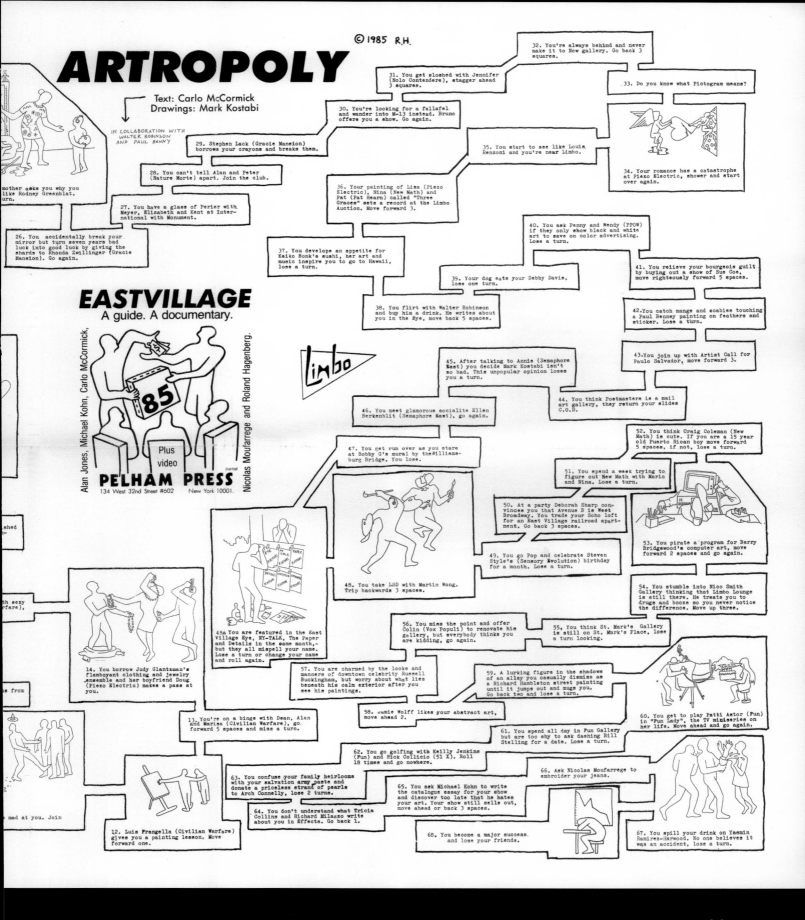

© 1985 R.H.

ARTROPOLY

Text: Carlo McCormick
Drawings: Mark Kostabi

IN COLLABORATION WITH
WALTER ROBINSON
AND PAUL BENNY

EASTVILLAGE
A guide. A documentary.

Alan Jones, Michael Kohn, Carlo McCormick,

Nicolas Moufarrege and Roland Hagenberg.

85

Plus
video

PELHAM PRESS
134 West 32nd Street #602   New York 10001.

Limbo

32. You're always behind and never make it to Now gallery. Go back 3 squares.

31. You get sloshed with Jennifer (Nolo Contendere), stagger ahead 3 squares.

33. Do you know what Pictogram means?

30. You're looking for a fallafel and wander into M-13 instead. Bruno offers you a show. Go again.

29. Stephen Lack (Gracie Mansion) borrows your crayons and breaks them.

35. You start to see like Louis Renzoni and you're near Limbo.

34. Your romance has a catastrophe at Piezo Electric, shower and start over again.

28. You can't tell Alan and Peter (Nature Morte) apart. Join the club.

36. Your painting of Lisa (Piezo Electric), Nina (New Math) and Pat (Pat Hearn) called "Three Graces" sets a record at the Limbo Auction. Move forward 3.

27. You have a glass of Perier with Meyer, Elizabeth and Kent at International with Monument.

26. You accidentally break your mirror but turn seven years bad luck into good luck by giving the shards to Rhonda Zwillinger (Gracie Mansion). Go again.

37. You develope an appetite for Keiko Bonk's sushi, her art and music inspire you to go to Hawaii, lose a turn.

40. You ask Penny and Wendy (PPOW) if they only show black and white art to save on color advertising. Lose a turn.

41. You relieve your bourgeois guilt by buying out a show of Sue Coe, move righteously forward 5 spaces.

39. Your dog eats your Debby Davis, lose one turn.

38. You flirt with Walter Robinson and buy him a drink. He writes about you in the Eye, move back 5 spaces.

42. You catch mange and scabies touching a Paul Benny painting on feathers and sticker. Lose a turn.

43. You join up with Artist Call for Paulo Salvador, move forward 3.

45. After talking to Annie (Semaphore East) you decide Mark Kostabi isn't so bad. This unpopular opinion loses you a turn.

44. You think Postmasters is a mail art gallery, they return your slides C.O.D.

46. You meet glamorous socialite Ellen Berkenblit (Semaphore East), go again.

52. You think Craig Coleman (New Math) is cute. If you are a 15 year old Puerto Rican boy move forward 5 spaces, if not, lose a turn.

47. You get run over as you stare at Bobby G's mural by the Williamsburg Bridge.

51. You spend a week trying to figure out New Math with Mario and Nina. Lose a turn.

50. At a party Deborah Sharp convinces you that Avenue B is West Broadway. You trade your Soho loft for an East Village railroad apartment. Go back 3 spaces.

53. You pirate a program for Barry Bridgewood's computer art, move forward 2 spaces and go again.

49. You go Pop and celebrate Steven Style's (Sensory Evolution) birthday for a month. Lose a turn.

48. You take LSD with Martin Wong. Trip backwards 3 spaces.

54. You stumble into Nico Smith Gallery thinking that Limbo Lounge is still there. He treats you to drugs and booze so you never notice the difference. Move up three.

48a You are featured in the East Village Eye, NY-TALK, The Paper and Details in the same month, but they all mispell your name. Lose a turn or change your name and roll again.

56. You miss the point and offer Colin (Vox Populi) to renovate his gallery, but everybody thinks you are kidding, go again.

55. You think St. Mark's Gallery is still on St. Mark's Place, lose a turn looking.

14. You borrow Judy Glantzman's flamboyant clothing and jewelry ensemble and her boyfriend Doug (Piezo Electric) makes a pass at you.

57. You are charmed by the looks and manners of downtown celebrity Russell Buckingham, but worry about what lies beneath his calm exterior after you see his paintings.

59. A lurking figure in the shadows of an alley you casually dismiss as a Richard Hambleton street painting until it jumps out and mugs you. Go back two and lose a turn.

60. You get to play Patti Astor (Fun) in "Fun Lady", the TV miniseries on her life. Move ahead and go again.

13. You're on a binge with Dean, Alan and Marisa (Civilian Warfare), go forward 5 spaces and miss a turn.

58. Jamie Wolff likes your abstract art, move ahead 2.

61. You spend all day in Fun Gallery but are too shy to ask dashing Bill Stelling for a date. Lose a turn.

62. You go golfing with Keilly Jenkins (Fun) and Rick Collicio (51 X). Roll 18 times and go nowhere.

63. You confuse your family heirlooms with your salvation army paste and donate a priceless strand of pearls to Arch Connelly, lose 2 turns.

66. Ask Nicolas Moufarrege to embroider your jeans.

65. You ask Michael Kohn to write the catalogue essay for your show and discover too late that he hates your art. Your show still sells out, move ahead or back 3 spaces.

64. You don't understand what Tricia Collins and Richard Milazzo write about you in Effects. Go back 1.

12. Luis Frangella (Civilian Warfare) gives you a painting lesson. Move forward one.

68. You become a major success. and lose your friends.

67. You spill your drink on Yasmin Ramirez-Harwood. No one believes it was an accident, lose a turn.

mother asks you why you like Rodney Greenblat.

...shed

...th sexy
...fare),

...s from

...mad at you. Join

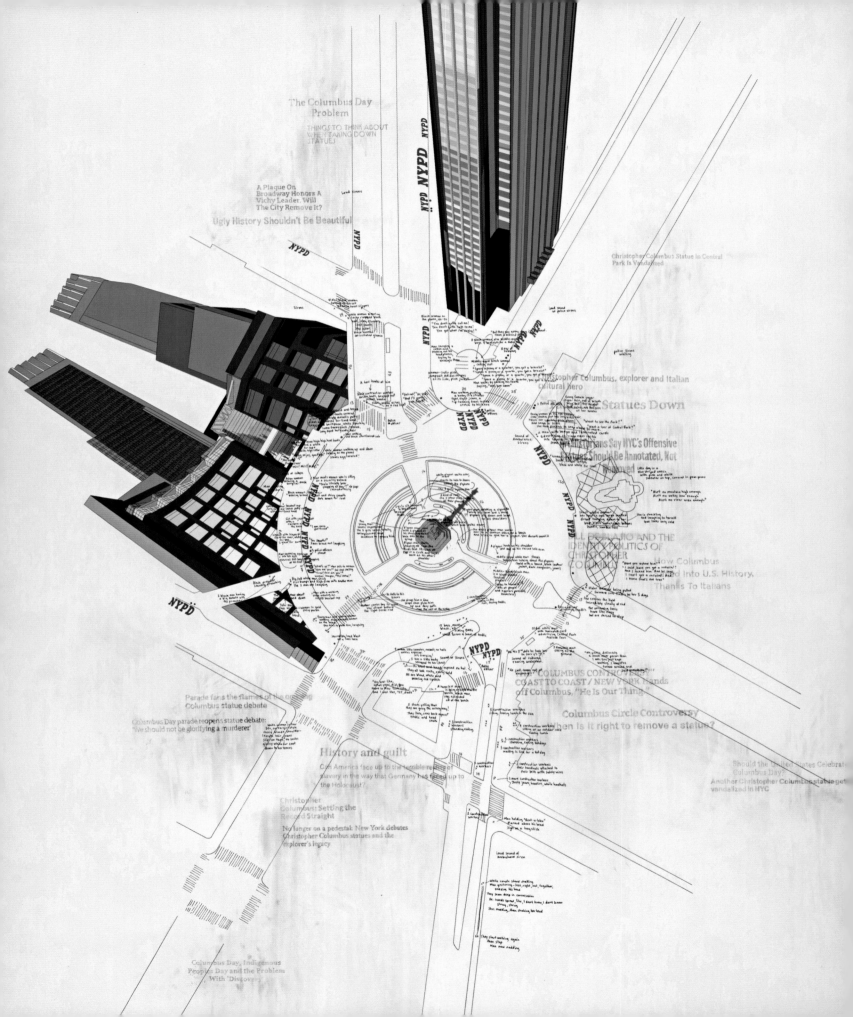

The New York Post in a Nutshell
A Monthly SPY Service Feature

The *Post's* editor-in-charge-of-composing-awful-headlines worked triple over-time. With his masterpieces, the trenchant MAN WHO SAWED OFF HEAD IS CUT OUT OF INSURANCE and the simpler DEAD MAN STARTS RIOT, he firmly estab-lished himself as one of the most twisted litterateurs since Céline. We await his next efforts with passionate longing. And guess which paper illustrated a story about a missing woman with a picture of her *dog*?
—*Adam-Troy Castro*

THE STORIES and their symbols

👁 SENSELESS TRAGEDIES		DEATH OF "FAT MAN"	
AIDS		ESCAPES FROM DEATH	
NAZIS		SEAN AND MADONNA	
☆ CELEBRITIES		DEAD FRIENDS & KIN OF CELEBS (OTHER THAN SEAN & MADONNA)	
DEAD CELEBRITIES			
😊 MANIACS		REAGAN'S NOSE	
MAFIA		KOCH'S STROKE	
DIRTY REDS		REAL-LIFE RAMBOS	
CHEESECAKE		BAD COPS	
PIT BULLS		ISLAMIC FANATICS	
HEROISM			

AUGUST

	1 S	2 S	3 M	4 T	5 W	6 T	7 F	8 S	9 S	10 M	11 T	12 W	13 T	14 F	15 S	16 S	17 M	18 T	19 W	20 T	21 F	22 S	23 S	24 M	25 T	26 W	27 T	28 F	29 S	30 S	31 M
FRONT-PAGE HEADLINE																															
FRONT-PAGE BLURB																															
BIG STORY																															
BURIED STORY																															
DEEPLY BURIED STORY																															
MAINLY CONFINED TO READERS' LETTERS																															

OPPOSITE AND PAGE 158

Larissa Fassler, *Columbus Circle, NYC II*, 2017–2018.
Berlin-based Canadian artist Larissa Fassler surveys Columbus Circle from varied perspectives—historical, architectural, anthropological, social, but mostly personal. Fassler's principal mapping tool is herself, walking, observing, listening, counting, taking notes about human behavior that she handwrites into the site plan. Shimmering in the background are headlines related to controversies that question the official narrative of Columbus and the "discovery" of America. Police oversee the busy scene.

ABOVE

Natasha Tibbott (design) and Adam-Troy Castro (text), *The New York Post in a Nutshell*, from *SPY*, August 1987.
SPY magazine kept close tabs on the *New York Post*, the city's tabloid, in this monthly feature. Designer Natasha Tibbott reminisces about the challenge of creating information graphics in the dawn of the computer age: "In the very earliest days of the Mac most of the type and art were Frankensteined together on the paste-up table. Alex Isley was the art director at the time, and he was not impressed with the handful of fonts that were available then. He actually wanted me to dig through Dover books to find the art, which was impossible to do considering the scale of reproduction. At first I drew some at 4x actual size with Rapidograph pens, and then I brought my wee-Mac SE with the postcard-size moni-tor into the offices in the Puck Building, running out repro to be cut and pasted into the layout. It seems like a blip now, but it took a few years to get all the parts of publication on the same platform."

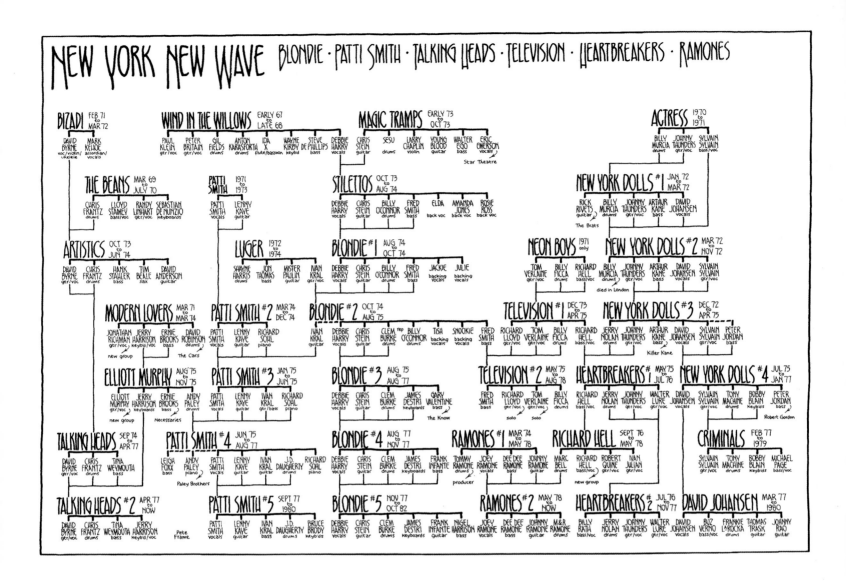

Peter Frame, *New York New Wave*, 1988.

For Peter Frame, a rock journalist and historian and the founder of *Zigzag* magazine, the tree structure solved the challenge of representing in a single compact graphic the tumultuous evolution of bands through breakups, switch-ups, reunions, and endless dramas. This one diagrams an especially rich period in New York's downtown music scene.

Sarah King, *Hip Hop Map of New York*, from *New York Magazine*, March 24, 2014.

Sarah King's map of Hip Hop in New York City is a mash-up that cleverly combines geography, language, and landmark buildings to tell a big story. Start at 1520 Sedgwick Avenue in the Bronx, "the official birthplace of Hip-Hop."

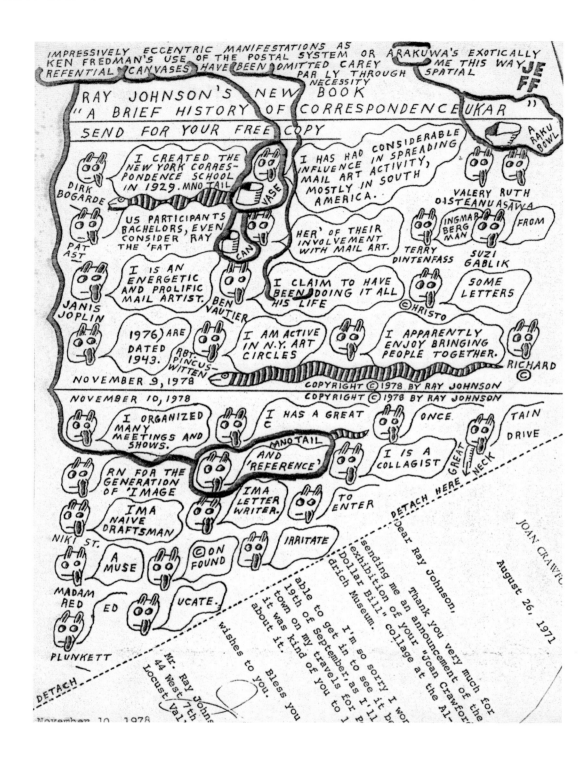

ABOVE

Ray Johnson, *A Brief History of Correspondence*, 1978.

The *New York Times* once described Ray Johnson as "New York's most famous unknown artist." Johnson encouraged artists, friends, acquaintances, and strangers to share their art through the postal system, creating, by the 1960s, a movement that he called the New York Correspondence School. This diagram, incorporating his avatar, a bunny head, offers a self-reflective account of his most influential project.

OPPOSITE

Adam Dant, *Jonathon Green's 100 Years of New York Tawk*, 2018.

Slang meets cartography in this collaboration of two specialists, lexicographer Jonathon Green and artist Adam Dant. The map connects Manhattan neighborhoods to speech balloons containing slang related to the backgrounds or pursuits of their inhabitants. Dant himself used to live in the Bowery, where "Hobo pictograms" are on display. According to Dant, "When they were riding the railways, they would scratch these signs in chalk on [the] wall. 'Bad dog here.' 'Kind lady will mend your clothes.'"

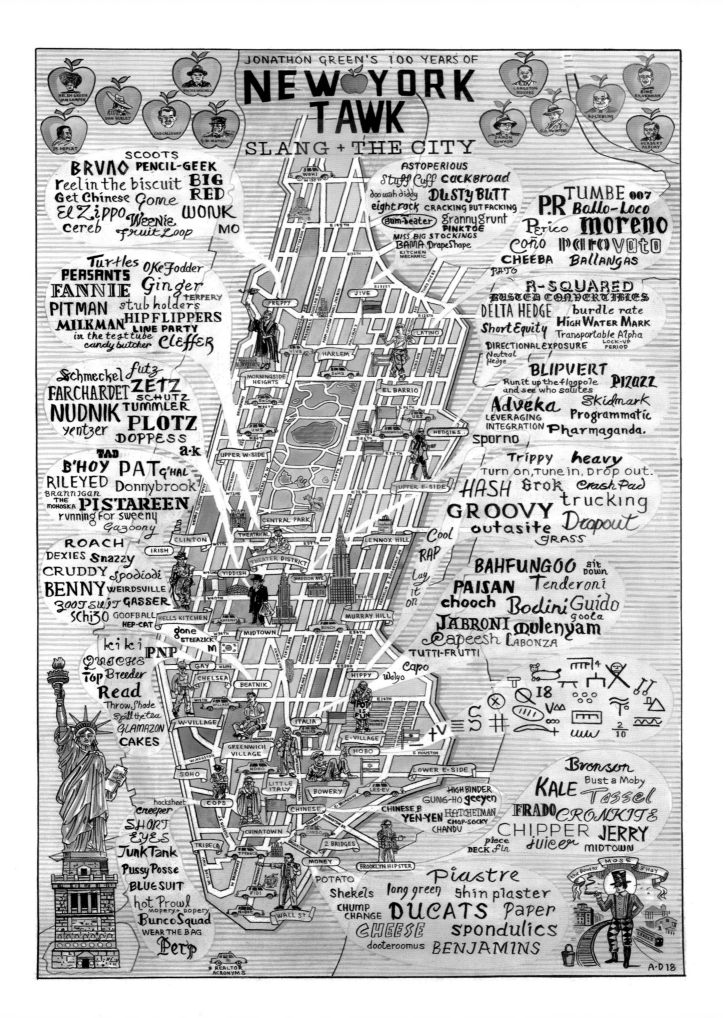

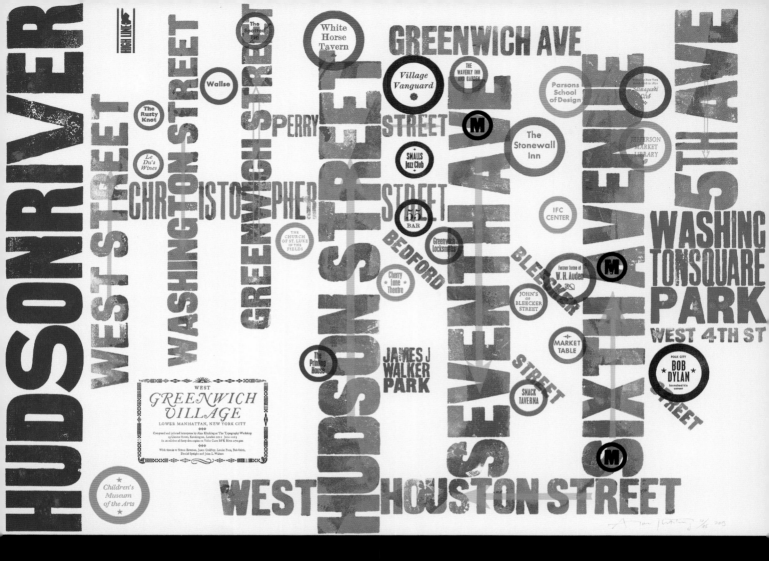

Alan Kitching, *West Greenwich Village*, 2013.

A visit to the city inspired Alan Kitching, a renowned London letter-press printer, to create this word map of Greenwich Village in antique wood type by a visit to the city. The map works on similar principles to a word cloud, except that in this case, the size and placement of the street names are dictated by the width and geographical position of the streets rather than the frequency of their names occurring in a text.

Lou Dorfsman, Herb Lubalin, and Tom Carnase, *Sketches for Gastrotypographicalassemblage*, 1965.

Gastrotypographicassemblage was known as the Great Wall at Black Rock, the CBS headquarters on Sixth Avenue, where it covered one thirty-five-foot-long wall of the cafeteria for more than twenty years. The three-dimensional mural, made of custom-milled wood type, was designed by CBS design director Lou Dorfsman working with typo-graphic maestros Herb Lubalin and Tom Carnase. Dorfsman consid-ered the massive frieze spelling out foods and food groups—from lamb chops to hasenpfeffer—his magnum opus, his "gift to the world." These sketches show three stages on the way to the final design.

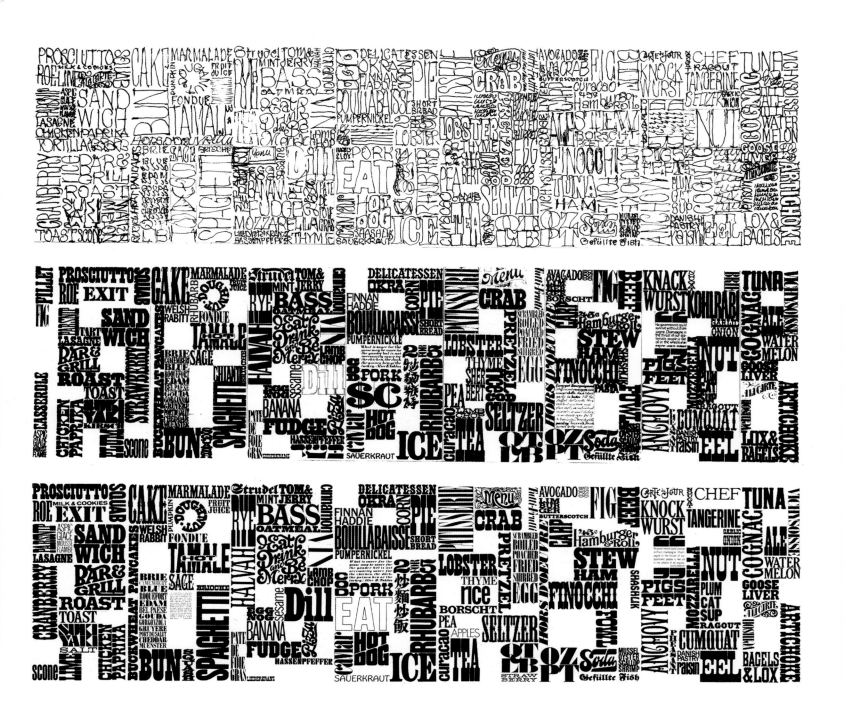

Derek Kim, *Times Square*, 2008.
Designer and illustrator Derek Kim's poster of Times Square is a tight arrangement of the logos of the biggest companies that advertised on its mammoth digital screens and billboards, organized by six business sectors: business/finance, media/entertainment, food/dining, retail/shopping, hotel/accommodations, and consumer electronics. This is how the global economy infiltrates New York's most populist public space.

OPPOSITE

Hamish Smyth, *New York City Subway*, 2015.
The New York City subway signage system designed during the late 1960s by Massimo Vignelli and Bob Noorda of Unimark International is part and parcel of the city's DNA. White Helvetica lettering on a black rectangle (although it was the reverse at the beginning) is enough to conjure the Big Apple in the minds of millions. In 2012, Hamish Smyth, inspired by work he was doing on an NYC pedestrian wayfinding system for the design firm Pentagram, decided to arrange in alphabetical sequence all 468 (at the time) station signs on a single poster, with only minor tweaks. The sprawling maze of the subway becomes at once understandable and pleasing in this ordered structure.

1 Av L · 2 Av F · 3 Av L · 3 Av-138 St 6 · 3 Av-149 St 2 5 · 4 Av-9 St F G R · 5 Av 7 · 5 Av-53 St E M · 5 Av-59 St N Q R · 6 Av L · 7 Av F · 7 Av B D E · 7 Av B Q · 8 Av L · 8 Av N · 8 St-NYU N R · 9 Av D · 14 St A C E · 14 St 1 2 3 · 14 St F M

14 St-Union Sq L N Q R 4 5 6 · 15 St-Prospect Park F G · 18 Av F · 18 Av N · 18 Av D · 18 St 1 · 20 Av N · 20 Av D · 21 St G · 21 St-Queensbridge F · 23 St C E · 23 St F M · 23 St 1 · 23 St 6 · 23 St N R · 25 Av N · 25 St R · 28 St 6 · 28 St 1 · 28 St N R · 30 Av N Q · 33 St 6

33 St-Rawson St 7 · 34 St-Herald Sq B D F M N Q R · 34 St-Penn Stn 1 2 3 · 34 St-Penn Stn A C E · 36 Av N Q · 36 St D · 36 St D N R · 39 Av N · 40 St-Lowery St 7 · 42 St-Bryant Park B D F M · 42 St-Port Authority Bus Terminal A C E · 45 St R

46 St M R · 46 St-Bliss St 7 · 47-50 Sts Rockefeller Center B D F M · 49 St N Q R · 50 St C E · 50 St D · 50 St 1 · 51 St 6 · 52 St 7 · 53 St R · 55 St D · 57 St F · 57 St-7 Av N Q R · 59 St N R · 59 St-Columbus Circle A C B D 1 · 61 St-Woodside 7 · 62 St D

63 Dr-Rego Park M R · 65 St M R · 66 St-Lincoln Center 1 · 67 Av M R · 68 St-Hunter College 6 · 69 St 7 · 71 St B C · 72 St B C · 72 St 1 2 3 · 74 St-Broadway 7 · 75 Av E F · 75 St-Elderts Lane Z · 77 St 6 · 77 St R · 79 St 1 · 79 St D · 80 St A

81 St-Museum of Natural History B C · 82 St-Jackson Hts 7 · 85 St-Forest Parkway J · 86 St R · 86 St B C · 86 St 1 · 86 St 4 5 6 · 88 St A · 90 St-Elmhurst Av 7 · 96 St B C · 96 St 1 2 3 · 103 St 1 · 103 St 6

103 St B C · 103 St-Corona Plaza 7 · 104 St A · 104 St J Z · 110 St 6 · 111 St 7 · 111 St A · 111 St J · 116 St 6 · 116 St B C · 116 St 2 3 · 116 St-Columbia University 1 · 121 St J Z

125 St 1 · 125 St 2 3 · 125 St 4 5 6 · 125 St A C B D · 135 St B C · 135 St 2 3 · 137 St-City College 1 · 138 St-Grand Concourse 4 5 · 145 St 3 · 145 St 1 · 145 St A C B D · 149 St-Grand Concourse 2 4 5

155 St C · 155 St B D · 157 St 1 · 161 St-Yankee Stadium B D 4 · 163 St-Amsterdam Av C · 167 St B D · 167 St 4 · 168 St A C 1 · 169 St F · 170 St 4 · 170 St B D · 174 St 2 5 · 174-175 Sts B D

175 St A · 176 St 4 · 181 St 1 · 181 St A · 182-183 Sts B D · 183 St 4 · 190 St A · 191 St 1 · 207 St 1 · 215 St 1 · 219 St 2 5 · 225 St 2 5 · 231 St 1 · 233 St 2 5 · 238 St 1

Alabama Av J · Allerton Av 2 5 · Aqueduct North Conduit Av A · Astor Pl 6 · Astoria Blvd N Q · Astoria-Ditmars Blvd D N R · Atlantic Av Barclays Ctr B Q 2 3 4 5 · Atlantic Av Barclays Ctr D N R · Atlantic Av L

Avenue H Q · Avenue I F · Avenue J Q · Avenue M Q · Avenue N F · Avenue P F · Avenue U F · Avenue U N · Avenue U Q · Avenue X F · Bay 50 St D · Bay Pkwy D · Bay Pkwy F · Bay Pkwy N

Bay Ridge-95 St R · Bay Ridge Av R · Baychester Av 5 · Beach 25 St A · Beach 36 St A · Beach 44 St A · Beach 60 St A · Beach 67 St A · Beach 90 St A S

Beach 98 St A S · Beach 105 St A S · Bedford Av L · Bedford Pk Blvd 4 · Bedford Pk Blvd B D · Bedford Pk Blvd Lehman College 4 · Bedford-Nostrand Avs G · Bergen St F · Bergen St 2 3 · Beverley Rd Q

Beverly Rd 2 5 · Brooklyn Bridge City Hall 4 5 6 · Bleecker St 6 · Borough Hall 2 3 4 5 · Botanic Garden S · Bowery J Z · Bowling Green 4 5 · Brianwood Van Wyck Blvd E F · Brighton Beach B Q · Broad Channel A S

Broad St J Z · Broadway G · Broadway N Q · Broadway Jctn A C J Z L · Bronx Park East 2 · Brook Av 6 · Buhre Av 6 · Burke Av 2 5 · Burnside Av 4 · Bushwick Av-Aberdeen St L · Broadway-Lafayette St B D F M · Canal St A C E

Canal St 1 · Canal St 6 · Canal St J Z · Canal St N Q R · Canarsie Rockaway Pkwy L · Carroll St F G · Castle Hill Av 6 · Cathedral Pkwy (110 St) 1 · Cathedral Pkwy (110 St) B C · Central Av M · Central Park North (110 St) 2 3

Chambers St 1 2 3 · Chambers St A C · Chambers St J Z · Chauncey St J Z · Christopher St Sheridan Sq 1 · Church Av 2 5 · Church Av B Q · Church Av F G · City Hall R · Clark St 2 3 · Classon Av G · Cleveland St L

Clinton-Washington Avs G · Clinton-Washington Avs C · Coney Island Stillwell Av D F N Q · Cortelyou Rd Q · Cortlandt St R · Court Sq G · Court Sq-23 St E M · Court St R · Crescent St J Z

Crown Heights Utica Av 3 4 · Cypress Av 6 · Cypress Hills J · DeKalb Av L · DeKalb Av B Q R · Delancey St-Essex St F M J Z · Ditmas Av F · Dyckman St 1 · Dyckman St A

E 143 St-St Mary's St 6 · E 149 St 6 · E 180 St 2 5 · East 105 St L · East Broadway F · Eastchester-Dyre Av 5 · Eastern Pkwy Brooklyn Museum 2 3 · Elder Av 6 · Elmhurst Av M R · Euclid Av A C

Far Rockaway Mott Av A · Flatbush Av Brooklyn College 2 5 · Flushing Av J M · Flushing Av G · Flushing-Main St 7 · Fordham Rd 4 · Fordham Rd B D · Forest Av M · Forest Hills-71 Av E F M R

Fort Hamilton Pkwy D · Fort Hamilton Pkwy N · Fort Hamilton Pkwy F G · Franklin Av C S · Franklin Av 2 3 4 5 · Franklin St 1 · Freeman St 2 · Fresh Pond Rd M · Fulton St G · Fulton St J Z · Fulton St 2 3 · Fulton St A C

Gates Av J Z · Graham Av L · Grand Army Plaza 2 3 · Grand Av-Newtown M R · Grand Central-42 St S 4 5 6 7 · Grand St B D · Grand St L · Grant Av A · Greenpoint Av G · Gun Hill Rd 5

Gun Hill Rd 2 · Halsey St J · Halsey St L · Harlem-148 St 3 · Hewes St J M · High St A C · Houston St 1 · Howard Beach JFK Airport A · Hoyt-Schermerhorn A C G · Hoyt St 2 3 · Hunters Point Av 7

Hunts Point Av 6 · Intervale Av 2 5 · Inwood 207 St A · Jackson Av 2 5 · Jackson Hts Roosevelt Av E F M R · Jamaica Center Parsons/Archer E J Z · Jamaica-Van Wyck E · Jamaica-179 St F · Jay St-MetroTech A C F R

Jefferson St L · Junction Blvd 7 · Junius St 3 · Kew Gardens Union Turnpike E F · Kings Hwy B Q · Kings Hwy N · Kings Hwy F · Kingsbridge Rd B D · Kingsbridge Rd 4 · Kingston Av 3

Kingston-Throop Avs C · Knickerbocker Av M · Kosciuszko St J · Lafayette Av C · Lexington Av-53 St E M · Lexington Av-59 St N Q R 4 5 6 · Lexington Av-63 St F · Liberty Av A · Livonia Av L · Longwood Av 6

Lorimer St L · Lorimer St J M · Marble Hill-225 St 1 · Marcy Av J Z M · Metropolitan Av L · Mets-Willets Point 7 · Middle Village Metropolitan Av M · Middletown Rd 6 · Montrose Av L · Morgan Av L · Morris Park 5

Morris Av-Soundview 6 · Mosholu Pkwy 4 · Mt Eden Av 4 · Myrtle Av J Z M · Myrtle-Willoughby Avs G · Myrtle-Wyckoff Avs L M · Nassau Av G · Neck Rd Q · Neptune Av F · Nereid Av 2 5 · Nevins St 2 3 4 5

New Lots Av 3 · New Lots Av L · New Utrecht Av N · Newkirk Plaza B Q · Newkirk Av 2 5 · Northern Blvd M R · Norwood-205 St D · Norwood Av J Z · Nostrand Av A C · Nostrand Av 3

Ocean Pkwy Q · Ozone Park Lefferts Blvd A · Park Pl S · Park Pl 2 3 · Parkchester 6 · Parkside Av Q · Parsons Blvd F · Pelham Bay Park 6 · Pelham Pkwy 5

Pelham Pkwy 2 5 · Pennsylvania Av 3 · President St 2 5 · Prince St N R · Prospect Av 2 5 · Prospect Av R · Prospect Park B Q S · Queens Plaza E M R · Queensboro Plaza N Q 7

Ralph Av C · Rector St 1 · Rector St R · Rockaway Av 3 · Rockaway Av C · Rockaway Blvd A · Rockaway Park Beach-116 St A S · Roosevelt Island F · St Lawrence Av 6 · Saratoga Av 3

Seneca Av M · Sheepshead Bay B Q · Shepherd Av C · Simpson St 2 5 · Smith-9 Sts F G · South Ferry 1 · Spring St 6 · Spring St C E · Steinway St M R · Sterling St 2 5 · Sutphin Blvd F

Sutphin Blvd-Archer Av JFK Airport E J Z · Sutter Av L · Sutter Av-Rutland Rd 3 · Times Sq-42 St N Q R S 1 2 3 7 · Tremont Av B D · Union St R · Utica Av A C · Van Cortlandt Park-242 St 1

Van Siclen Av 3 · Van Siclen Av C · Van Siclen Av J Z · Vernon Blvd-Jackson Av 7 · W 4 St-Wash Sq A C E B D F M · W 8 St-NY Aquarium F Q · Wakefield-241 St 2 · Wall St 2 3 · Wall St 4 5 · West Farms Sq East Tremont Av 2 5

Westchester Sq East Tremont Av 6 · Whitehall St South Ferry R · Whitlock Av 6 · Wilson Av L · Winthrop St 2 5 · Woodhaven Blvd M R · Woodhaven Blvd J Z · Woodlawn 4 · World Trade Center E · York St F · Zerega Av 6

New York City   **Subway**

The Literary Map of N.Y.

ALGONQUIN HOTEL

ABOVE

Linda Ayriss, *The Literary Map of New York*, 1988.

Posed like movie stars at a grand premiere, standing under the awning of the Algonquin Hotel, a legendary literary watering hole on West 44th Street, the stars of this map are the writers who called Manhattan home. Plot your own tour by following the number-speckled cityscape.

OPPOSITE

Randy Cohen and Nigel Holmes, *A Literary Map of Manhattan*, from the *New York Times Book Review*, 2005.

Writer Randy Cohen and information designer Nigel Holmes crowd-sourced many of the entries on their Manhattan map showing where New Yorkers from literature might have lived, worked, or played. Where else than Manhattan's Central Park might the eponymous heroine of Kay Thompson's *Eloise* cross paths with Holden Caulfield, the young antihero of J. D. Salinger's *Catcher in the Rye*?

The New York Times Book Review

A LITERARY MAP OF MANHATTAN

Here's where imaginary New Yorkers lived, worked, played, drank, walked and looked at ducks. By Randy Cohen and Nigel Holmes.

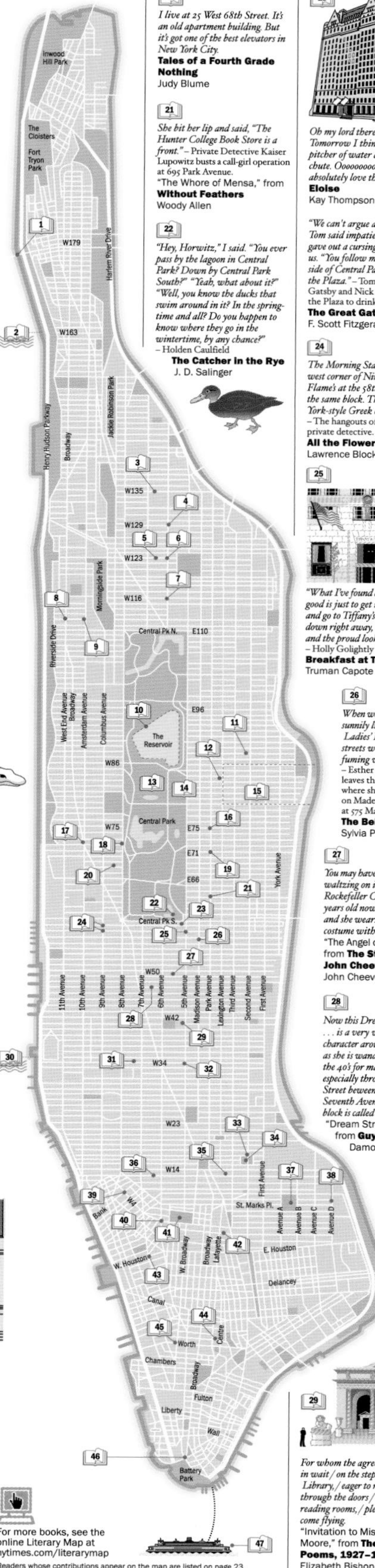

1

I will always remember when the stars fell down around me and lifted me up above the George Washington Bridge. . . . I can wear it like a diamond necklace.
Tar Beach
Faith Ringgold

2

"Congratulations," the young man said, "the sum of $425 is yours." He led Cornelius before the microphone. "Now before I pay you, will you tell us your name and address." "Cornelius Schmidt," whispered Cornelius (the whisper, but not the words, resounded in the microphone), "845 West 163rd Street."
"Screeno," from **In Dreams Begin Responsibilities and Other Stories**
Delmore Schwartz

3

I am the only colored student in my class. / The steps from the hill lead down into Harlem, / through a park, then I cross St. Nicholas, / Eighth Avenue, Seventh, and I come to the Y, / the Harlem Branch Y, where I take the elevator / up to my room, sit down, and write this page.
– A City College student (the Y is at 180 West 135th Street).
"Theme for English B," from **Selected Poems**
Langston Hughes

4

The colored patrons of Harlem's Dew Drop Inn on 129th Street and Lenox Avenue were having the times of their lives that crisp October night.
The Real Cool Killers
Chester Himes

5

"I understand there was a funeral three days ago at our Ephesus Church at 101 West 123rd Street. Why don't you get in touch with Elder Wiggins there?" "Thank you," Cross said.
The Outsider
Richard Wright

6

"Didn't I see it with my own eyes? About 8 o'clock down on Lenox and 123rd this paddy slapped a kid for grabbing a Baby Ruth and the kid's mama took it up and then the paddy slapped her and that's when hell broke loose."
Invisible Man
Ralph Ellison

7

For six months Raul diligently appeared before the door of the rooming house where she lived, on Lenox Avenue and 116th Street.
– Lydia España, former Cuban society girl, future American cleaning lady, is courted by her husband-to-be.
Empress of the Splendid Season
Oscar Hijuelos

8

Struggling to get a grip on my emotions, I went out and splurged on a meal at the Moon Palace.
– Chinese restaurant and Columbia student hangout, formerly at 112th and Broadway.
Moon Palace
Paul Auster

9

Dave ran up the hill past the choir buildings through the Dean's Garden, November-sad in the downpour, and climbed a flight of concrete steps that led into the Cathedral itself. – The Cathedral Church of St. John the Divine, at 112th and Amsterdam.
The Young Unicorns
Madeleine L'Engle

10

Ottenburg . . . floundered across the drive through a wild spring snowstorm. When he reached the reservoir path, he saw Thea ahead of him, walking rapidly against the wind. Except for that one figure, the path was deserted. She looked like some rich-pelted animal, with warm blood, that had run in out of the woods. – Two friends circle the Central Park Reservoir.
The Song of the Lark
Willa Cather

11

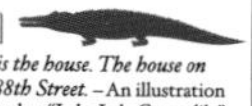

This is the house. The house on East 88th Street. – An illustration reveals that "Lyle, Lyle Crocodile" lives at No. 236.
The House on East 88th Street
Bernard Waber

12

We were putting a stakeout on 109 East 84th Street, a lone town house pinned between giant doorman apartment buildings, in and out of the foyers of which bicycle deliverymen with bags of hot Chinese flitted like tired moths.
Motherless Brooklyn
Jonathan Lethem

13

The telescope was pointed toward the southeast, where a thicket of maples bordered the Great Meadow. She could only be there. Yes, now he saw: the telescope looked toward a leafy notch and through it to the summit of one of the little alps which overlook the Pond. – Will Barrett first sees Kitty Vaught on the (misnamed) Great Lawn in Central Park.
The Last Gentleman
Walker Percy

14

She decided that her leaving home would not be just running from somewhere but would be running to somewhere. To a large place, a comfortable place . . . . And that's why she decided upon the Metropolitan Museum of Art.
– Claudia, age 12, finds a hideout.
From the Mixed-Up Files of Mrs. Basil E. Frankweiler
E. L. Konigsburg

15

This alligator was pinto: pale white and seaweed black. – Benny Profane, hunting alligators in the sewers "between Lexington and the East River and between 86th and 79th Streets."
V.
Thomas Pynchon

16

His tongue seemed stuck to the roof of his mouth. "Name?" "Sherman McCoy." It was barely a whisper. "Address?" "816 Park Avenue."
The Bonfire of the Vanities
Tom Wolfe

17

The Ansonia . . . looks like a baroque palace from Prague or Munich enlarged 100 times, with towers, domes, huge swells and bubbles of metal gone green from exposure, iron fretwork and festoons. – 2109 Broadway, the inspiration for the Hotel Gloriana, where Tommy Wilhelm and his father, Dr. Adler, live.
Seize the Day
Saul Bellow

18

"Have you ever seen the Dakota?" "The what?" He nodded. "If you'd ever seen it, you'd remember that name." – Simon Morley hears about the time-traveling apartment building at 72nd Street and Central Park West.
Time and Again
Jack Finney

19

Once I'm on the subway to school I pull out the blue folder, which has my pay envelope paper-clipped inside. Mrs. X, 721 Park Avenue, Apt. 9B New York, N.Y. 10021.
The Nanny Diaries
Emma McLaughlin and Nicola Kraus

20

I live at 25 West 68th Street. It's an old apartment building. But it's got one of the best elevators in New York City.
Tales of a Fourth Grade Nothing
Judy Blume

21

She bit her lip and said, "The Hunter College Book Store is a front." – Private Detective Kaiser Lupowitz busts a call-girl operation at 695 Park Avenue.
"The Whore of Mensa," from **Without Feathers**
Woody Allen

22

"Hey, Horwitz," I said. "You ever pass by the lagoon in Central Park? Down by Central Park South?" "Yeah, what about it?" "Well, you know the ducks that swim around in it? In the springtime and all? Do you happen to know where they go in the wintertime, by any chance?"
– Holden Caulfield
The Catcher in the Rye
J. D. Salinger

23

Oh my lord there's so much to do. Tomorrow I think I'll pour a pitcher of water down the mail chute. Ooooooooooooo I absolutely love the Plaza.
Eloise
Kay Thompson

"We can't argue about it here," Tom said impatiently, as a truck gave out a cursing whistle behind us. "You follow me to the south side of Central Park, in front of the Plaza." – Tom, Jordan, Daisy, Gatsby and Nick take a suite at the Plaza to drink mint juleps.
The Great Gatsby
F. Scott Fitzgerald

24

The Morning Star's on the northwest corner of Ninth and 57th; the Flame's at the 58th Street end of the same block. They're both New York-style Greek coffee shops.
– The hangouts of Matt Scudder, private detective.
All the Flowers Are Dying
Lawrence Block

25

"What I've found does the most good is just to get into a taxi and go to Tiffany's. It calms me down right away, the quietness and the proud look of it."
– Holly Golightly
Breakfast at Tiffany's
Truman Capote

26

When we came out of the sunnily lit interior of the Ladies' Day offices, the streets were gray and fuming with rain.
– Esther Greenwood leaves the magazine where she works (based on Mademoiselle, then at 575 Madison).
The Bell Jar
Sylvia Plath

27

You may have seen my mother waltzing on ice skates in Rockefeller Center. She's 78 years old now but very wiry, and she wears a red velvet costume with a short skirt.
"The Angel of the Bridge," from **The Stories of John Cheever**
John Cheever

28

Now this Dream Street Rose . . . is a very well-known character around and about, as she is wandering through the 40's for many a year, and especially through West 47th Street between Sixth and Seventh Avenues, and this block is called Dream Street.
"Dream Street Rose," from **Guys and Dolls**
Damon Runyon

29

For whom the agreeable lions lie in wait / on the steps of the Public Library, / eager to rise and follow through the doors / up into the reading rooms, / please come flying.
"Invitation to Miss Marianne Moore," from **The Complete Poems, 1927–1979**
Elizabeth Bishop

30

In my wallet was a supply of engraved cards reading Archie Goodwin, with Nero Wolfe, 922 West 35th Street. – The Wolfe Pack prefers 454 West 35th, another address Wolfe uses.
The Silent Speaker
Rex Stout

31

Dean had already left. Carlo and I saw him off at the 34th Street Greyhound station. – The old Greyhound terminal was at 244-248 West 34th Street.
On the Road
Jack Kerouac

32

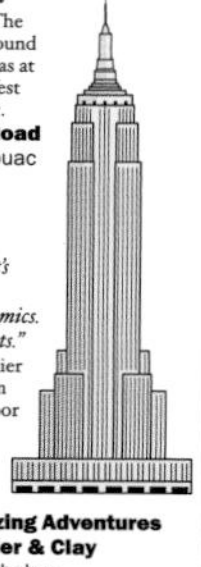

"The outfit's called Empire Comics. New tenants."
– Joe Kavalier moves in on the 25th floor of the Empire State Building.
The Amazing Adventures of Kavalier & Clay
Michael Chabon

33

I got to Kreizler's house, at 283 East 17th Street, a few minutes early, white-tied and caped.
– The narrator "enters into conspiracy" with Lazlo Kreizler, the alienist.
The Alienist
Caleb Carr

34

It was . . . one week after Commencement, when Kay Leiland Strong, Vassar '33 . . . was married to Harald Petersen, Reed '27, in the chapel of St. George's Church. . . . Outside, on Stuyvesant Square, the trees were in first leaf.
The Group
Mary McCarthy

35

On a January evening of the early 70's, Christine Nilsson was singing in "Faust" at the Academy of Music in New York.
– Newland Archer first glimpses the Countess Ellen Olenska at 126 East 14th Street (later the Palladium, now a New York University dormitory).
The Age of Innocence
Edith Wharton

36

"What's your number?" said Mrs. Vance. "Thirteenth Street," said Carrie reluctantly. "112 West."
Sister Carrie
Theodore Dreiser

37

It is an incredibly weird sound, man, the likes of which no one in Tompkins Square Park has ever heard. – Horse Badorties plans his Love Concert.
The Fan Man
William Kotzwinkle

38

There were four rooms in the flat they lived in. There were eight windows. Some faced 9th Street. Some faced Avenue D.
– David Schearl's family finds a new apartment.
Call It Sleep
Henry Roth

39

The apartment on Bank Street was ideally arranged for keeping out of each other's way, yet each could use the other as protection against encroachments of ladies.
– Frederick and Murray, roommates near 4th Street and Bank.
The Locusts Have No King
Dawn Powell

40

I can feel the heat closing in, feel them out there making their moves, setting up their devil doll stool pigeons, crooning over my spoon and dropper I throw away at Washington Square Station, vault a turnstile and two flights down the iron stairs, catch an uptown A train.
Naked Lunch
William S. Burroughs

41

The doctor built himself a handsome modern wide-fronted house, with a big balcony before the drawing room windows, and a flight of white marble steps ascending to a portal which was also faced with white marble. In front . . . was the square . . . and round the corner was the more august precinct of the Fifth Avenue.
Washington Square
Henry James

They went and sat a good deal in the softening evenings among the infants and dotards of Latin extraction in Washington Square.
– The March family takes its ease.
A Hazard of New Fortunes
William Dean Howells

42

I went to the room in Great Jones Street, a small crooked room, cold as a penny. . . . I thought of opening the window and shouting: "Fire! Hey, Fire!" The great doors of the firehouse would slowly come open. – Bucky Wunderlick looks out on Engine Co. #33, Ladder 9, from 35 Great Jones.
Great Jones Street
Don DeLillo

43

They agree to go to the Film Forum on Sunday afternoon, to see the Antonioni double feature that Lydia and Gerald have recently been to and recommended over dinner.
The Namesake
Jhumpa Lahiri

44

The impending Thaw trial was not the only excitement down at the Tombs. Two of the guards in their spare time had fashioned new leg irons that they claimed were better. . . . To prove it they challenged Harry Houdini himself to put them to the test.
Ragtime
E. L. Doctorow

45

Doesn't he know that what I do for a living is I'm good? "Civil Service," I answered, pointing across to 30 Worth. Mister Modesty. – Alexander Portnoy, assistant commissioner for the New York City commission on human opportunity.
Portnoy's Complaint
Philip Roth

46

His story begins in New York, on the corner of Broadway and Battery Place, the most disheveled, God-forsaken, not-for-profit corner of New York's financial district. On the 10th floor, the Emma Lazarus Immigrant Absorption Society greeted its clients.
The Russian Debutante's Handbook
Gary Shteyngart

47

We were very tired / we were very merry / we had gone back and forth / all night on the ferry.
"Recuerdo," from **Early Poems**
Edna St. Vincent Millay

There now is your insular city of the Manhattoes, belted round by wharves as Indian isles by coral reefs — commerce surrounds it with her surf. Right and left, the streets take you waterward. Its extreme down-town is the Battery, where that noble mole is washed by waves, and cooled by breezes, which a few hours previous were out of sight of land. Look at the crowds of water-gazers there.
Moby-Dick, Herman Melville

For more books, see the online Literary Map at nytimes.com/literarymap

Readers whose contributions appear on the map are listed on page 23.

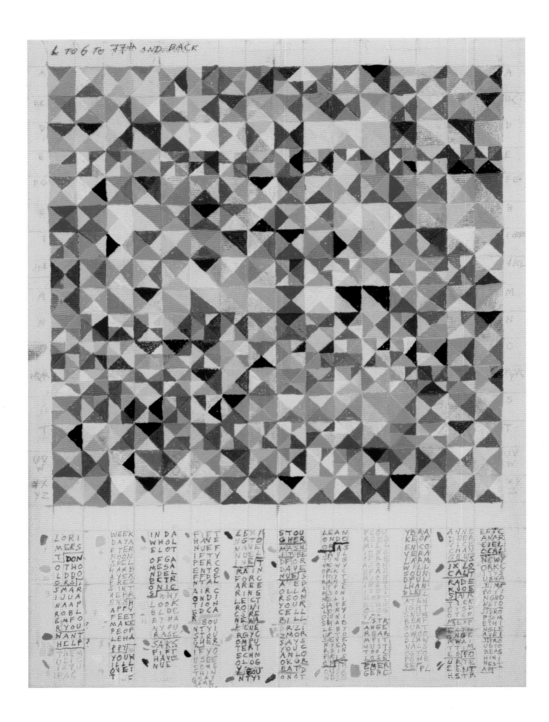

ABOVE
Leslie Roberts, *L to 6 to 77th and Back*, 2014.
Roberts diagrams a subway ride—a colorful jumble of station names, advertising slogans, public service announcements, and much, much more.

OPPOSITE
Shana Agid, *Call a Wrecking Ball to Make a Window*, 2012. Title borrowed from L. B. Thompson.
Artist/designer and activist Shana Agid created a book in the form of a folding map to explore routes taken and spaces made by queer people in New York City from the 1970s through the 2000s. The routes, keyed to decades, trace trajectories taken by queer writer and artist David Wojnarowicz, mapped from his writings, along with Agid's own trajectories. The text combines the personal and the historical to evoke, in Agid's telling, "a fantastic landscape in which these lives overlap through the geography and infrastructure of the city and the bodies of the characters."

Call a Wrecking Ball
to Make a Window

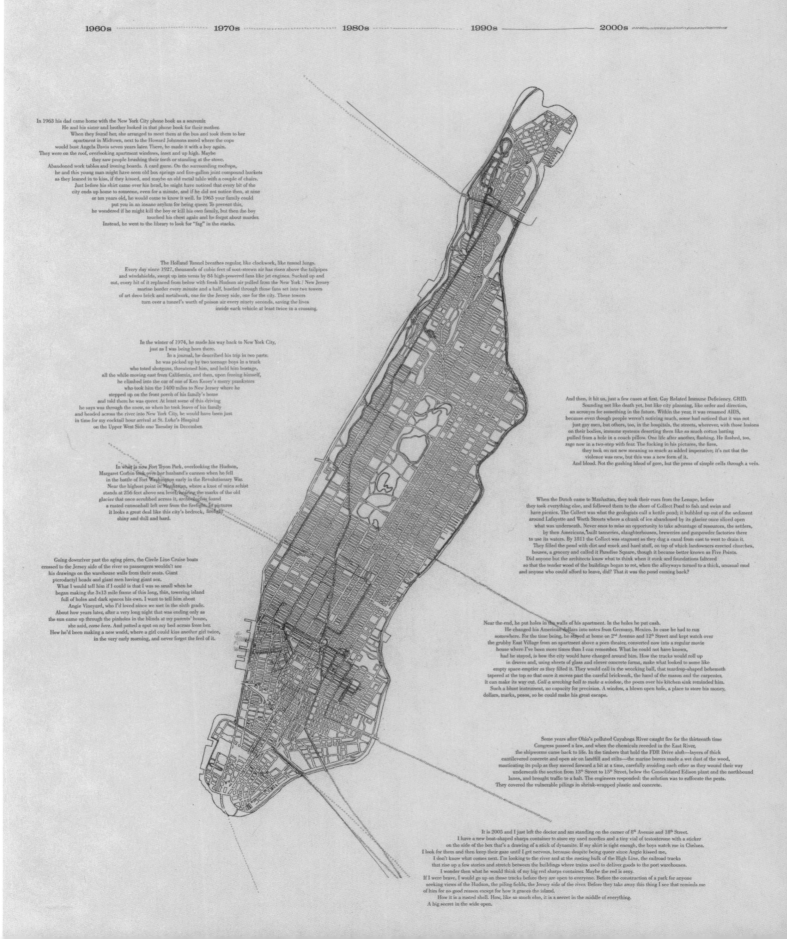

In 1963 his dad came home with the New York City phone book as a souvenir.
He and his sister and brother looked in that phone book for their mother.
When they found her, she arranged to meet them at the bus and took them to her
apartment in Midtown, next to the Howard Johnsons motel where the cops
would bust Angela Davis seven years later. There, he made it with a boy again.
They were on the roof, overlooking apartment windows, inset and up high. Maybe
they saw people brushing their teeth or standing at the stove.
Abandoned work tables and ironing boards. A card game. On the surrounding rooftops,
he and this young man might have seen old box springs and five-gallon joint compound buckets
as they leaned in to kiss, if they kissed, and maybe an old metal table with a couple of chairs.
Just before his shirt came over his head, he might have noticed that every bit of the
city ends up home to someone, even for a minute, and if he did not notice then, at nine
or ten years old, he would come to know it well. In 1963 your family could
put you in an insane asylum for being queer. To prevent this,
he wondered if he might kill the boy or kill his own family, but then the boy
touched his chest again and he forgot about murder.
Instead, he went to the library to look for "fag" in the stacks.

The Holland Tunnel breathes regular, like clockwork, like tunnel lungs.
Every day since 1927, thousands of cubic feet of soot-strewn air has risen above the tailpipes
and windshields, swept up into vents by 84 high-powered fans like jet engines. Sucked up and
out, every bit of it replaced from below with fresh Hudson air pulled from the New York / New Jersey
marine border every minute and a half, hustled through those fans set into two towers
of art deco brick and metalwork, one for the Jersey side, one for the city. These towers
turn over a tunnel's worth of poison air every ninety seconds, saving the lives
inside each vehicle at least twice in a crossing.

In the winter of 1974, he made his way back to New York City,
just as I was being born there.
In a journal, he described his trip in two parts:
he was picked up by two teenage boys in a truck
who toted shotguns, threatened him, and held him hostage,
all the while moving east from California, and then, upon freeing himself,
he climbed into the car of one of Ken Kesey's merry pranksters
who took him the 1400 miles to New Jersey where he
stepped up on the front porch of his family's home
and told them he was queer. At least some of this driving
he says was through the snow, so when he took leave of his family
and headed across the river into New York City, he would have been just
in time for my cocktail hour arrival at St. Luke's Hospital
on the Upper West Side one Tuesday in December.

In what is now Fort Tryon Park, overlooking the Hudson,
Margaret Corbin took over her husband's cannon when he fell
in the battle of Fort Washington early in the Revolutionary War.
Near the highest point in Manhattan, where a knot of mica schist
stands at 256 feet above sea level, bearing the marks of the old
glacier that once scrubbed across it, archaeologists found
a rusted cannonball left over from the firefight. In pictures
it looks a great deal like this city's bedrock, fireball,
shiny and dull and hard.

Going downriver past the aging piers, the Circle Line Cruise boats
crossed to the Jersey side of the river so passengers wouldn't see
his drawings on the warehouse walls from their seats. Giant
pterodactyl heads and giant men having giant sex.
What I would tell him if I could is that I was so small when he
began making the 3x13 mile frame of this long, thin, towering island
full of holes and dark spaces his own. I want to tell him about
Angie Vineyard, who I'd loved since we met in the sixth grade.
About how years later, after a very long night that was ending only as
the sun came up through the pinholes in the blinds at my parents' house,
she said, come here. And patted a spot on my bed across from her.
How he'd been making a new world, where a girl could kiss another girl twice,
in the very early morning, and never forget the feel of it.

And then, it hit us, just a few cases at first. Gay Related Immune Deficiency. GRID.
Sounding not like death yet, but like city planning, like order and direction,
an acronym for something in the future. Within the year, it was renamed AIDS,
because even though people weren't noticing much, some had noticed that it was not
just gay men, but others, too, in the hospitals, the streets, wherever, with those lesions
on their bodies, immune systems deserting them like so much cotton batting
pulled from a hole in a couch pillow. One life after another, flashing. He flashed, too,
rage now in a two-step with fear. The fucking in his pictures, the fires,
they took on not new meaning so much as added imperative; it's not that the
violence was new, but this was a new form of it.
And blood. Not the gushing blood of gore, but the press of simple cells through a vein.

When the Dutch came to Manhattan, they took their cues from the Lenape, before
they took everything else, and followed them to the shore of Collect Pond to fish and swim and
have picnics. The Collect was what the geologists call a kettle pond; it bubbled up out of the sediment
around Lafayette and Worth Streets where a chunk of ice abandoned by its glacier once sliced open
what was underneath. Never ones to miss an opportunity to take advantage of resources, the settlers,
by then Americans, built tanneries, slaughterhouses, breweries and gunpowder factories there
to use its waters. By 1811 the Collect was stagnant so they dug a canal from east to west to drain it.
They filled the pond with dirt and muck and hard stuff, on top of which landowners erected churches,
houses, a grocery and called it Paradise Square, though it became better known as Five Points.
Did anyone but the architects know what to think when it stunk and foundations faltered
so that the tender wood of the buildings began to rot, when the alleyways turned to a thick, unusual mud
and anyone who could afford to leave, did? That it was the pond coming back?

Near the end, he put holes in the walls of his apartment. In the holes he put cash.
He changed his American dollars into notes from Germany, Mexico. In case he had to run
somewhere. For the time being, he stayed at home on 2nd Avenue and 12th Street and kept watch over
the grubby East Village from an apartment above a porn theater, converted now into a regular movie
house where I've been more times than I can remember. What he could not have known,
had he stayed, is how the city would have changed around him. How the trucks would roll up
in droves and, using sheets of glass and clever concrete forms, make what looked to some like
empty space emptier as they filled it. They would call in the wrecking ball, that teardrop-shaped behemoth
tapered at the top so that once it moves past the careful brickwork, the hand of the mason and the carpenter,
it can make its way out. Call a wrecking ball to make a window, the poem over his kitchen sink reminded him.
Such a blunt instrument, no capacity for precision. A window, a blown open hole, a place to store his money,
dollars, marks, pesos, so he could make his great escape.

Some years after Ohio's polluted Cuyahoga River caught fire for the thirteenth time
Congress passed a law, and when the chemicals receded in the East River,
the shipworms came back to life. In the timbers that hold the FDR Drive aloft—layers of thick
cantilevered concrete and open air on landfill and stilts—the marine borers made a wet dust of the wood,
masticating its pulp as they moved forward a bit at a time, carefully avoiding each other as they wound their way
underneath the section from 13th Street to 15th Street, below the Consolidated Edison plant and the northbound
lanes, and brought traffic to a halt. The engineers responded: the solution was to suffocate the pests.
They covered the vulnerable pilings in shrink-wrapped plastic and concrete.

It is 2005 and I just left the doctor and am standing on the corner of 8th Avenue and 18th Street.
I have a new boat-shaped sharps container to store my used needles and a tiny vial of testosterone with a sticker
on the side of the box that's a drawing of a stick of dynamite. If my shirt is tight enough, the boys watch me in Chelsea.
I look for them and then keep their gaze until I get nervous, because despite being queer since Angie kissed me,
I don't know what comes next. I'm looking to the river and at the rusting bulk of the High Line, the railroad tracks
that rise up a few stories and stretch between the buildings where trains used to deliver goods to the port warehouses.
I wonder then what he would think of my big red sharps container. Maybe the red is sexy.
If I were brave, I would go up on those tracks before they are open to everyone. Before the construction of a park for anyone
seeking views of the Hudson, the piling fields, the Jersey side of the river. Before they take away this thing I see that reminds me
of him for no good reason except for how it graces the island.
How it is a rusted shell. How, like so much else, it is a secret in the middle of everything.
A big secret in the wide open.

CHAPTER SIX

WE
HEART
NY

A DIAGRAM—CHART, MAP, OR GRAPH—MIGHT NOT SEEM TO BE the most humanistic form of art or visual communication. Data is defined in the *Merriam-Webster Dictionary* as "factual information (such as measurements or statistics) used as a basis for reasoning, discussion, or calculation." This does not sound warm and cuddly—or even ironic and coy. But we have already seen that data visualization can be fun. In this chapter is a wellspring of brisk, playful diagramming that juggles abstract, personal, and emotive ideas. Expressiveness sneaks into cartograms, pie charts, tables, and elevations. These forms are used as storytelling tools that reveal the complexities of living in the city.

I ♥ NY, the logo designed by Milton Glaser, was introduced in 1977 at the nadir of Manhattan's modern history—and made "heart" a verb (page 198). The advertising campaign it crowned proved to be just the right inspirational trigger. The rebus represented the feelings of New Yorkers across the boroughs and it was adopted quickly and enthusiastically. Although Glaser's was a novel approach, the heart representing an aspect of New York was a venerable concept. Take the 1950 Hudson Tube Recreation Guide by Amelia Opdyke Jones (page 200), which guaranteed that riders would be delivered to the heart of the city on time and stress free. A map in the shape of heart—a tribute to Glaser's I ♥ NY designed by Zero Per Zero—says in no uncertain terms that New Yorkers will love the speed and convenience of riding the subway (page 201).

It is always comforting to know we can look either comically or realistically into those aspects of the city that seem forbidding and closed. Roz Chast's 1990 vision of layers of garbage, sewage, broken pipes, and other malfunctioning infrastructure (alligators included) that reside under 38th Street is deceptively pleasant (page 205). In a similar vein, Seymour Chwast's Dantean representation of "Hi-Rise Hell" offers up a hilarious, and cautionary, vision of lives lived way above ground and high on the hog (page 204). On the other hand, in his *Frozen Assets* (1931), the Mexican muralist Diego Rivera strips away facades to express a darker feeling about the city, without the insulating warmth of humor (page 209).

A different kind of imagination is at play in two diagrams illustrating what could be considered unsettling scenarios. Saul Steinberg's 1987 *The New Jersey War* (page 212) posits, albeit humorously, a battle plan in the event that New Jersey's military forces invaded and occupied parts of Manhattan. Inconceivable? Maybe. Maybe not! Anything is possible in the diagrammatic arena. Opposite is a less witty what-if scenario, a startling "diagrammatic photograph" showing the "twelve-mile range over which our new dreadnought could scatter death and destruction" from the *New-York Tribune* in 1909 (page 213). In the image, the battleship USS *Delaware* is stationed outside the Narrows in New York Bay, lobbing shells into the metropolitan area. What if, indeed?

I ♥ NY

MORE THAN EVER

BE GENEROUS. YOUR CITY NEEDS YOU. THIS POSTER IS NOT FOR SALE.

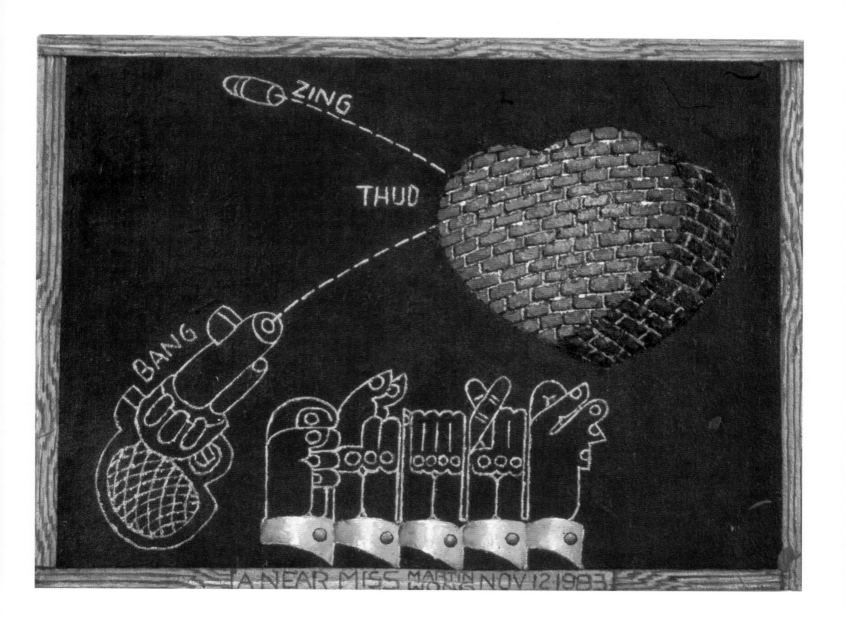

OPPOSITE

Milton Glaser, *I ♥ NY More Than Ever*, 2001.

Neither Milton Glaser nor anyone else anticipated how popular
I ♥ NY—the logo he sketched in a taxi in 1977 for a marketing campaign for New York State—would become. In the wake of September
11, the logo took on an entirely unexpected relevance. Discerning
this within hours of the tragedy, Glaser set about augmenting the
original in a poster with a message of determination that expressed
both pain and hope.

ABOVE

Martin Wong, *A Near Miss*, 1983.

The motifs at play here make this work unmistakably Martin Wong's.
The intense textural brickwork and the American Sign Language–
inspired typeface (spelling the word "sharp") were essential parts
of the Chino-Latino artist's visual language when portraying scenes
of 1980s tenement life in Loisaida. A bullet bouncing off a brick
heart might as well be a metaphor for the vibrant resilience within
this harsh urban environment.

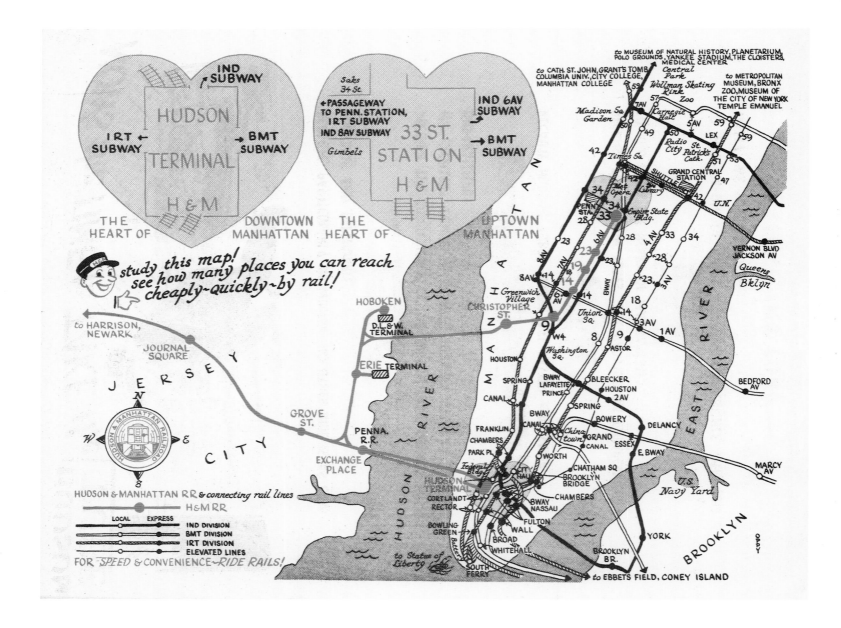

Amelia Opdyke Jones, *Hudson Tube Recreation Guide*, c. 1950.

Manhattan gets two hearts, one for downtown (Hudson Terminal) and another for uptown (33rd Street Station), in this map-cum-ad for the Hudson & Manhattan Railroad between Manhattan and New Jersey. Renamed PATH in 1962, the line is often called the Hudson Tubes after the tunnels under the river. Inside these hearts are the chambers leading to the connecting arteries of the subway. Signing as Oppy is artist Amelia Opdyke Jones, known as the "Subway Surrealist" for her subway etiquette posters and said to have invented the term "litterbug," a play on the 1940s popular dance "jitterbug."

Zero Per Zero, *NYC Pink*, 2014.

The map becomes the symbol in this "tourist-optimized version" of the subway map by Kim Ji-Hwan and Jin Sol of Seoul design studio Zero Per Zero. The five boroughs merge into one big, pink, heart-shaped island, a clear nod to Milton Glaser's popular creation.

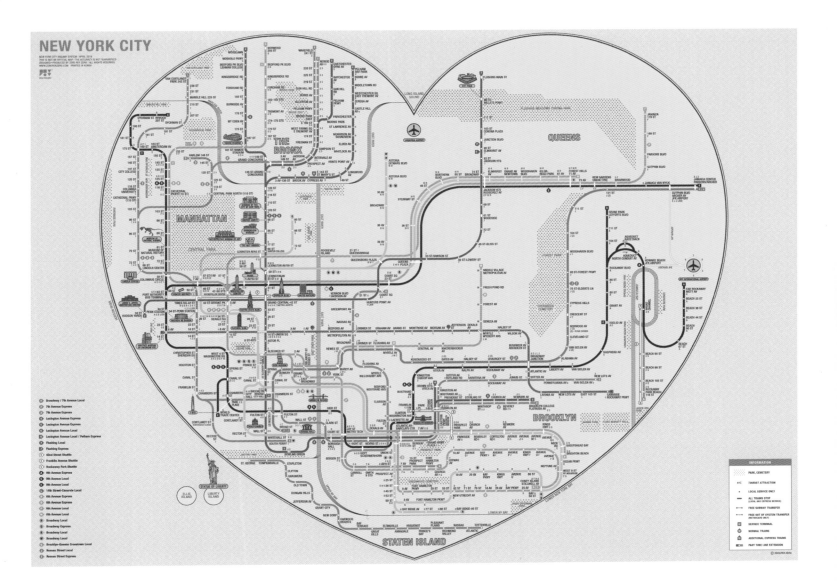

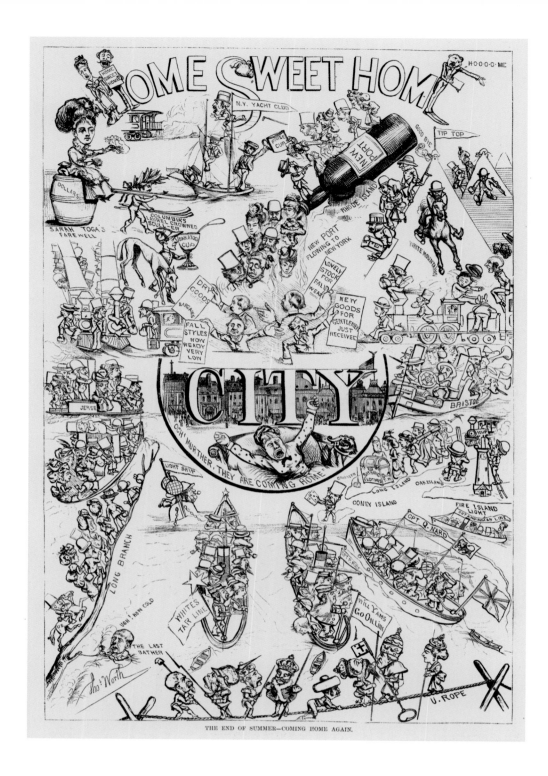

Thomas Worth, *The End of Summer—Coming Home Again*, from *Harper's Weekly*, September 19, 1874.
Conspicuous for their absence in this comic celebration of the annual September return of the hoi polloi to the city from their far-flung resorts—"Sarah Toga," "New Port," "U. Rope," as well as the White Mountains, Fire Island, and Long Branch—are the Hamptons, not yet a summer destination in 1874. Otherwise, it's déjà vu all over again: "Och' murther, they are coming home."

Christoph Niemann, *Fall at MoMA. Plan Accordingly*, 2009.
Invited to update an infographic of 1940—a simple cross section of MoMA that used the Isotype language of pictorial symbols to visualize an "average day at the museum"—Niemann invented a dynamic space where typography, works of art, and museum visitors interact playfully.

Fall at MoMA.
Plan Accordingly.

ILLUSTRATION BY CHRISTOPH NIEMANN

Free MoMA Audio Guides

Free WiFi – Follow MoMA on Twitter, Facebook, and YouTube

Free Daily Gallery Talks

MoMA MiXX Dance Parties

MoMA Courses

MoMA.guide Digital Kiosks

Free Admission for Kids 16 & Under

OOF

Drinks at The Bar Room

Fine Dining at The Modern

The Sculpture Garden

The MoMA Design Store

MoMA Books

Member Discounts at Every MoMA Store

Daily Film Screenings

P.S.1 Contemporary Art Center— Only 2 Stops Away and Free with MoMA Admission

Lectures and Conversations

Identify 38 artworks from the collection above (answers at MoMA.org/fall).

OPENING:

New Photography 2009: Walead Beshty, Daniel Gordon, Leslie Hewitt, Carter Mull, Sterling Ruby, Sara VanDerBeek
SEP 30–JAN 11

Paul Sietsema
SEP 30–FEB 15

Projects 91: Artur Zmijewski
OCT 28–JAN 4

Bauhaus 1919–1933: Workshops for Modernity
NOV 8–JAN 25

Tim Burton
NOV 22–APR 26

Gabriel Orozco
DEC 13–MAR 1

ONGOING:

In & Out of Amsterdam: Travels in Conceptual Art, 1960–1976
THROUGH OCT 5

Ron Arad: No Discipline
THROUGH OCT 19

Looking at Music: Side 2
THROUGH NOV 30

Monet's Water Lilies
THROUGH APR 12

P.S.1:

Opening Day Celebration: Fall Exhibitions
SUN, OCT 25, 12:00–6:00 PM

1969 OCT 25–APR 5

Between Spaces
OCT 25–APR 5

100 Years (version #1, ps1, nov 2009) NOV 1–APR 5

FILM:

Spike Jonze: The First 80 Years
OCT 8–18

To Save and Project: The Seventh MoMA International Festival of Film Preservation
OCT 24–NOV 15

MoMA Presents: John Cassavetes's *A Woman Under the Influence*
OCT 24–30

PROGRAMS & EVENTS:

DANCE PARTY
MoMA MiXX
SAT, SEP 26, 8:00 PM

CONVERSATIONS WITH CONTEMPORARY ARTISTS
With James Welling, Jan Dibbets
MON, OCT 5, 6:30 PM

BAUHAUS LAB
Hands-on workshops for visitors of all ages
NOV 8–JAN 25

FREE TEEN NIGHTS
Free pizza, films, artist workshops, and more
FRIDAYS STARTING OCT 9, 4:00–8:00 PM

EAT
**Casual Lunch at Cafe 2
Tea for Two at Terrace 5
Fine Dining at The Modern**

SHOP
Books, Gifts, Exhibition Catalogues & More at the MoMA Design Store and MoMAstore.org

JOIN
Members skip the lines and see exhibitions first. MoMA.org/membership

THE MUSEUM OF MODERN ART
11 WEST 53 STREET
MoMA.ORG/FALL

Seymour Chwast, *Hi-Rise Hell*, 2007.

A New Yorker's vision of hell: name droppers, bad wallpaper, men who keep the toilet seat up, no hot water, and other outrages. Soon after this windup, Seymour Chwast segued to illustrating Dante's *Divine Comedy*.

Roz Chast, *Under 38th Street*, cover for *The New Yorker*, October 1, 1990.

Chast's comic cross section, a layered, imaginative mix of myth, reality, and miscellany, excavates the strata beneath East 38th Street—it's a great way to entertain and perhaps calm the mind fretting over what cannot be seen yet is vital to the city.

Although artist Florine Stettheimer was deeply embedded in avant-garde circles in Manhattan, her Cathedral cycle, largely executed during the Great Depression, maps an upper-middle-class world of comfort and culture without a hint of distress. Many of its dependable touchstones are still potent symbols of continuity: Tiffany's; the Stock Exchange; the Met and MoMA; and Broadway theaters (many of which have been restored to their former glory).

TOP LEFT
Florine Stettheimer, *The Cathedrals of Art*, 1942.

TOP RIGHT
Florine Stettheimer, *The Cathedrals of Fifth Avenue*, 1931.

LEFT
Florine Stettheimer, *The Cathedrals of Broadway*, 1929.

OPPOSITE
Florine Stettheimer, *The Cathedrals of Wall Street*, 1939.

Diego Rivera, *Frozen Assets*, 1931.
In stark contrast to Stettheimer, the Mexican muralist Diego Rivera mapped Depression-era New York City with anger and foreboding, pushing its formidable infrastructure of transport and skyscrapers into the background. Front and center are the assets that built the city: labor and capital. Each is in its own prison, for all intents and purposes frozen.

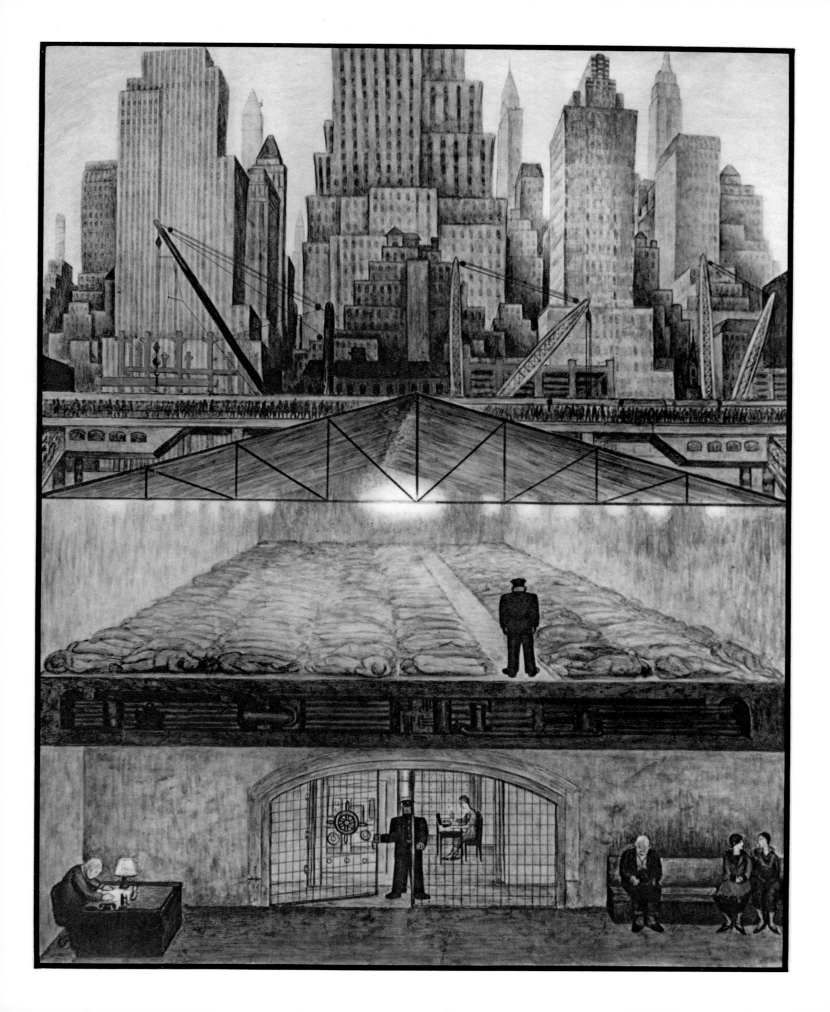

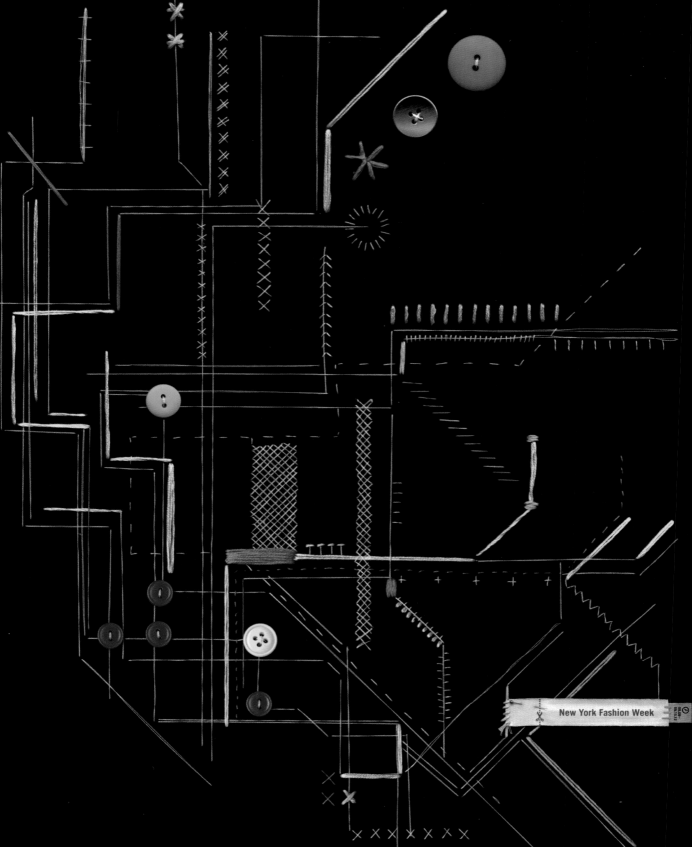

New York Fashion Week

OPPOSITE
Jiin Kim, *New York Fashion Week*, November 2011.
To promote Fashion Week, recent design-school graduate Jiin Kim
recreated the New York City subway map in thread and buttons for
a series of posters.

ABOVE
Jean Tinguely, sketch for *Homage to New York*, 1960.
The Swiss artist Jean Tinguely masterminded a legendary performance
at the Museum of Modern Art in 1960: Assisted by Robert Rauschenberg and other artists and engineers, he built a machine that destroyed
itself. *Homage to New York* celebrated the city as pure energy that
dissipated itself in heat and light—at least until the New York Fire
Department showed up and put a stop to the festivities.

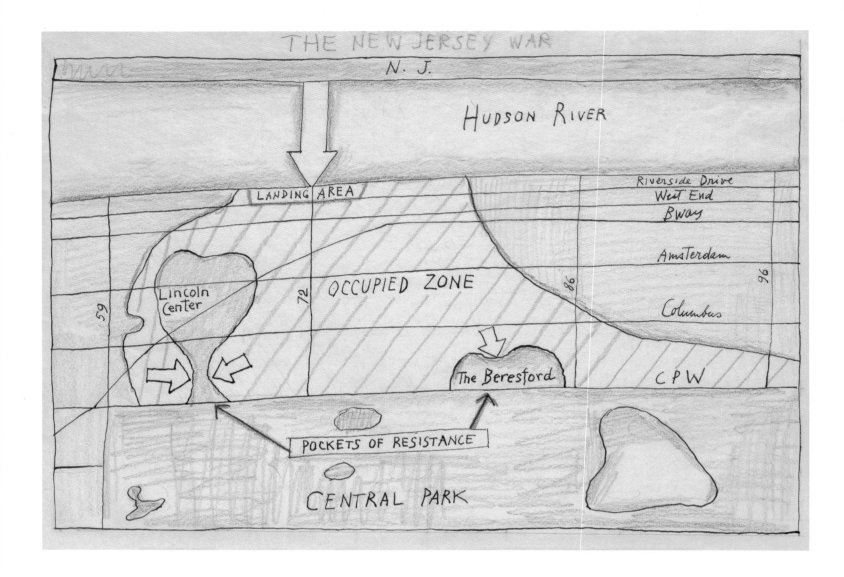

ABOVE

Saul Steinberg, *The New Jersey War*,
from *The New Yorker*, February 23, 1987.

Steinberg was loyal both to New York and his comic imagination. This
make-believe war, with its amphibious landing on Manhattan's Upper
West Side, poked fun at some easy targets, but also engaged the artist's
allegiance to the imaginary "pockets of resistance" valorously defend-
ing their city.

OPPOSITE

Twelve-Mile Range over Which Our New Dreadnought
***Could Scatter Death and Destruction*, from the**
***New-York Tribune*, October 31, 1909.**

Every now and then, the popular press is used to advance a truly
bizarre fantasy.

TWELVE-MILE RANGE OVER WHICH OUR NEW DREADNOUGHT COULD SCATTER DEATH AND DESTRUCTION.

Besides demonstrating last week, by attaining a speed of 21.98 knots, that she is the fastest first class battleship ever made, the Delaware has the most powerful battery in the service. From each of her ten 12-inch guns of the largest type she can throw a shell weighing 870 pounds to a distance of twelve miles, or from below the Narrows, down the Bay, into City Hall Park and a little beyond. After traversing 9,000 yards these shells can still penetrate eleven inches of solid steel.

KEY TO THIS DIAGRAMMATIC PHOTOGRAPH.

1, Fort Tompkins; 2, Fort Wadsworth; 3, Staten Island; 4, the Narrows; 5, Fort Lafayette; 6, Upper Bay; 7, St. George; 8, Kill van Kull; 9, Bergen Point; 10, Newark Bay; 11, Newark; 12, New Jersey; 13, Passaic River; 14, Hackensack River; 15, Bedlow's Island; 16, Ellis Island; 17, Jersey City; 18, Hoboken; 19, Manhattan; 20, Weehawken; 21, Hudson River; 22, the Battery; 23, Governor's Island; 24, East River; 25, Brooklyn Bridge; 26, Manhattan Bridge; 27, Williamsburg Bridge; 28, Bay Ridge; 29, Fort Hamilton; 30, Bath Beach; 31, Benson-nurst; 32, Prospect Park; 33, West Brighton; 34, Gravesend Bay; 35, Norton's Point; 36, Lower Bay; 37, the battleship Delaware; 38, a 12-inch shell.

RIGHT

Andrew Kuo, *Select Shows at Roseland Ballroom, 1992–95*, 2014.

In the early 1990s the Roseland Ballroom on West 52nd Street was one of the best places in New York to hear and see music. Here, in a tour de force of remembrance, artist Andrew Kuo rates twenty-three shows he saw there when he was a high-school music fan two decades earlier, including Nirvana, the Beastie Boys, Pavement, and Hole.

OPPOSITE

Andrew Kuo, *New York State of Mind*, 2018.

Andrew Kuo's diagramming of the essence of Manhattan is made up of personal and idiosyncratic observations that appear to be scattershot but will nonetheless ring true to many New Yorkers.

1. The Beastie Boys, fIREHOSE 5/23/92
2. The Beastie Boys, Rollins Band 11/7/92
3. The Ramones, Overwhelming Colorfast 11/11/92
4. Sonic Youth, the Boredoms 11/24/92
5. Dinosaur Jr., Lunachicks, Gumball 4/2/93
6. Nirvana, the Jesus Lizard 7/23/93
7. Fugazi, the Spinanes, Unrest 9/23/93
8. Fugazi, Jawbox, Mecca Normal 9/24/93
9. Bad Religion, Green Day, Seaweed 10/1/93
10. Radiohead, Belly 10/9/93
11. Rage Against the Machine 11/4/93
12. Nirvana, the Breeders, Half Japanese 11/15/93
13. The Smashing Pumpkins 11/24/93
14. The Ramones, Frank Black 4/1/94
15. Nine Inch Nails, Marilyn Manson 5/14/94
16. Red Hot Chili Peppers 8/19/94
17. Pavement, Guided by Voices 10/15/94
18. Dinosaur Jr., Kyuss 10/28/94
19. Sugar, Velocity Girl 11/12/94
20. Hole 2/15/95
21. Weezer, Archers of Loaf 3/28/95
22. Ned's Atomic Dustbin 8/18/95
23. The Mighty Mighty Bosstones 10/27/95

If a machine sent people back in time just once, I would go back for this show.

A combination of nostalgia, joy and sadness that this won't ever happen again.

Just to make it more interesting, I try to remember it as great instead of just good.

It seems more fun now than the long, sweaty, crowded night it was at the time.

All I can think about is the TV I missed while I was standing at this show.

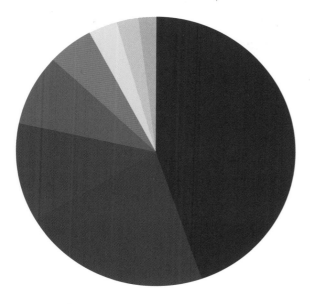

TO CONSIDER WHEN EATING IN NEW YORK CITY

The best meals are the ones that make you want to take a shower afterwards.

Eating a utility slice while waiting in line for destination pizza is a snack hack.

Shame happens only when you tell your dinner friends that you're not that hungry.

If you've never been anywhere else, tacos and sushi are better here than there.

Knowing about germs won't help you in the quest of anything that's truly delicious.

Never settle for anything that isn't at least a $6 noodle soup on Bowery and Bayard.

Everything bagels provide the essential vitamins needed for sprinting after the J train.

Brunch is for the underachievers who believe there's usually only 3 meals in a day.

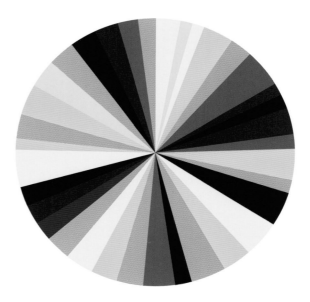

THOUGHTS ON A SUBWAY ON 7/30/2018

9:28am   9:56am

It's all about the difference between being late and not knowing the time.

Always have a dollar for someone who probably likes the same things you do.

You're on your way to anywhere if you pick a tropical song and close your eyes.

Seeing a person with the book that you'll never read is as good as reading it.

Phones were invented so we wouldn't have to worry about talking or smiling.

Never having a car means you'll never have to worry about being alone.

Shorter, straighter rides should either be cheaper or more expensive than the others.

Falling asleep means you're a hard worker and not that you watched all the TV.

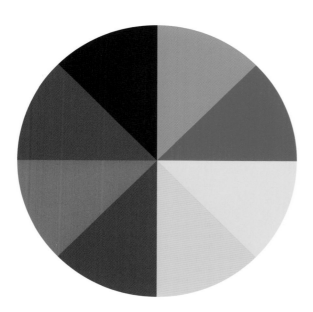

FOR THE BEST NEW YORK LIFE

Wear the right footwear for dodging snappy dogs and scooters.

Meditate regularly to prepare for common supermarket drama.

Remember the coldest January days during the middle of August.

Expect everyone to tell you or act like they're late for something.

Always know where a semi-respectable bathroom is at any time.

Accept conversations about how the neighborhood used to be.

Skip everything that isn't walking to new and exotic street foods.

Celebrate this as the center of the center-of-the-universe universe.

Nicholas Felton, *The Feltron 2008 Atlas*, 2008.

Nicholas Felton, whose design studio Feltron focuses on translating quotidian data into meaningful experiences, distills a year of his life into a map whose form echoes Buckminster Fuller's Dymaxion projection of the world. Fuller's map linked all of the Earth's landmasses into one continuous island; here, the island universe is Felton himself, who contains New York, rather than vice-versa.

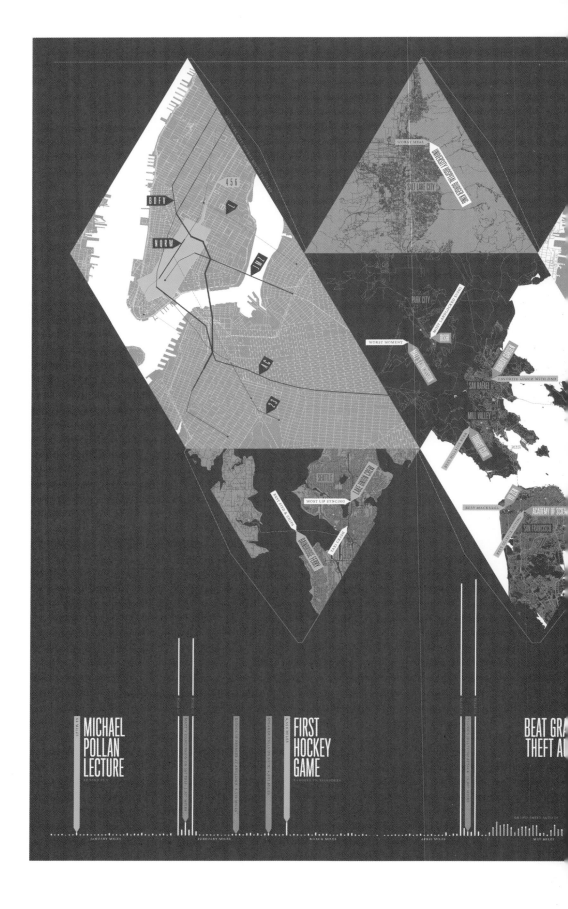

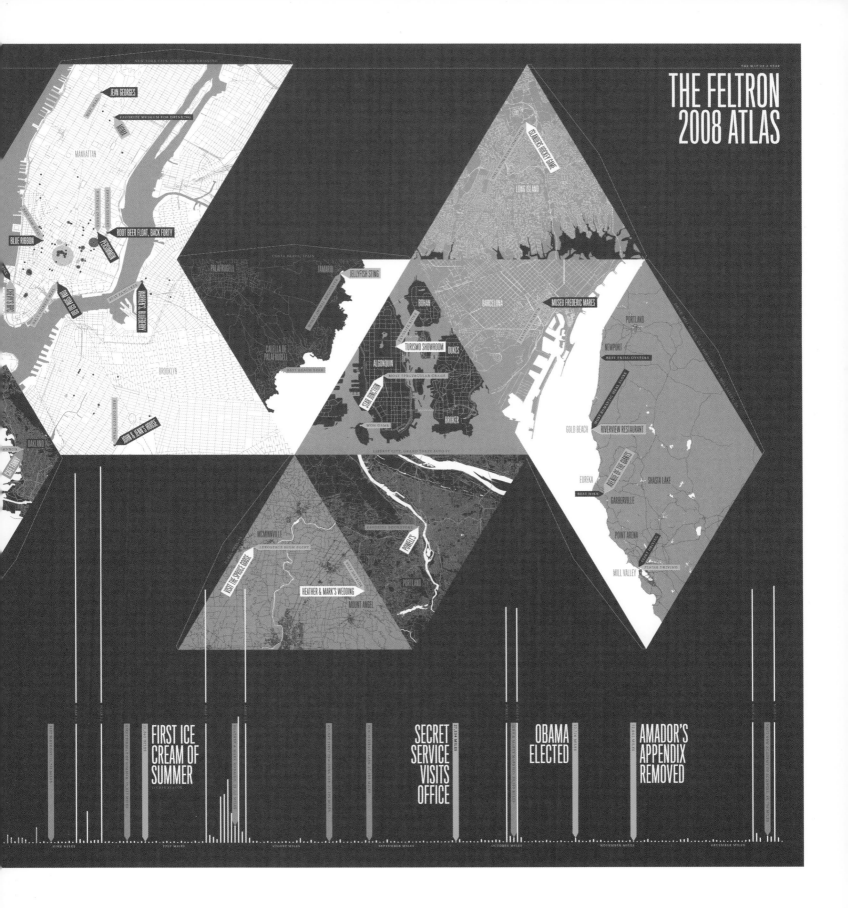

THE FELTRON
2008 ATLAS

FIRST ICE
CREAM OF
SUMMER

SECRET
SERVICE
VISITS
OFFICE

OBAMA
ELECTED

AMADOR'S
APPENDIX
REMOVED

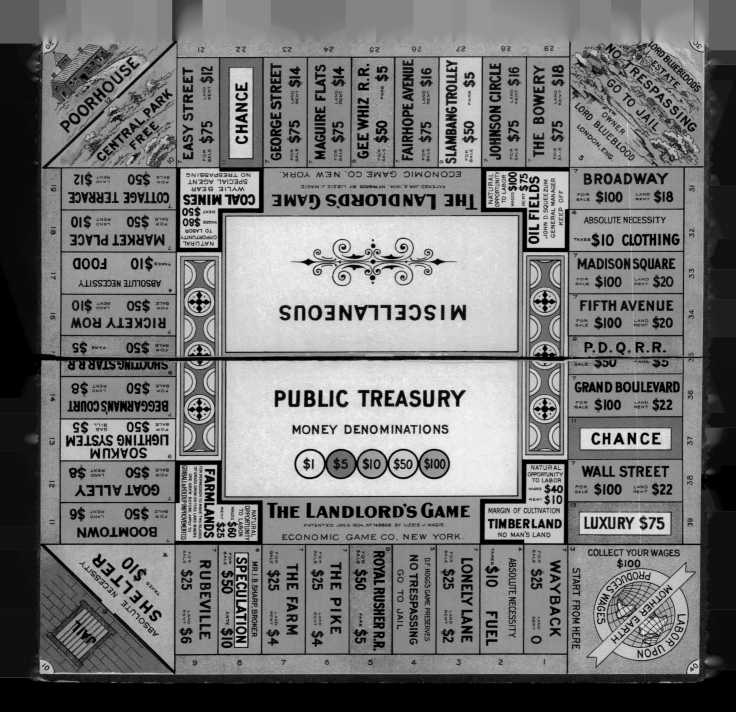

The Landlord's Game board (1906) with the following spaces and labels:

POORHOUSE

CENTRAL PARK FREE

EASY STREET — FOR SALE $75 — LAND RENT $12

CHANCE

GEORGE STREET — FOR SALE $75 — LAND RENT $14

MAGUIRE FLATS — FOR SALE $75 — LAND RENT $14

GEE WHIZ R.R. — FARE $5 — $50

FAIRHOPE AVENUE — FOR SALE $75 — LAND RENT $16

SLAMBANG TROLLEY — FARE $5 — $50

JOHNSON CIRCLE — FOR SALE $75 — LAND RENT $16

THE BOWERY — FOR SALE $75 — LAND RENT $18

NO TRESPASSING — GO TO JAIL — LORD BLUEBLOOD'S ESTATE — OWNER LORD BLUEBLOOD LONDON, ENG.

COTTAGE TERRACE — FOR SALE $50 — LAND RENT $12

MARKET PLACE — FOR SALE $50 — LAND RENT $10

FOOD — TAXES $10 — ABSOLUTE NECESSITY

RICKETY ROW — FOR SALE $50 — LAND RENT $10

SHOOTING STAR R.R. — FARE $5 — $50

BEGGARMAN'S COURT — FOR SALE $50 — LAND RENT $8

SOAKUM LIGHTING SYSTEM — GAS BILL $5 — FOR SALE $50

GOAT ALLEY — FOR SALE $50 — LAND RENT $8

BOOMTOWN — FOR SALE $60 — LAND RENT $6

COAL MINES — WAGES $80 TO LABOR — NATURAL OPPORTUNITY — FOR SALE $50 RENT $50

WYLIE BEAR SPECIAL AGENT — NO TRESPASSING

ECONOMIC GAME CO. NEW YORK.

PATENTED JAN. 5, 1904, NO. 748626 BY LIZZIE J. MAGIE

THE LANDLORD'S GAME

OIL FIELDS — NATURAL OPPORTUNITY TO LABOR — WAGES $100 — RENT $75 — JOHN D. SQUEEZUM GENERAL MANAGER — KEEP OFF

BROADWAY — FOR SALE $100 — LAND RENT $18

ABSOLUTE NECESSITY — TAXES $10 CLOTHING

MADISON SQUARE — FOR SALE $100 — LAND RENT $20

FIFTH AVENUE — FOR SALE $100 — LAND RENT $20

P.D.Q. R.R. — SALE $50 — FARE $5

GRAND BOULEVARD — FOR SALE $100 — LAND RENT $22

CHANCE

WALL STREET — FOR SALE $100 — LAND RENT $22

LUXURY $75

FARMLANDS — FOR PERMISSION TO MAKE TWO BLADES OF GRASS GROW ON THIS LAND WHERE ONE GREW BEFORE, APPLY TO CORRAL & HOLDUP IMPROVEMENT CO. — NATURAL OPPORTUNITY TO LABOR — WAGES $25 — RENT $25

TIMBERLAND — MARGIN OF CULTIVATION — NO MAN'S LAND

NATURAL OPPORTUNITY TO LABOR — WAGES $40 — RENT $10

MISCELLANEOUS

PUBLIC TREASURY — MONEY DENOMINATIONS — $1 $5 $10 $50 $100

THE LANDLORD'S GAME — PATENTED JAN. 5, 1904, NO. 748626 BY LIZZIE J. MAGIE — ECONOMIC GAME CO., NEW YORK.

RUBEVILLE — FOR SALE $25 — LAND RENT $6

SPECULATION — FOR SALE $50 — WAGES $10 — ANTE $10

MR. I. B. SHARP, BROKER

THE FARM — FOR SALE $25 — LAND RENT $4

THE PIKE — FOR SALE $25 — LAND RENT $4

ROYAL RUSHER R.R. — FOR SALE $50 — FARE $5

D.F. HOGG'S GAME PRESERVES — NO TRESPASSING — GO TO JAIL

LONELY LANE — FOR SALE $25 — LAND RENT $2

FUEL — TAXES $10 — ABSOLUTE NECESSITY

WAYBACK — FOR SALE $25 — LAND RENT 0

START FROM HERE

COLLECT YOUR WAGES $100 — PRODUCES MOTHER EARTH WAGES — LABOR UPON

JAIL — SHELTER — TAXES $10 — ABSOLUTE NECESSITY

…gie, *The Landlord's Game*, 1906.

…s after the Civil War, the skyrocketing value of Manhattan …enriched many landlords. In 1903, Lizzie Magie, a color-…t of various pursuits, created the Landlord's Game to help …the ideas of reformer Henry George, who believed that land …common property and proposed land-tax policies that would, …eturn rent to the renter—an idea that many of today's Man-…might applaud. In Magie's game, the only land in America …able than Wall Street was an oil field. Ironically, her creation …e game of Monopoly, incubator of many a young landlord…

OPPOSITE AND PAGE 196

Post Office Game, 1897.

As a goal, delivering the mail might seem like a comedown fro…ing Wall Street, but Parker Brothers believed that Post Office …enable players to "become familiar with the location of the im…streets and buildings of New York." The gameboard offers one…more charming, if naïve, maps in this book.

POST OFFICE GAME

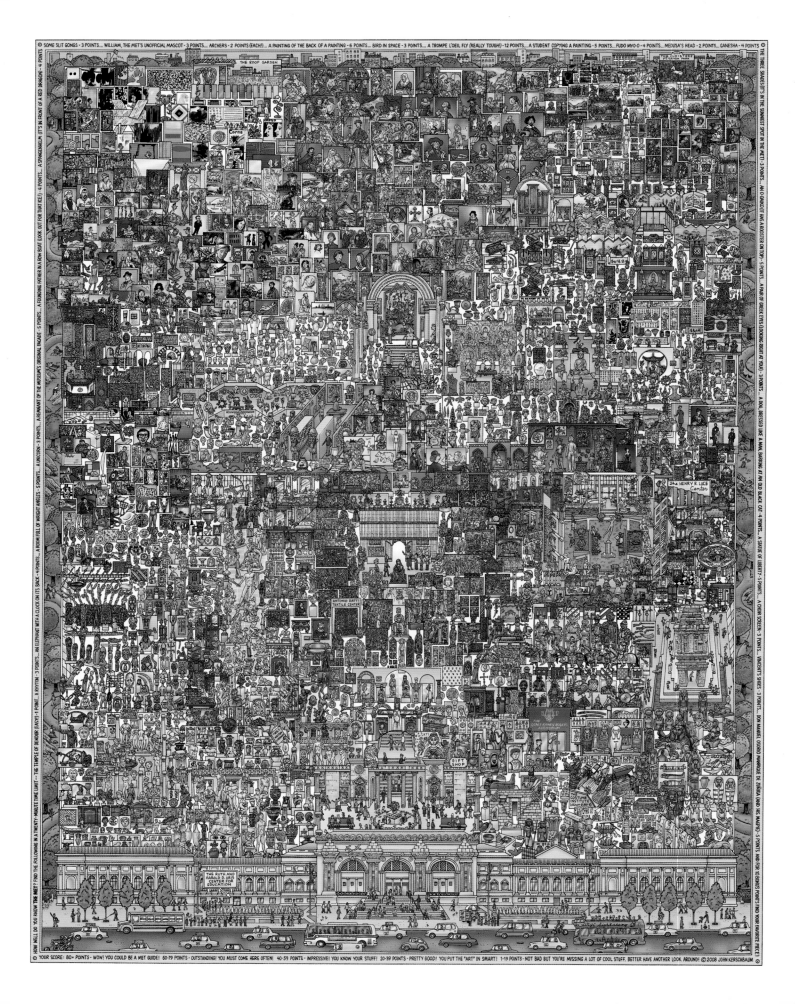

OPPOSITE

John Kerschbaum, *The Metropolitan Museum of Art Family Map*, 2008.

The fruit of many years work, John Kerschbaum's map of the Metropolitan Museum of Art is almost too much of a muchness. Presented as a game where the winner must find the most works of art from a list in a set time period, this map intentionally frustrates efficient wayfinding. Instead, it conveys the kaleidoscopic plenitude of an encyclopedic museum.

ABOVE

Jane Mount, *Ideal Bookshelf 364: NYC*, 2011.

Jane Mount's popular paintings are based on the associative mapping that anyone with a bookshelf can do. This kind of arranging is extremely personal, and Mount's challenge is to create a not-obvious group of titles that everyone can appreciate. Here, we are invited to imagine *Breakfast at Tiffany*'s Holly Golightly sharing a bench with Patrick Bateman of *American Psycho*.

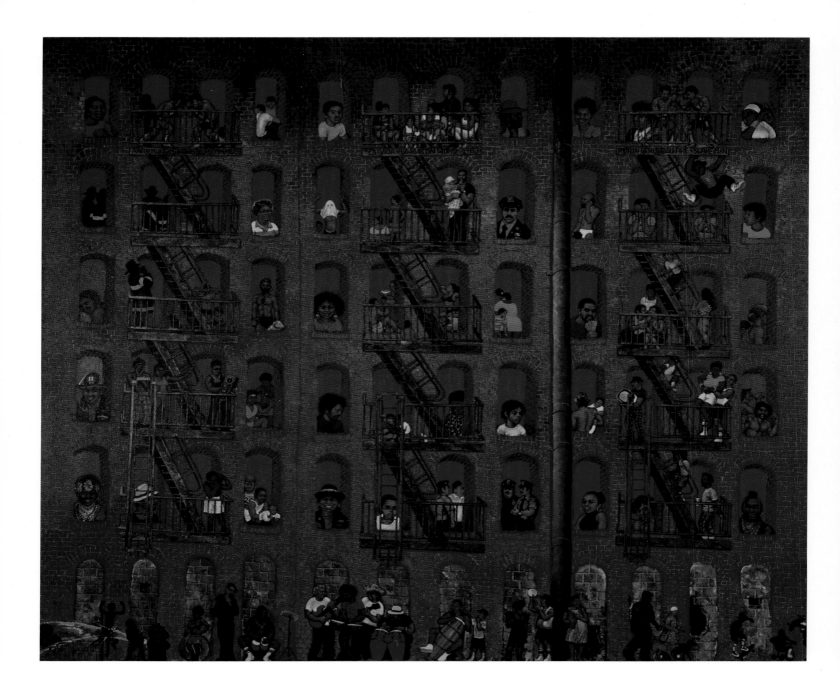

ABOVE

Martin Wong, *La Vida*, 1988.

A stylized fortress-like tenement frames Wong's celebration of the 1980s in Loisaida, the spirited Latino community centered on Avenue C in the Lower East Side. Here, too, cultural history is shot through with personal history: Among the graffiti artists DAZE, Sharp, and LA2, are writer Amiri Baraka, actor Mr. T, and Wong's stock cast of firefighters and boxers. Miguel Piñero, his collaborator and lover, who had died a few months before this painting was made, appears three times, making the scene a buoyant commemoration of the poet and playwright.

OPPOSITE

Faith Ringgold, *The Bitter Nest, Part II: The Harlem Renaissance Party*, 1988.

Artist Faith Ringgold's narrative quilt cycle about a family in Harlem during the 1920s was, in her words, a "fantasized adaptation of real life." Here, at a dinner party that is also a diagram of Harlem Renaissance luminaries, including Alain Locke, Countee Cullen, Langston Hughes, and Aaron Douglas, a domestic drama unfolds: Celia, soon to become a doctor (lower left), is embarrassed by her flamboyant and artistic mother, Cee Cee, lower right, a stand-in for Ringgold. Both of these conflicted figures are encouraged in their aspirations by the struggles of their dinner guests.

Nancy Chunn, *9/11*, 2002–2004.

Nancy Chunn's vivid visual storytelling is a dark satire of our absurd times. Appropriated symbols, pictograms, and pop culture references animate a grid—a cross between storyboard and board game—portraying the culture of fear after 9/11.

Eduardo Paolozzi, *Wittgenstein in New York*, from the *As Is When* portfolio, 1965.

Pop artist Eduardo Paolozzi diagrams an encounter in New York between the philosophers Ludwig Wittgenstein and Norman Malcolm, via a collage of printed ephemera from his vast personal collection.

I went to New York to meet Wittgenstein at the ship. When I first saw him I was surprised at his apparent physical vigour. He was striding down the ramp with a pack on his back, a heavy suitcase in one hand, cane in the other.

John Holmstrom, *The Ramones in New York City!*, 2016.

John Holmstrom, co-founder of *Punk* magazine, helped create the punk aesthetic in New York City. He traces the Ramones' trajectory from Forest Hills to CBGB in this biographical cartogram, a tribute drawn for the band's Queens Museum retrospective.

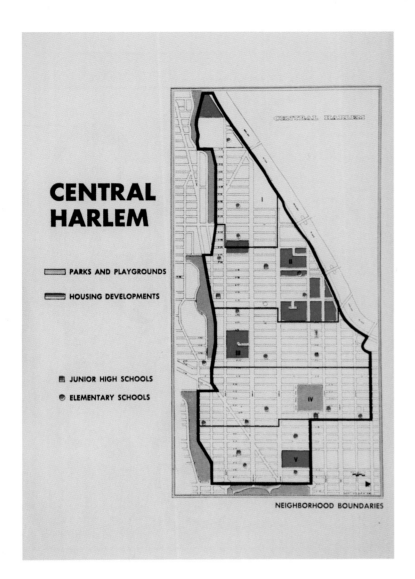

Tony Millionaire, *Harlem Renaissance: 100 Years of History, Art and Culture*, 2001. Concept by Marc H. Miller and design by Kevin Hein.

Harlem, the walking tour.

Pages from *Youth in the Ghetto and the Blueprint for Change (Harlem Youth Report #5)*, 1964.

The powerful six-hundred-page report released in 1964 by Harlem Youth Opportunities Unlimited (HARYOU), *Youth in the Ghetto: A Study of the Consequences of Powerlessness and a Blueprint for Change*, was summarized for younger readers in a comic book—"the voice of Harlem Youth Unlimited"—published by Custom Comics Inc. The free comic contained a very different map of Harlem from the previous one, as well as graphic treatments of themes in the larger report.

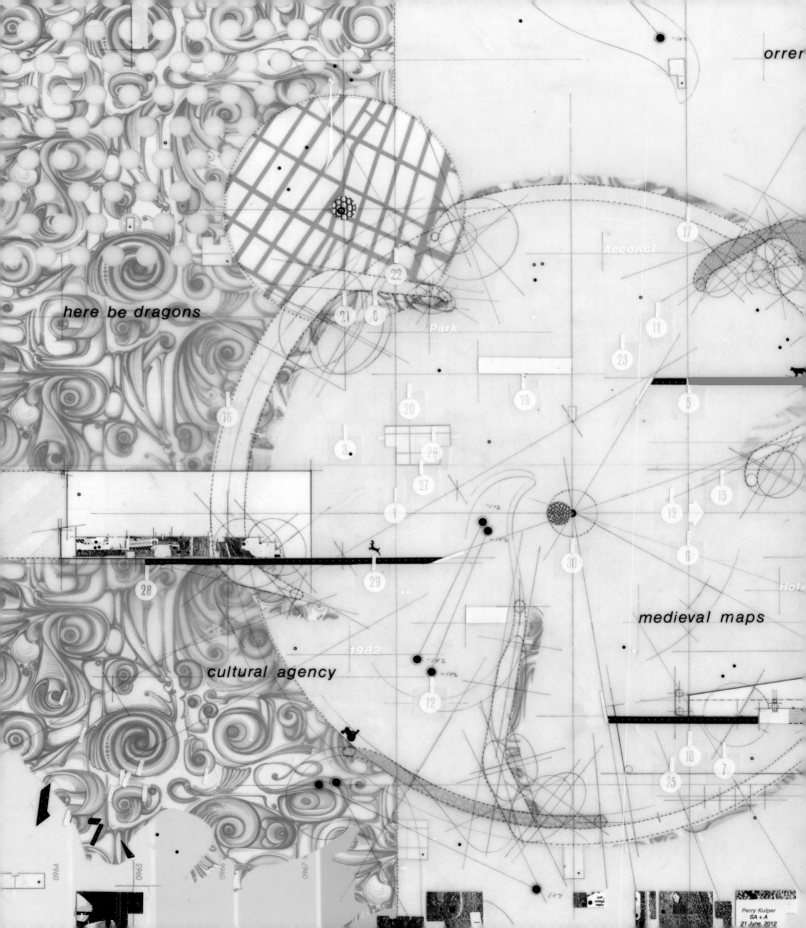

orrer

here be dragons

Acconci

Park

medieval maps

1982

cultural agency

Hol

Perry Kulper
SA + A
21 June, 2012

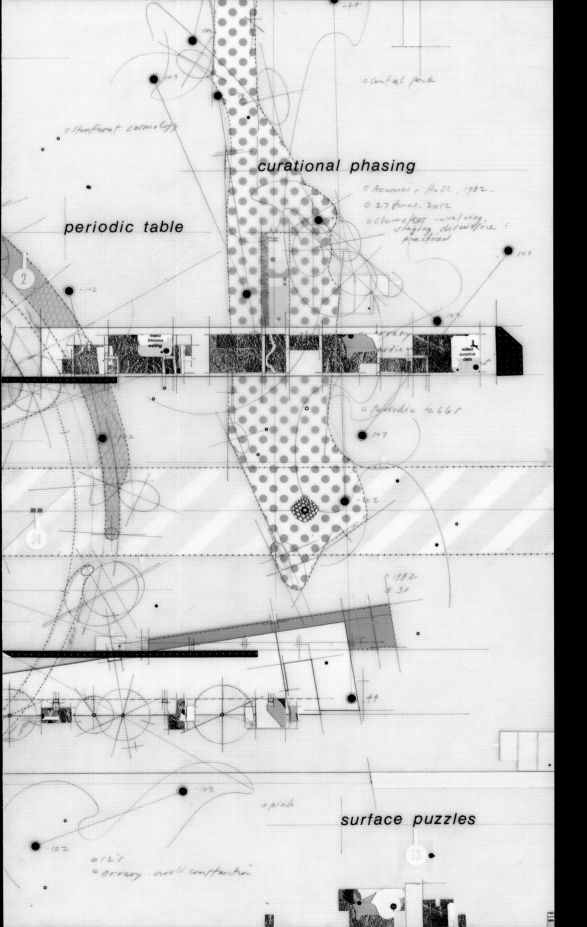

curational phasing

periodic table

surface puzzles

Perry Kulper, *Storefront,
A Cosmology*, 2012.

Art galleries are vital nodes for transmitting ideas in Manhattan. For an exhibition about architectural drawings, Storefront for Art and Architecture commissioned thirty drawings of its gallery space at 97 Kenmare Street in Manhattan: This one, by architect Perry Kulper, found a fresh visual language to capture the fluid relations of an art gallery with place, time, society, history, and culture.

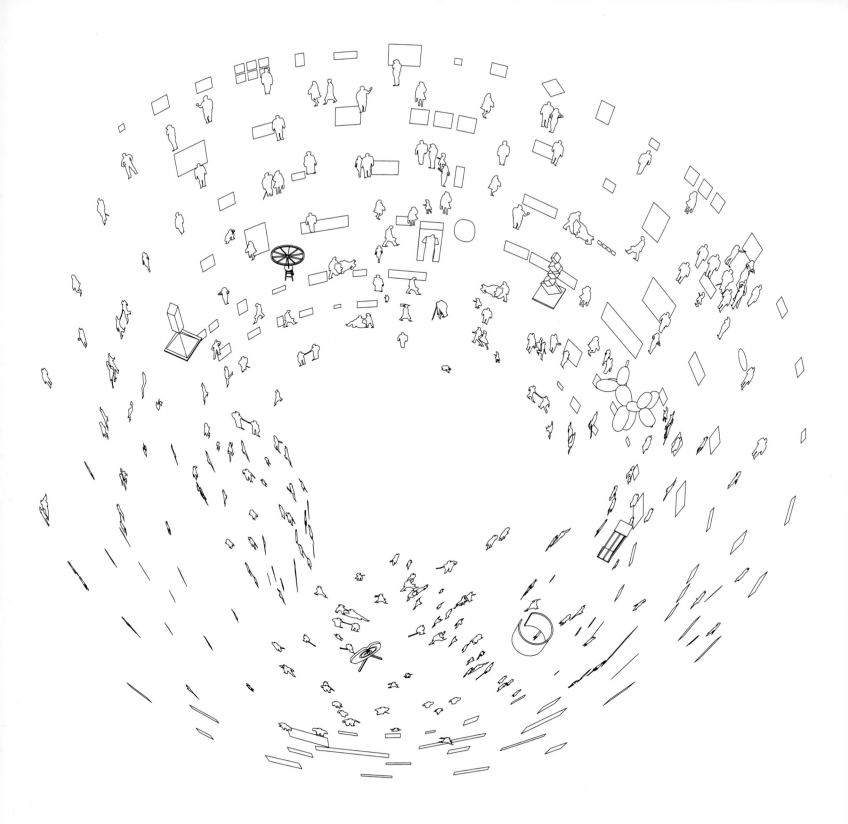

SO – IL, *Zenith Nadir*, 2009.

For some Manhattanites, the Guggenheim's spiral is the true heart of the island. Here, in architecture studio SO – IL's elegant diagrams of the view looking up from the ground and down from the top, the physical mass of Frank Lloyd Wright's rotunda has been inexplicably erased, leaving museum visitors and art floating in space.

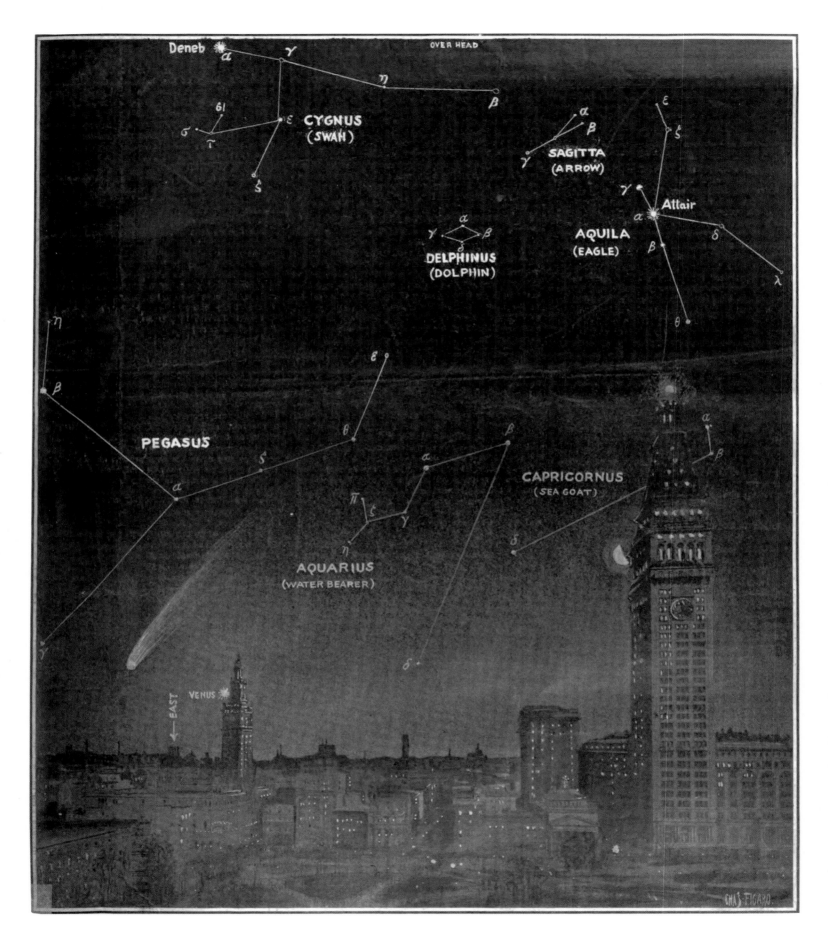

Charles Figaro, *Haley's Comet at Its Brightest*, from *Scientific American*, April 16, 1910.

Of all celebrity visitors to Manhattan, Haley's Comet was the most heavenly. More than a century ago, the city and the universe met as equals in the pages of *Scientific American*. Rising above the sometimes-grim realities of science and technology, and the plague of superstition, the mind is filled with wonder. Sadly, in reality the city's bright lights all but block out the luminous stars and planets.

BIBLIOGRAPHY

Adler, Phoebe, Tom Howells, and Duncan McCorquodale, eds. *Mapping New York*. London: Black Dog Publishing, 2009.

Andersen, Kurt, Graydon Carter, and George Kalogerakis. *Spy: The Funny Years*. New York: Miramax Books, 2006.

Ascher, Kate. *The Works: Anatomy of a City*. New York: Penguin Press, 2007.

Auster, Paul. *City of Glass: The Graphic Novel*. Adaptation by Paul Karasik and David Mazzucchelli. New York: Picador, 2004.

Baker, Nicholson, and Margaret Brentano. *The World on Sunday: Graphic Art in Joseph Pulitzer's Newspaper (1898-1911)*. New York: Bulfinch Press, 2005.

Blake, Art M. *How New York Became American, 1890-1924*. Baltimore: Johns Hopkins University Press, 2006.

Brosterman, Norman. *Out of Time: Designs for the Twentieth-Century Future*. New York: Harry N. Abrams, 2000.

Burrington, Ingrid. *Networks of New York: An Illustrated Field Guide to Urban Internet Infrastructure*. Brooklyn: Melville House, 2016.

Chast, Roz. *Going into Town: A Love Letter to New York*. New York: Bloomsbury, 2017.

Christianson, Scott. *100 Diagrams That Changed the World: From the Earliest Cave Paintings to the Innovation of the iPod*. London: Batsford, 2014.

Chwast, Seymour, and Steven Heller, eds. *The Art of New York*. New York: Harry N. Abrams, 1983.

Cohen, Paul E., and Robert T. Augustyn. *Manhattan in Maps: 1527-1995*. New York: Rizzoli, 1997.

Cooke, Lynne, Karen Kelly, and Barbara Schröder, eds. *Max Neuhaus: Times Square, Time Piece Beacon*. New York: Dia Art Foundation, 2009.

Cooper, Becky. *Mapping Manhattan: A Love (and Sometimes Hate) Story in Maps by 75 New Yorkers*. New York: Harry N. Abrams, 2013.

Dant, Adam. *Living Maps: An Atlas of Cities Personified*. San Francisco: Chronicle Books, 2018.

DeGraff, Andrew, and A. D. Jameson. *Cinemaps: An Atlas of Great Movies*. Philadelphia: Quirk Books, 2017.

Eisner, Will. *Will Eisner's New York: Life in the Big City*. New York: W.W. Norton & Company, 2006.

Fitzpatrick, Tracy. *Art and the Subway: New York Underground*. New Brunswick: Rutgers University Press, 2009.

Futurist Depero: 1913-1950. Madrid: Fundación Juan March, 2014.

Goldin, Greg, and Sam Lubell. *Never Built New York*. New York: Metropolis Books, 2016.

Goldsmith, Kenneth. *Capital: New York, Capital of the 20th Century*. Brooklyn: Verso Books, 2015.

Harmon, Katharine. *You Are Here NYC: Mapping the Soul of the City*. Hudson: Princeton Architectural Press, 2016.

Homberger, Eric. *The Historical Atlas of New York City, Third Edition: A Visual Celebration of 400 Years of New York City's History*. New York: St. Martin's Griffin, 2016.

Koolhaas, Rem. *Delirious New York: A Retroactive Manifesto for Manhattan*. New York: Monacelli Press, 1994.

Kuo, Andrew. *What Me Worry*. Bologna: Damiani, 2010.

Kuper, Peter. *Drawn to New York: An Illustrated Chronicle of Three Decades in New York City*. Oakland: PM Press, 2013.

Lynch, Kevin. *The Image of the City*. Cambridge: The MIT Press, 1960.

Mackay, Donald A. *The Building of Manhattan*. Mineola: Dover Publications, 2010. First published 1987 by Harper & Row (New York).

McGuire, Richard. *Here*. London: Hamish Hamilton, 2014.

Muratyan, Vahram. *Paris Versus New York: A Tally of Two Cities*. Camberwell: Viking, 2012.

New York Transit Museum. *Subway Style: 100 Years of Architecture & Design in the New York City Subway*. New York: Harry N. Abrams, 2004.

Page, Max. *The Creative Destruction of Manhattan, 1900-1940*. Chicago: University of Chicago Press, 1999.

Pericoli, Matteo. *Manhattan Unfurled*. Edinburgh: Canongate, 2002.

Pyle, Nathan W. *NYC Basic Tips and Etiquette*. New York: William Morrow, 2014.

Rendgen, Sandra. *Information Graphics*. Edited by Julius Wiedemann. Köln: Taschen, 2018.

Robinson. *New York Line by Line: from Broadway to the Battery*. New York: Universe Publishing, 2009.

Rosenberg, Daniel, and Anthony Grafton. *Cartographies of Time: A History of the Timeline*. New York: Princeton Architectural Press, 2013.

Rothman, Julia. *Hello NY: An Illustrated Love Letter to the Five Boroughs*. San Francisco: Chronicle Books, 2014.

Sanderson, Eric W. *Mannahatta: A Natural History of New York City*. New York: Harry N. Abrams, 2013.

Sasek, M. *This Is New York*. New York: Universe, 2009.

Scher, Paula. *Make It Bigger*. New York: Princeton Architectural Press, 2005.

Scudiero, Maurizio, and David Leiber. *Depero Futurista & New York: Futurism and the Art of Advertising*. Rovereto: Longo, 1987.

Shaw, Paul. *Helvetica and the New York City Subway System: The True (Maybe) Story*. Cambridge: The MIT Press, 2011.

Tobocman, Seth. *War in the Neighborhood*. New York: Shadow Press, 2016.

Tufte, Edward R. *Envisioning Information*. Cheshire: Graphics Press, 1990.

Tufte, Edward R. *The Visual Display of Quantitative Information*. Cheshire: Graphics Press, 1983.

Tufte, Edward R. *Visual Explanations: Images and Quantities, Evidence and Narrative*. Cheshire: Graphics Press, 1997.

Weitzman, David. *A Subway for New York*. New York: Farrar, Straus and Giroux, 2005.

Wertz, Julia. *Tenements, Towers & Trash: An Unconventional Illustrated History of New York City*. New York: Black Dog & Leventhal Publishers, 2017.

Other sources/websites:

archives.nyc

archive.org

artgallery.yale.edu

barronmaps.com

bigthink.com/strange-maps

boweryboyshistory.com

brainpickings.org

cooperhewitt.org

davidrumsey.com

digital.library.cornell.edu

digitalcollections.nypl.org

ephemeralnewyork.wordpress.com

eyemagazine.com

geographicus.com

gothamist.com

harpers.org

johnnycakebooks.com

justseeds.org

loc.gov

longstreet.typepad.com

lubalin100.com

moma.org

museoreinasofia.es

newyorker.com

nycurbanism.com

nytimes.com

placesjournal.org

raremaps.com

renzopicasso.com

skyscraper.org

tagfinearts.com

tate.org.uk

visualaids.org

visualizingnyc.org

INDEX

ACKNOWLEDGMENTS

We would like to give a huge amount of thanks to Eric Himmel, our editor at Abrams Books, whose enthusiasm for this project has been invaluable. Thanks also to John Gall for his support early in this project. Thanks to Danielle Youngsmith, the book's designer, for her wonderful work, as well as Deb Wood, creative director; Anet Sirna-Bruder, production director; and Glenn Ramirez, managing editor at Abrams Books. Thanks to Christoph Niemann for his superb jacket design.

We are indebted to all the artists, designers, architects that made this book possible by generously sharing their work.

Many resources were scoured to achieve this marvelous collection of rare vintage and contemporary material. Thank you to the galleries, libraries, and other key sources that formed part of this treasure trove.

Also, a big tip of the hat to J.J. Sedelmaier for his generous access to some of his archival material.

Much gratitude goes to all to the following who have provided us with essential materials:

Aaron Silverman & Molly Maguire

Adam Brown & Anne Boissonnault (Trisha Brown Dance Company)

Alexander Tochilovsky (Herb Lubalin Study Center of Design and Typography, Cooper Union)

Anja Sieber-Albers (UAA Ungers Archiv für Architekturwissenschaft)

Barry Lawrence Ruderman & Jorge Chavez (Barry Lawrence Ruderman Antique Maps)

Beth Kleber (Milton Glaser Design Study Center, School of Visual Arts)

Brandon Rumsey (David Rumsey Map Collection)

Chris Mullen

Denne J. Wesolowski (Digital Content Library, University of Minnesota)

Ellen Moon & Christopher Leich (Hugh Ferriss family)

Flora Smith (TopFoto)

Hobby Limon (TAG Fine Arts)

Irwin Chusid (JimFlora.com)

Jan Bresnick & Lynn Leibowitz (Matthew Leibowitz family)

Janet Hicks (Artists Rights Society)

Jeff Roth

Jim Heimann

Ken Friedman

Laura Ten Eyck (Argosy Gallery)

Lee Wallender

Louise Peck & Bob Saich (Advanced Graphics London)

Luigi Berio (L'Archivio Renzo Picasso)

Maurizio Scudiero (Archivio Depero)

Micaela Frank (P•P•O•W)

Nicholson Baker

Norman Brosterman

Rossy Mendez & Ken Cobb (New York City Department of Records and Information Services)

Ryan Mungia

Sarah Copplestone & Raffaella Fletcher (Alan Fletcher Archive)

Silvia Cecere Neuhaus (Estate Max Neuhaus)

Sophie Moiroux & Kai Vollmet (Studio Maria Thereza Alves)

Thomas Forsyth (landlordsgame.info)

Tom Geismar

Vince Ruvolo (Ronald Feldman Fine Arts)

—Antonis Antoniou and Steven Heller

A very special thank you to Itxaso Corral Arrieta and Maria and Georgios Antoniou for their unwavering encouragement throughout this project.

—Antonis Antoniou

CREDITS

2-3: Library of Congress.

16-17: The New York Public Library, Lionel Pincus and Princess Firyal Map Division.

19: The New York Public Library, Lionel Pincus and Princess Firyal Map Division.

20: Norman B. Leventhal Map & Education Center.

24: Cooper Hewitt, Smithsonian Design Museum / Art Resource, New York.

26-27: Museum of the City of New York. 39.380.2.

29: Library of Congress, *Chronicling America:* Historic American Newspapers.

30: Courtesy of Norman Brosterman.

32: Photo: akg-images.

33: Library of Congress.

35: Courtesy Argosy Gallery.

36: Used with permission of Chronicle Books LLC, San Francisco. Visit ChronicleBooks.com. © 2018 Adam Dant / Artists Rights Society (ARS), New York / DACS, London.

37: Courtesy Geographicus Rare Antique Maps, www.geographicus.com.

38: © Ungers Archiv für Architekturwissenschaft UAA.

39: © The Saul Steinberg Foundation/Artists Rights Society (ARS), New York.

40 right: © TopFoto.

43: © Maxwell J Roberts. Reproduced with permission, all rights reserved.

51: Reprinted by permission of Black Dog & Leventhal, an imprint of Hachette Book Group, Inc.

60: David Rumsey Map Collection, www.davidrumsey.com.

61: Cornell University, PJ Mode Collection of Persuasive Cartography.

62: Courtesy Nicholson Baker.

63 bottom: Library of Congress, *Chronicling America:* Historic American Newspapers.

64: Courtesy Nicholson Baker.

65: David Rumsey Map Collection, www.davidrumsey.com.

69: Archivio Renzo Picasso, Genova.

74: Library of Congress, *Chronicling America:* Historic American Newspapers.

75 left: Library of Congress, *Chronicling America:* Historic American Newspapers.

75 right: Library of Congress, *Chronicling America:* Historic American Newspapers.

76-77: Courtesy Chris Mullen.

80 top: Library of Congress.

80 bottom right: Library of Congress, *Chronicling America:* Historic American Newspapers.

82: Page from J. Clarence Davies scrapbook. Museum of the City of New York. X2012.61.34.53.

83: Private collection © The Saul Steinberg Foundation/Artists Rights Society (ARS), New York.

86: Library of Congress.

87: Courtesy of Archivio Depero, MART, Rovereto. © 2018 Artists Rights Society (ARS), New York / SIAE, Rome.

91: Courtesy J. J. Sedelmaier.

92: From *Cinemaps* (Quirk Books, 2017).

94: © Trisha Brown, Trisha Brown Archive, New York.

98-99: Courtesy Jim Heimann and Ryan Mungia.

101-103: Archivio Renzo Picasso, Genova.

109: © The Saul Steinberg Foundation/Artists Rights Society (ARS), New York.

116-117 top: The New York Public Library.

120: Cornell University, PJ Mode Collection of Persuasive Cartography.

121: David Rumsey Map Collection, www.davidrumsey.com.

122-123: Library of Congress, Geography and Map Division.

125: Courtesy Jim Heimann and Ryan Mungia.

126: Library of Congress.

127: Cooper Hewitt, Smithsonian Design Museum / Art Resource, New York.

130: Courtesy Jim Heimann and Ryan Mungia.

140: From the exhibition "Maria Thereza Alves: Seeds of Change: New York—A Botany of Colonization," photo: Nick Ash.

142-143: © Kate McLean 2017 and NYC Department of Transportation DOT Art/Summer Streets.

144: Library of Congress, *Chronicling America:* Historic American Newspapers.

153 bottom: Copyright © 2014 by Nathan W. Pyle. Reprinted by permission of HarperCollins Publishers.

156-157: © Condé Nast.

158-159: Image courtesy of the artist and Galerie Jérôme Poggi. Photo: Hans-Georg Gaul.

160: The New York Public Library, Lionel Pincus and Princess Firyal Map Division.

161: The New York Public Library, Lionel Pincus and Princess Firyal Map Division.

162: Library of Congress, Prints and Photographs Division.

164 bottom: Library of Congress, *Chronicling America:* Historic American Newspapers.

166 top: Library of Congress.

166 bottom: Library of Congress, Work Projects Administration Poster Collection.

167: Library of Congress.

170 bottom: Courtesy of Archivio Depero, MART, Rovereto. © 2018 Artists Rights Society (ARS), New York / SIAE, Rome.

171: Based on text by the Call to Action working group of the Zuccotti Park General Assembly.

172: © Raffaella Fletcher.

176: © The Museum of Modern Art/Licensed by SCALA / Art Resource, New York. © 2018 George Maciunas Foundation / Artists Rights Society (ARS), New York.

177: © The Museum of Modern Art/Licensed by SCALA / Art Resource, New York.

180-181: Image courtesy Barry Lawrence Ruderman Antique Maps Inc.

182: Image courtesy of the artist and Galerie Jérôme Poggi. Photo: Hans-Georg Gaul.

186: © The Ray Johnson Estate.

187: © 2018 Adam Dant / Artists Rights Society (ARS), New York / DACS, London / Image courtesy of TAG Fine Arts.

188: Courtesy of Advanced Graphics London.

192: Courtesy of Molly Maguire and Aaron Silverman.

199: Courtesy of the Estate of Martin Wong and PPOW, New York.

200: Steven Rappaport Collection, 2012.27.1.50; New York Transit Museum.

206-207: Metropolitan Museum of Art, New York. Gift of Ettie Stettheimer, 1953.

209: © 2018 Banco de México Diego Rivera Frida Kahlo Museums Trust, Mexico, D.F. / Artists Rights Society (ARS), New York.

211: © The Museum of Modern Art/Licensed by SCALA / Art Resource. © 2018 Artists Rights Society (ARS), New York / ADAGP, Paris.

212: Beinecke Rare Book and Manuscript Library, Yale University. © The Saul Steinberg Foundation/Artists Rights Society (ARS), New York.

218: © LandlordsGame.Info 2014.

219: The Liman Collection. ID 1992.12.16, New-York Historical Society.

222: Courtesy of the Estate of Martin Wong and PPOW, New York.

223: Smithsonian American Art Museum, Washington, DC / Art Resource, New York. © 2018 Faith Ringgold, member Artists Rights Society (ARS), New York.

224: Courtesy the artist and Ronald Feldman Gallery, New York.

225: Presented by Rose and Chris Prater through the Institute of Contemporary Prints 1975. © Tate, London / Art Resource, New York © ARS, New York. © Trustees of the Paolozzi Foundation, Licensed by DACS / Artists Rights Society (ARS), New York 2018.

228: © 2001 Ephemera Press.

229: New York Municipal Archives.

PAGES 2-3:

**Charles Hart (lithographer) and Joseph Koehler (printer),
The City of Greater New York, 1905.**
Panoramic maps, a popular genre during the nineteenth century, provided
a romanticized vision from an imagined bird's-eye view of the changing urban
landscape during the industrial age. In this print that works as a cartogram
thanks to its distorted perspective, Park Row, with its imposing wall of buildings that were home to New York's newspapers, is greatly exaggerated. Park
Row was the hub of the imagery that shaped Manhattan, including many
of the diagrams that appear throughout this book.

Editor: Eric Himmel
Designer: Danielle Youngsmith
Production Manager: Sarah Masterson Hally

Library of Congress Control Number: 2020931054

ISBN: 978-1-4197-4760-1
eISBN: 978-1-64700-170-4

Printed and bound in China
10 9 8 7 6 5 4 3 2 1

Abrams books are available at special discounts when purchased in quantity
for premiums and promotions as well as fundraising or educational use.
Special editions can also be created to specification. For details, contact
specialsales@abramsbooks.com or the address below.

Abrams® is a registered trademark of Harry N. Abrams, Inc.

ABRAMS The Art of Books
195 Broadway, New York, NY 10007
abramsbooks.com